Open Systems for Better Business—Something Ventured, Something Gained

Trademarks

The following company names are registered trademarks. Company names are expressed in the form most commonly used in the text of the book. Amdahl, American Express, Apple, AT&T, Blue Cross and Blue Shield, Borland, Bull, Canon, Convex, DEC, Deloitte & Touche LLP, Fujitsu, G2 Research Inc., General Motors, Hewlett-Packard, Hitachi, IBM, Intel, KMart, Magnavox, Microsoft, Motorola, Nordstromís, Novell, Oracle Corporation, Sears, Roebuck, and Co., Stratus, Sun, SunSoft, Sybase, Transarc, Unisys, Wal-Mart, WordPerfect, Xerox, and Zenith.

The following products are licensed trademarks of Apple Computer, Inc.: Apple, Chicago, Macintosh, and Power Macintosh.

The following products are licensed trademarks of Digital Equipment Company (DEC): Alpha, AXP, DEC, DECdas, Digital, OpenVMS, PDP, ULTRIX, VAX, XUI Toolkit Application Programming Interface.

The following products are licensed trademarks of Hewlett-Packard: HP, HP-UX and OPENVIEW.

The following products are licensed trademarks of International Business Machines (IBM): AS/400, DRDA, ES/9000, S/370, MVS/ESA, MVS/SP, MVS/XP, OS2, PS/1, PS/2, PS/ValuePort, RISC System/6000, System/360, and ThinkPad.

The following product is a licensed trademark of the Massachusetts Institute of Technology (MIT): Kerberos.

The following products are licensed trademarks of Microsoft: Microsoft Access, Microsoft At Work, Microsoft Excel, Microsoft Powerpoint, Microsoft Windows, Microsoft Word, MS-DOS, Tempus, Win32, and Windows.

The following product is a licensed trademark of Novell Corporation: UNIX.

The following products are licensed trademarks of the Object Management Group (OMG): CORBA and Object Request Broker.

The following products are licensed trademarks of the Open Software Foundation (OSF): ANDF, OSF/Motif, OSF/1, and OSF DCE (Distributed Computing Environment).

The following product is a licensed trademark of the Oracle Corporation: ORACLE TOOLS.

The following products are licensed trademarks of Sun Computers: NeWS, NFS, OPENLOOK, Solaris, and SunOS 5.0.

The following products are licensed trademarks of X/Open Co. Ltd.: CAE, Spec 1170, X/Open and XPG.

The following product is a joint trademark of Apple, Hewlett-Packard and IBM: Taligent.

The following product is a joint trademark of IBM and Microsoft: DOS.

Open Systems for Better Business—Something Ventured, Something Gained

Ann Senn

 VAN NOSTRAND REINHOLD
I(T)P A Division of International Thomson Publishing Inc.

New York • Albany • Bonn • Boston • Detroit • London • Madrid • Melbourne
Mexico City • Paris • San Francisco • Singapore • Tokyo • Toronto

Printed in the United States of America
For more information, contact:

Van Nostrand Reinhold
115 Fifth Avenue
New York, NY 10003

International Thomson Publishing GmbH
Königswinterer Strasse 418
53227 Bonn
Germany

International Thomson Publishing Europe
Berkshire House 168-173
High Holborn
London WCIV 7AA
England

International Thomson Publishing Asia
221 Henderson Road #05-10
Henderson Building
Singapore 0315

Thomas Nelson Australia
102 Dodds Street
South Melbourne, 3205
Victoria, Australia

International Thomson Publishing Japan
Hirakawacho Kyowa Building, 3F
2-2-1 Hirakawacho
Chiyoda-ku, 102 Tokyo
Japan

Nelson Canada
1120 Birchmount Road
Scarborough, Ontario
Canada M1K 5G4

International Thomson Editores
Campos Eliseos 385, Piso 7
Col. Polanco
11560 Mexico D.F. Mexico

1 2 3 4 5 6 7 8 9 10 QEBFF 01 00 99 98 97 96 95 94

Library of Congress Cataloging-in-Publication Data
Senn, Ann
    Open systems for better business : something ventured, something
gained / Ann Senn.
        p. cm.
    Includes bibliographical and index.
    ISBN 0-442-01911-4
    1. Information technology—Management. 2. Management information
systems—Costs. 3. Information storage and retrieval systems—Business.
I. Title.
HD30.2.S46 1994
658.4' 038—dc20   94-33081
                                                   CIP

Project Management: Raymond T. Campbell • Art Director: Jo-Ann Radin-Campbell • Production:
mle design, 562 Milford Point Road, Milford, CT 06460

Table of Contents

Preface

Wisdom is meaningless until your own experience has given it meaning...and there is wisdom in the selection of wisdom.

—*Bergen Evans*

The information capabilities of a business, along with its business processes, people, and corporate culture shape its competitive strengths (and weaknesses) in the marketplace. Companies have invested millions of dollars in their information capabilities. Large companies invest many millions of dollars each year in their information systems.

In many ways, companies find their past technology investments limiting rather than enabling them to respond to the business marketplace. Companies need to be able to change: change their business, change their business processes, and change the information they circulate through the organization. They need to be able to drive down costs and improve the quality of their products and services. They also need the ability to grow—not in big "add-another-mainframe-processor" units of growth, but in smaller, lumpy, more frequent increments.

Bottom line—businesses need flexibility from their systems and an array of options from which they can choose how to proceed.

We are at a point where (finally!) business and technology meet.

Open Systems are about choice—the freedom to opt into and out of vendor product lines and architectures, freedom to swap products and platforms, freedom to choose from a greater variety of applications, tools, and other technologies. With this freedom comes power—the power to drive down the unit costs of technology and information services and the power to improve the information capabilities of the business in ways that were not possible before.

But choice requires decisions. And the decisions in an open systems environment are complex. There is no disputing the fact that an open, distributed computing environment is more complex to define, design, manage, and evolve than the more traditional, "primary-vendor" computing environment. Selecting and integrating technologies is hard.

I visited Lithuania in 1990. It was under Soviet rule at the time, and the Lithuanian freedom movement was just beginning. A Lithuanian friend was showing me around his home city, Vilnius, the capital of Lithuania. We stopped in a department store so that I could experience "shopping" in the Soviet Union. The department store was barren by U.S. standards. Most of the shelves were empty. Departments were separated by dirty, paper-thin curtains. The Lithuanian took me into the men's department to show me the meager assortment of goods and explained, much to his surprise, that day was a good day—the store had a pair of slacks in his size (one pair!). There was no choice, but there was a product—brown, straight-legged trousers size "48" cut from a thin wool blend. We bought the slacks and moved on to a toy store, looking for a birthday present for his son. The toy store had perhaps 20 different types of toys—all simple, cheap plastic things: a pail and shovel, an ugly plastic doll with no clothes, a plastic hammer, a bag of colored plastic balls. That was shopping in Lithuania. No choice. The stores were government run. My friend's new pants and the xylophone I bought for his son's birthday were products of a "supply-side" system, planned and regulated by state administrators. You bought what was available, if you needed it.

"Hard currency" stores were a different matter. They were set up for visitors and the lucky locals (such as black marketers) who could pay with foreign currency. Entering a hard currency store was like entering a different world. Although the selection was still limited by Western standards, shelves were stocked (!) with good quality, foreign imports. Hard currency stores carried such essential items as windshield wipers, towels, men's shirts, and winter boots, which rarely showed up on the shelves of a state-run store. Items in hard currency stores were available only to a privileged few.

A year later, my Lithuanian friend came to the United States for a visit. We went shopping in Minneapolis to buy some presents for his family. He wanted a microwave oven. I took him to an electronics superstore and he stared, eyes glazed over, at the long wall of microwave ovens. He walked from model to model and demanded to know the differences between them. Weakly, I tried to describe some feature differences, but beyond the obvious, I wasn't much help. He then wanted to know why there were so many competing products if they delivered essentially the same functionality. And, how in the world did we ever make a choice between them? I began, slowly, to explain advertising, product literature, salespeople, and the ultimate decision tool in the world of consumer items, *Consumer Reports*. He was dumbfounded. We left the store without a microwave. We had the same difficulty trying to buy clothes for his children and a few presents for his wife. He could not express his desires to narrow our search. And, he could not make a choice. He had no frame of reference to work from, no decision criteria. His life experiences had not prepared him for a world that offered him such an array of choices.

Open systems confront us with a similarly bewildering array of choices. We can choose applications, tools, operating software, and platforms from a growing number of suppliers. The industry is moving *from* a "supply side" market—where technology choice was limited to compatible products within a given vendor line, where technology was meted out to us as the vendor developed and made it available—where we bought what was available if we needed it. We are moving *to* a "demand-side" market—where we can choose from a variety of products from different vendors and where the next time we choose, we can select a different vendor's product, if we like.

Yes, choice gives us more freedom and power than ever, but choice also makes our technology decisions infinitely more complex.

Like the Lithuanian who needed a different frame of reference, a different set of experiences to make a choice from a wall of microwaves, we too need a different frame of reference and new decision criteria to arm ourselves in the technology marketplace. Many organizations that I know of and work with are struggling to take advantage of the changes in technology. In that struggle they raise two questions most frequently:

How can we implement open systems?

How can we control/manage our costs as we invest in our future?

Even just two years ago, the most frequently asked question was probably "*Why* should we consider open systems—what would we gain?" Today's concern with the two *how* questions signals that times have truly changed.

But, these two *how* questions are difficult to answer. There is no one way, no one answer, and no easy route to open systems. And, as the chapter on definitions and disinformation in this book explains, "open systems" cannot be achieved. Open systems are not a state-of-being-at-a-point-in-time type of thing. "Openness" is a continuum. There is only more open and less open. And, at the same time, "totally open" (if there were such a thing), probably wouldn't be desirable. We live in a world where industry standards and proprietary technology both have their place. And, they will both add value to the marketplace for the foreseeable future.

About This Book...

The goal of this book is to help business leaders and managers to understand the role of open systems in designing distributed information systems and the issues involved with introducing and evolving open systems in an organization. Ultimately, the objective is to help organizations make the difficult technology direction decisions and take advantage of the choices open to them.

The intent of the material is to provide a vendor-neutral, standards organization-neutral introduction to:

- The characteristics of an open computing environment and "degrees of openness" that may exist

- The reasons for implementing (or avoiding) open systems

- The open systems marketplace

- The technology and standards

- The role of the operating system in an open environment

- The "open" direction of several major technology vendors and guidelines on how to assess the "openness" of vendors

- Special information protection issues in an open environment

- The experiences of organizations implementing open systems

    The material also attempts to provide a perspective on:

- The impact of open systems architecture on IS and other parts of the organization

- Where to start planning and creating an open computing environment

This book is an attempt to provide some guidance on the *how* questions. The book is written for both non-technical and technical audiences. Each chapter is relatively self-contained so you should feel free to skip around the book (although arguments do build upon the work contained in previous chapters). Detailed discussions of standards and standards organizations are set off in the text giving you more control over the level of detail you want to absorb.

The structure of the book also gives you some control over what you want to read. Chapters 1 and 2 introduce business and technology issues. Chapters 3 and 4 introduce open systems and the benefits, risks, and costs of open systems to understand why organizations should consider them. Chapters 5-7 portray a perspective on technology and the marketplace. This perspective gives a frame of reference to help formulate the new decision criteria necessary to make technology and product choices. Chapters 8-10 explore the impact of open systems on the business, the end users of technology, and the IS organization. Chapters 11-13 share some experiences of organizations undertaking open systems strategies and compile advice to organizations pondering the question of *how* to implement open systems. The appendices contain descriptions of standards organizations and standards along with a glossary of terminology.

Because the market and technology are changing so rapidly, the information presented is meant to lend some *structure* to the analysis of standards and vendor offerings and serve as an example of how to do the analysis. It is *not* the book's intention to present a detailed analysis of standards, vendor offerings, and options.[1]

And above all, the opinions expressed in this book are my own. They do not necessarily reflect the opinions of Deloitte & Touche LLP, the various companies contributing their experiences, or any standards organization or vendor on the subject of open systems. They are offered to help lend perspective on a very confusing and confused subject.

---

[1] While every attempt has been made in this book to wade through misinformation, identify statement sources, and repeat and attribute statements to organizations only when they were printed in publications under that organization's control, please do not rely on specific vendor and standard information presented in this paper. Check with vendors, standards bodies, and other sources directly for more reliable, up-to-date information.

Acknowledgments

It is truly amazing, when preparing a work of any size or importance, to look back on how many people become involved over the life of the project. This book is no exception. Many people participated in its development: some volunteered, some were drafted, some were coerced, and some didn't even know they contributed—but they did. I would like to take a moment to thank the many people: professional colleagues, friends, relatives, graphics support, administrative personnel, librarians, and publishing staff who helped create this book. It is impossible to name everyone—so many people played a part.

To all of you who contributed, thank you.

And, a very special thanks to:

Bill Atkins—National Practice Advisor, Information Technology Consulting, Deloitte & Touche LLP. Bill is the sponsor of this project and has given it a tremendous amount of support. Projects like these can prematurely age authors and sponsors alike. (*Thanks for your partnership and vision.*)

Charles Popper, Ian Miller, and Richard Bakunas of Merck, Gordon Kerr of Hyatt, and Dave Ellis and Beach Clark Jr. of Home Depot. Charles, Ian, Richard, Gordon, Dave and Beach all contributed candid descriptions of the experiences their respective companies have had with open systems. They also spent a significant amount of time discussing their personal views, insights and concerns about the technology, business and human issues associated with open systems. These men are visionaries in their fields—accomplished business leaders and technologists. And, it is clear that their companies are benefiting from their service. (*Thank you for your candor, your advice and your time.*)

John White—Manager of Technology Supplier Relations at Honeywell. John contributed several careful readings of drafts of this document and many lively, spirited arguments over the direction of parties involved in open systems and interpretations of their statements. He also contributed the experience of Honeywell with open systems. John is a proficient and impressive technologist, an avid mathematician, a staunch believer in the future of open systems, and a master of abstract extension and juxtaposition of theories about life, technology, mathematics, and literature. (*Thank you for your wit and creativity.*)

Fran Reich—a partner at Townsend Consulting. Fran read the original whitepaper on open systems and decided that it should be a book. It is because of her vision that this project has become published. (*Thank you for your foresight, time and advice.*)

Harry B. DeMaio and William H. Murray. Harry is a colleague at Deloitte & Touche's Wilton, CT Computer Audit and Security group, specializing in Information Protection. Harry was drafted to write a chapter about information protection in an open computing environment and (quite cheerfully) struggled to condense his thoughts about the subject into two chapters. Now it looks as if Harry will be writing a full book on the topic. Harry in turn would like to thank William, executive consultant to Deloitte & Touche for assistance with concepts and ideas on information protection in open systems.(*Thanks for your ideas and flowing prose.*)

Raj Joshi, Ben Boller, Romil Bahl—colleagues at Deloitte & Touche in Dallas. Raj, Ben and Romil were drafted to review and report on the open strategies of technology vendors. The Dallas team combed through voluminous piles of mind-numbing detail provided by technology vendors in pursuit of a vision of the current status of technology products and confirmation of the open directions of vendors. (*Thank you for your insight, diligence and fortitude.*)

Seth Montgomery—a colleague at Deloitte & Touche, Minneapolis. Seth deciphered the contents of aging, scribbled lists of standards organizations and standards, and contacted both formal and informal groups around the world, looking for developments, current status, and future directions of standards organizations and standards. Seth contributed to the chapters and compiled the appendices on standards organizations and standards. (*Thank you for your careful attention, long hours and persistence.*)

Dave Scouler—a professional colleague and neighbor. Dave read several drafts, contributed ideas and generally lent insight as the manuscript evolved. Dave is a pragmatic practitioner, a clear thinker, and an accomplished sailor. It is difficult at times to decipher from an observed course, the influence of wind (natural direction), current (flow, turbulence, or undertow) and navigation (purposeful steering). Sometimes, having a sailor on your team provides a unique perspective. (*Thank you for your clarity of thought and time.*)

Jane Cross-Cella, Mark Verbeck, Gary Adams and other Deloitte & Touche practitioners; Mindy Braselton (former Deloitte & Touche); and many other professional associates...There are many people, associates and colleagues, who contributed their ideas, their views and thoughts, and their time. Several patiently read several versions of the manuscript, pointing out incomprehensible logic, languishing points, and just plain boring passages. (*Thank you all for your ideas and assistance, and especially for your tact.*)

Deloitte & Touche Librarians: Rick Reynen, Therese Cotillas and Dan Mesnik; Ann Hogan and the Minneapolis Deloitte & Touche Graphics Staff; Ralph Dumain, Archivist/Librarian, CLR James Institute. Rick, Therese and Dan provided tremendous support throughout the project. They dug up everything from U.S. Bureau of Census statistics, histories of the motorcar and facsimile machines, to quotes given only vague descriptions of subject and author, to detailed material on technologies and organizations. Rick, Therese and Dan never questioned a request for information, even when they couldn't see the slightest of relevance to the topic at hand. Ralph was a bottomless source of information on Esperanto and other esoteric, but relevant topics. Ann and the graphics staff have suffered through several versions of this project over several years. (*Thank you for your speediness, quality and creativity.*)

VNR Publishing: Dianne Littwin, senior editor, Jo-Ann Campbell, of mle design, and countless others. Dianne, Jo-Ann, and many others from VNR contributed their time and energy to bring this project to life. (*Thank you for your spirit, artistry, and attention to detail.*)

And, a very, very special thanks to:

Mark Ambrosen—my husband, who supported me throughout the effort even though it meant late, late nights, lost weekends, dealing with a grumpy dog Misha (after Misha kept me company through the wee hours of the morning), and having to run out and buy a new laser printer in the middle of the project. (*Thank you for your support. We, and Misha, will finally get some sleep.*)

This project has been an incredible learning experience for me. I hope it provides some portion of that value back to the reader.

Chapter 1

Introduction

"Where shall I begin, please your Majesty?" he asked.
"Begin at the beginning," the King said, gravely,
"and go on till you come to the end: then stop."

—Lewis Carroll

> Changes in the business marketplace are causing us to challenge old thoughts on what a business is, how it competes, and how it uses information technology. As the business changes, the Information Systems/Information Technology (IS/IT or IS) function must also change. Where it once played a supporting role, technology today is becoming not only an enabler of business strategies, but also a driver in defining new business competitive capabilities. Therefore, IS can no longer just continue to do what it was doing, just better. It must now change the game it is playing—and in the process, do things better, faster, and less expensively. Systems are an enabler of significant business change. Open systems are an enabler of significant IS change.

The business world that organizations face today is much different from that of a decade ago. Companies long thought to be invincible (General Motors, IBM, Sears Roebuck, American Express, KMart, and many others) are struggling to survive in markets that have been turned upside down.

The upheaval in the business world is epitomized by stories found in several major industries in the U.S.:

* In 1970, the steel industry in the United States produced 70% of the steel in the world. Today, it produces less than 12%. [Donovan, 1993]

* In 1970, the U.S. dominated more than 80% of the world market for automobiles. By 1992, this number was less than 40%. [Donovan, 1993]

* In 1993, Toyota employed 38,000 people to build roughly four million cars. GM needed 800,000 employees to build eight million cars in the same period of time. Moreover, GM's cars had three times as many defects per 100 units rolling off the manu-

facturing line, and took four times as long to go from product design to market introduction. [Donovan, 1993]

- After tax profits of American manufacturers dropped 18% between 1981 and 1990, from $101.3 billion to $91.8 billion. About 1.2 million jobs were lost in the manufacturing sector between 1980 and 1990. [Rukeyser, 1991]

- GM's biggest supplier isn't a steel manufacturer or a tire maker. Instead, it's Blue Cross and Blue Shield. Two of the fastest growing areas in the service economy are business services and health services. [Rukeyser, 1991]

- Today, over 75% of American workers are employed in service producing industries. This is in sharp contrast to the beginning of the 20th century when about 73% of the population worked in agriculture and blue collar occupations, or even in 1952 when 58.6% were employed in services. For the first time in history, most Americans do not produce the things we all need to live. [Rukeyser, 1991]

- Electronics has become one of the world's fastest growing industries. The U.S. electronics industry has grown from $200 million in 1927 to $266 billion in 1990. Sales of electronic products grew 50% faster than the rest of the economy during the 1980's and the U.S. electronics industry now rivals the chemical, auto, and steel industries in size. [Rukeyser, 1991]

- In the electronics industry, foreign competition severely undercut U.S. rivals in the mid 1980's. In 1979, six American companies made television sets. Today, only one, Zenith, is left. Similarly, U.S. manufacturers supply less than 10% of the VCRs sold in America. Today in the U.S. there are 201 million television sets reaching 98% of all households. VCRs are in 65% of homes, up from 20% in 1984. [Rukeyser, 1991]

- AT&T deftly avoided what many analysts thought was imminent demise after it cut a deal in 1982 with the U.S. Justice department as a 1974 anti-trust suit moved towards trial. AT&T spun off its 22 operating phone companies and retained the competitive business of long distance service and equipment manufacturing. Through the economic staying power of a large advertising budget, massive layoffs, divestitures, and cost slashing, the telecommunications giant managed to hold most of its marketshare, grow its revenue, and keep earnings in the black. [Rukeyser, 1991]

The Changing Business Environment

Changes such as these in the business environment are forcing companies to re-invent themselves just to survive. One factor forcing these make-overs is increased competition, worldwide. The competition may come from companies within the marketplace (intra-market) or from new entries outside the marketplace (inter-market). (See Figure 1.1.)

FACTORS IN THE BUSINESS ENVIRONMENT

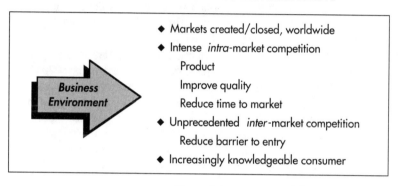

♦ Markets created/closed, worldwide

♦ Intense *intra*-market competition

Product

Improve quality

Reduce time to market

♦ Unprecedented *inter*-market competition

Reduce barrier to entry

♦ Increasingly knowledgeable consumer

Figure 1.1

In today's business world, for instance, the intra-market competitive focus is on products and services—feature differentiation, speed to market, quality, and price. And competition in these areas comes from different sources. While businesses are casting an eager eye on new market opportunities, they are also maintaining a careful watch for new competitors in their own backyard. It is increasingly true that competition may come from sources that may not have seemed even a remote possibility several years ago.

Another factor forcing businesses to reinvent themselves is the new breed of consumer. The new age consumer is much more selective in choosing products and services than those of previous generations. S/he has a great deal of information about competitor products and the competition in general. And, s/he is much more knowledgeable about features, functions, manufacturing processes, assembly processes, touch-up processes, distribution channels, markups, markons, markdowns, gross margins, and costs in general. This consumer is definitely a tough customer.

How is business responding? As competition heats up, and the rate of change speeds up, and customers become more discriminating, we are seeing a growing number of business partnerships—organizations teaming together, collaborating on products and services. The partnership concept is more picturesquely described in terms of a "virtual organization." A "virtual organization" is based on partnership contributions to a specific product or service. Partnerships may be formed *within* or *between* organizations, but are always formed to create or provide a specific product or service.

In early 1983, Hewlett-Packard (HP) engineers in Boise, Idaho, set out to develop a desktop laser printer for the office market. Back then, the prevailing model for computer printers was the so-called "impact" or "daisy-wheel printer," which was affordable but disappointing in quality. The cheapest laser printer, used only with mainframe computers, cost more than $100,000. HP engineers were anxious to get a product to the market. In the interest of speed, they bucked the "not invented here" culture of HP. They designed the electronic formatting components of its printers, using Motorola chips, had Microsoft and others write the software, and had Canon assemble some of the final product in Japan.

Astonishingly, by the following year's spring Comdex computer show, HP introduced its first LaserJet printer for $3,495—a desktop machine that instantly shifted the industry paradigm and at the same time altered HP's own accepted rules of how to do business.

The results were hard to challenge: HP seized the top spot in the new desktop laser printing market, where it remains today. HP sells more laser printers annually in the U.S. than the other 127 suppliers put together. It is estimated to have a 54% world market share. HP's Boise Printer Division makes up 40% of the firm's income prior to taxes.

The experience changed the company. [Huey, 1991; Design, 1994]

The strengthening partnership between suppliers and manufacturers in a variety of industries is a good example of the virtual organization. Suppliers are participating with manufacturers in early product conceptualization, design, and planning to smooth development and delivery capabilities, and to manage product costs together.

"Virtual organizations" pay less attention to organizational structures and boundaries, and more attention to the value each partner adds to the end-product or service, whatever it is.

The bottom line? Today's business environment requires organizations to constantly reinvent themselves to survive. We are coming to realize that the only sustainable advantage is the ability to continuously change—to continuously, and quickly, respond to new business situations and demands in the market.

Change: Today's Business Challenge

The key to continuous change lies in our ability to perpetually evolve our business processes, our people, and our information systems. (See Figure 1.2.) Businesses are mastering this "evolution process" by learning how to learn, when to learn, and how much to learn. Business Process Reengineering (BPR) and Total Quality Management (TQM) are just two of the many corporate make-over programs taking the business world by storm. Radical, fundamental, discontinuous change followed by continual, incremental improvement is proving to be an effective formula for re-establishing competitive positions and responding to market shifts. The challenge, of course, is in developing business processes, systems capabilities, and people that are flexible, capable and willing to change.

TODAY'S BUSINESS CHALLENGE
CONTINUAL METAMORPHOSIS

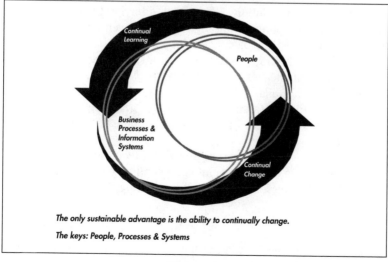

Figure 1.2

The IS Crisis

Some IS[1] organizations across the country and around the world are immersed in this kind of evolving, radical change. Many others, however, are embattled in crisis.

In the past, IS was established to manage technology. IS quizzed the business on its direction and needs, selected technology, developed huge systems, and implemented them. Little attention was paid to the end-user in this process, and the users revolted. They did not like complex screens, funky keyboard commands, and inconsistent, confusing user interfaces. They wanted systems that were easier to comprehend and use. The new battle cry became "user involvement" and IS set out to work with the end users. Decisions about what to build were pushed down from executive business management to key user departments and key users. Business unit budgets swelled to accommodate the new direct responsibility for systems support of their activities. Flush budgets and squeaky wheels got the attention of the systems department. As systems functionality accumulated, IS spent an increasing amount of time operating and supporting the systems. And along with systems support, IS added to its growing responsibilities the task of managing long lists of user requests and the difficult job of allocating scarce resources. IS grew. But, demand far outstripped supply. As the IS organization grew, its management ranks filled out and overhead costs swelled.

With these ever-increasing IS backlogs and costs, users began to seek alternative solutions. They started buying their own technology, personal computers, midrange systems, even mainframes, their own software, and their own technology services.

Today, with IS backlogs, lead times, and expenditures at a record high, businesses are understandably up in arms about the value of IS. IS is similarly distraught over its inability to keep up with rising demand for its services, and the growing departmental computing fiefdoms that will ultimately become its responsibility to integrate.

Basically, within many organizations, technology leadership is being fumbled. In the past, technology vendors provided technology leadership. Businesses bought both technology and their technolo-

---

[1]Throughout the book, we will use "IS" as an abbreviation for the internal Information Systems/Information Technology group(s) of an organization.

gy direction directly from vendors. Through open systems, technology direction is being passed from individual technology vendors to the industry as a whole. And, control over the technology direction within the business is being passed from the primary technology vendor servicing the business to IS. Within the industry, technology direction is being assumed by industry standards bodies and vendor consortia. Within many businesses, however, the transfer of control over the technology direction is being lost. Decisions—affecting the scope and functionality of applications, and ultimately affecting technology investments—are being made at lower and lower levels in both the user and IS organizations. Ultimately, a cohesive view and strategy for the overall technology direction is left unattended and unmanaged.

Today's IS Challenge—Into the Fire!

Another factor intensifying the crisis is that, while demand for IS is growing, IS budgets are flat or declining. At the same time, businesses are issuing a new challenge to IS: sharpen the business competitiveness, deliver significant new functionality, build systems that can be continually changed, integrate business units and work teams, and do all this while driving down unit costs and managing the risk to the business. (See Figure 1.3.)

Business Challenges to IS

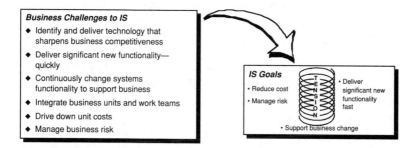

Figure 1.3

Obviously IS cannot win at the game it is playing. So it is time to change the game.

In the past, IS has assumed the role of technology owner in the organization. As a technology owner, IS evaluated, selected, and purchased technology, and planned, designed, and built applications. Essentially, the IS function translated business needs into technology. IS also set the priorities. This was the most expedient way to get technology into the organization and probably the only way to get it up and running given the mysteries and idiosyncrasies of technology. And, given the state of technology, businesses really had no choice but to dedicate a function to ministering to it. But, today's technology is much more usable, and much more ubiquitous in business operations. And, today's user is much more technology savvy and demanding of both technology and IS. The new challenge is to change IS from being the sole owners of technology to being *advisors* on how to use technology. The change effectively boils down to redefining the role of IS and increasing the quality and *value* of IS service, increasing the *volume* of services, changing the infrastructure, and investing in the future—while at the same time, driving down the unit cost of service.

A tall order.

In many respects the IS department is assuming the "hot seat" as a function that is absolutely required to create business change and is often a barrier to it. The CIO is assuming the "hottest seat" at the management round table.[2] IS initiatives in the past might be characterized as "getting out of the trees and above the forest"— looking up from the technology idiosyncrasies and problems to understand the business issues the technology is to solve. While the approach does get you further (your actions are better related to the business issues) the problem is that you tend to continue to do the same things. You are still in the same environment—you see the same trees, just more of them. A different approach is to reevaluate what IS is doing and try something different—such as "jump out of the frying pan and into the fire." It may be hot, but at least you have changed your environment.

At the same time there is a very real challenge being issued back to users and the business. The issues around information and technology are more complex than ever. Technology is more complex, systems are more complex, and business needs are tougher to

---

[2]The Deloitte & Touche LLP annual CIO Survey of *Leading Trends in Information Systems* reported that the CIO turnover rate in the U.S. increased from 14% in 1991 to 17.5% in 1992 to 18.8% in 1993.

anticipate and plan for. Users, business leaders and IS all need to work together to redefine their respective roles and responsibilities.

"Open systems" are a tool in the IS "kit bag" for managing the cost of technology and easing the integration burden. Open systems also makes things possible that otherwise would be either technically impossible or so uneconomical to be effectively impossible. At the root of open systems are goals to support the sharing of information, eliminating reinvention and redundancy through componentization and reuse, and developing common views of things and common ways of doing things to minimize the learning curve generally associated with technology. These goals hold as true and useful in building and integrating systems as they do in purchasing technology.

Where Business and Technology (Finally!) Meet

Using technology is not a business advantage in its own right. Using technology *well* is the deciding factor. Companies that compete effectively in rapidly changing markets are doing so by using technology to rapidly change themselves—to continually improve and change their business and decision processes as market conditions change.

Using technology well is not as simple as selecting and implementing "best of breed" technology products. Instead, it means understanding where technology can be used to improve or change the organization. Robert Benjamin of the Sloan Management School observes that with the support of technology, an organization can:

- Move the locus of knowledge and hence the power in an organization

- Change the time dimensions of business processes and decisions

- Enable new organizational constructs [Benjamin, 1992]

But using technology well means understanding that technology can both enable and complicate organizational change. To use technology well, organizations need to transform themselves into learning, "information-driven" entities, able to assess technology developments, envision the benefit to the business, and assimilate beneficial technology developments—quickly and effectively. For most organizations that means significant change. And, for most organizations, that means changing how they view technology and its role in defining and shaping the organization's products, services, and structure.

The futures of business and technology are beginning to converge. With this convergence, we are seeing a respective recognition of need and value. A business manager becomes part programmer as s/he writes spread sheet macros, queries a corporate database, and formats custom reports and presentations. An IT staff member becomes part business strategist as s/he joins with business counterparts to build linked business and technology plans. A CIO joins the executive management team as s/he brainstorms with other executives on the future of the marketplace, the business, and the technology needed to make it happen.

There are few subjects as important to the future competitiveness of an organization, to the viability of whole industries, and to the economic well being of countries, as information systems. And there are few topics within systems that are as hotly debated and full of misinformation and emotion as open systems. But, even as battles rage on, in many respects, the open systems war has been won. Open systems followers are no longer viewed as "oddball." Instead, the purveyors and supporters of proprietary systems are now on the defense.

A prime reason for the shift is that technology is becoming a driver in business strategy. Use of technology can hold the key to competitiveness of the business organization. Open systems are an enabler for dramatically increasing the usability and flexibility of systems as well as driving down the unit operating costs of IS.

As we are coming to the realization that open systems simply "must be," the market is taking a wild, confused path towards open systems. Standards organizations are embarking on what often ends up to be parallel, competitive development efforts. Standards are being defined at the same time as technology products that "support" the standards are being developed. Vendors are waging wild competitive wars, forming alliances to promote products that both *comply with* and *compete with* standards. David House, of Intel, made a poignant observation a few years ago that is still holds true today:

> *The oldest marketing technique in the world is to create confusion if you are losing. There are a lot of companies spending a lot of money to create confusion.*
>
> —David L. House, Intel Corp., commenting on the open systems marketplace [Verity, 1991]

The one thing the marketplace is succeeding at is creating confusion. But, it is not as bad as it looks at first blush. There is good news. Users are banding together to try to make sense of the industry and inject some influence over its direction. Real progress is being made. Real products exist. Although the market still has a long way to go, it has already come a long distance.

The Open Systems Marketplace

Ultimately, open systems are all about implementing a base of systems capabilities that works, is economical, and provides a stable foundation for adding more functionality as business computing needs grow and change. The only way an organization can provide this kind of foundation is by being in tune with the direction of the technology market, rather than with the direction of a given technology vendor. For organizations without unique, specific technology needs, the best way to proceed is to implement technology that adheres to and supports industry standards and the direction of the industry as a whole (using *de jure* "specifications" or *de facto* "products").

Staying in tune with the open systems technology market isn't easy. But, we can describe the market in terms of a few key components. (See Figure 1.4.)

THE OPEN SYSTEMS INDUSTRY

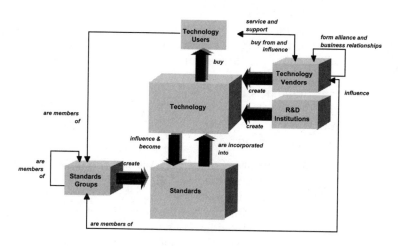

Figure 1.4

In brief, these components are:

- **Standards**—At the foundation of open systems are industry standards that define component functionality and interaction between components of a computing environment. Standards can be written by organizations established specifically for the purpose of creating technology standards, or written by vendors as specifications for using their products or creating "like" products. When standards exist, technology products can be created that are "compliant" with the standards, thereby allowing the products to work together, using functionality and interfaces defined by the standards.

- **Technology**—Technology products are developed by vendors and research institutions. Technology products generally lead standards—that is, technology products are often in effect "proofs of concept" of standards. Technology products that are innovative and popular often become *de facto* standards. The specifications for popular technology products may be subsequently formalized into industry standards. When formal industry specifications exist, products can be certified as "compliant with" the industry standards.

- **Standards bodies and influencers**—Standards organizations, consisting of independent industry participants, vendors, and users, work to define the need for industry standards, and the standards themselves. Some standards organizations work at a base level, defining individual technology standards. Some organizations have undertaken the charter of integrating formal standards into frameworks consisting of many standards that identify and define the component functionality of distributed computing environments. Other organizations concern themselves primarily with defining *requirements* for standards.

- **Technology vendors**—Vendors create technology products. They participate as members of standards organizations in defining and integrating standards. Additionally, vendors form informal alliances with other technology vendors and participate in more formal vendor consortia to select and support products that they hope will become *de facto* standards.

- **Research and Development** (R&D)—Research and development facilities and academic institutions, such as MIT and Berkeley, are technology innovators. As part of their research activities, they develop new technologies and often receive funding from technology vendors or government agencies.

- **Technology users**—Users implement technology in their organizations. Technology users also define requirements for technology and standards as members of formal and informal standards organizations.

The Era of Connectivity is Upon Us

At some levels, open systems exist. Real products are in real use, today. At other levels, a lot of work yet needs to be done. And, it is not always clear *by whom?* Regrettably, a master blueprint for the evolution of technology does not exist. Of even more concern is the reality that the path through technology creation, selection, and evolution is such that choices made upstream limit others down the line.

However, one thing is clear. Open systems are *the only path for distributing computing resources.* No single vendor can do it all. Multi-national organizations are already dealing with the complexities of distributed computing and multi-vendor environments. Organizations with a high percentage of "knowledge workers" are struggling with how to design distributed access to corporate information. Information technology paradigms are being smashed, and a new era of connectivity is emerging. Fifteen or twenty years from now, we will look back on this time as being pivotal in redefining the role of technology in organizations, and perhaps, in defining the organization itself.

Open systems is a philosophy, an attitude, a characteristic of systems. Open systems is inviting in its simplicity, but beneath the simplicity (and indeed supporting the simplicity) is a complex and difficult reality.

Chapter 2

Information Systems in Perspective—Smashing OLD Paradigms

There is one thing stronger than all the armies in the world; and that is an idea whose time has come.

—*Victor Hugo*

Anyone who has begun to think places some portion of the world in jeopardy.

—*John Dewey*

Our views on information technology are evolving along with our views on business. We are entering the era of connectivity—focused on linking computing resources together into workgroups, integrated business flows and inter-enterprise "virtual organizations." Open systems architecture provides the foundation for this enterprise connectivity.

The challenge to evolve continuously requires a willingness to break free of old paradigms or patterns of thought or behavior. Although the phrase "paradigm shift" has been widely used, the term aptly describes the challenge. Paradigms are useful in developing an understanding of things. We use paradigms to understand and manage complexity. For example, we operate within a paradigm when we drive a car:

- We drive on the right (in the U.S.)

- We stop at red, go at green

- We go slow in residential areas, fast on highways, and so on

In this case, stepping out of the paradigm actually endangers us.

Sometimes, however, paradigms are as limiting as they are helpful. And sometimes paradigms need to be shifted because of new discoveries, developments and understanding.

For over a thousand years we believed that earth was at the center of the universe and ignored all common sense signs to the contrary—such as the sun seeming to "rise" in the east and "set" in the west. We explained away observable phenomena contrary to our belief as true "happenings" in the heavens. Because of the fundamental error in our belief, we couldn't keep calendars in sync with astronomical observations and consequently built complicated mathematical formulas, "epicycles," to correct for the deviations.

The "earth at the center of the universe" theory was also at the center of our religious belief system and it was considered heresy to challenge the concept. This complication made it particularly difficult and dangerous for scientists and philosophers to challenge the theory—even to themselves. Rational thought and logic were no match for belief and religion. Belief and religion led science. Finally, Copernicus supplied the mathematics and later Galileo the telescope, to prove, once and for all, that the earth rotated around the sun. (And those messy epicycle calculations weren't needed anymore.)

In another example of paradigm smashing, an ancient Chinese Tao philosopher, Chuang-tse, when criticizing the narrow view of followers of the competing Confucius doctrine wrote, "A well-frog cannot imagine the ocean, nor can a summer insect conceive of ice. How then can a scholar understand the Tao? He is restricted by his own learning." [Hoff, 1992]

Though we are aware of historical struggles between logic and "accepted fact," it is tough to recognize the paradigms within which we, ourselves, operate. One of my coworkers is fond of saying, "The fish doesn't know the water in which it swims." (This is obviously a very deep philosophical statement.) But, tough as it is to recognize paradigms, in order to create significant change, we need to be aware of the restrictions they place on our thinking.

Today, many organizational "well-frogs" are dreaming of salt water, sun and palm trees. As these well-frogs breathe life into those dreams, traditional business relationships and operational paradigms are blown away. For example:

Old paradigm—Retailers buy products from manufacturers, then promote them and present them to customers for sale.

New paradigm—Retailers are an extended distribution arm for manufacturers. Many major retailers (e.g.,

KMart, WalMart) are asking manufacturers to manage shelf space for them, participate in advertising, and share (or even assume) the risk of inventory. In some cases, payment is transferred from the retailer to the manufacturer when the product is sold, rather than when it is received from the manufacturer.

Old paradigm—Consumers buy products from retailers.

New paradigm—The consumer catalog business has grown more than 7%, more than doubling in sales to about $60 billion in 1992. In 1993, catalog sales grew 12%-15% from a year earlier, more than double the overall growth rate of retail sales. [Investor's, 1994]

Old paradigm—Automobile manufacturers *manufacture* automobiles and are vertically integrated to design, create, and assemble all of the components of an automobile.

New paradigm—The automobile manufacturer's job will be managing the integration of the vehicle, selecting suppliers, building relationships, and managing the overall process. Suppliers will be involved throughout the process from the very earliest stages of planning and design. Suppliers and automobile manufacturers together become links in the chain, from raw materials to finished product.

Old paradigm—Banks in the United States are financial intermediaries that earn their income by making loans and accepting deposits.

New paradigm—The role of financial intermediary is increasingly usurped by financial markets. Banks, meanwhile, are becoming fee-for-service providers. In 1989 a typical regional bank earned 17% of its income from fees, by 1992 fee income represented 38%. [Springfield, 1993]

As the marketplace continues to change, there will be more paradigm smashing. When organizations ask questions like: "What business are we in?," "What is our competitive edge in that business?," and "What are our core competencies?" and answer those questions honestly, paradigms begin to crumble. Traditional notions of "vertical integration" and market dominance, for instance, are replaced with seemingly radical notions of "partnership" and niche market targeting. New paradigms are created to reflect the new reality.

Technology Infrastructures Mirror Corporate Infrastructures

Nowhere is paradigm smashing more visible than in the use of technology. For years corporate information and technology architectures duplicated hierarchical corporate operational structures in their design, growth, and evolution. The predominant technology architecture found in large organizations today was originally designed to support centralized authority and decision-making. This architecture summarized operational and accounting data together into corporate information systems. Corporate management reviewed the summary and used it to set high-level direction. Tracy Kidder wrote of this use of technology:

> *Computers probably did not create the growth of conglomerates and multinational corporations, but they certainly have abetted it. They make fine tools for the centralization of power, if that's what those who buy them want to do with them. They are handy greed extenders.*
>
> [Kidder, *The Soul of a New Machine*, 1982]

But, old hierarchical reporting structures are crumbling as the old business paradigms they served are smashed. Organizations are scrambling to respond to new business situations. In the process, they are often finding that their old information systems stand as an almost insurmountable barrier to change (often to their great surprise). Systems built to support the old hierarchical corporate structure, with their "function" domains and "result of operations" reporting focus, are not well suited to support information sharing, work flow management, process tracking, and "right now" process status inquiries. Increasingly, therefore, old hierarchical systems architectures and the infrastructures that support them are being replaced with structures supporting a more "horizontal" view of business activities.

"Horizontal" information architectures emphasize integration of business activities into workflows sharing access to common information. A short-term goal of a "horizontal" architecture is to help an organization be more responsive to uncommon or unanticipated business situations by distributing operational business decisions and supporting information closer to the business situation. A longer-term goal is to build flexibility into information systems architectures to help an organization be more aware of market shifts and demands, and more "agile" in its response.

Our Philosophy of Computing is Evolving

In other words, as our corporate infrastructures are changing, our views of computing and the role of technology in the organization are also changing—fundamentally. (See Figure 2.1.)

THE EVOLUTION OF TECHNOLOGY IN BUSINESS

	Centralized Capabilities and Operations		Distributed Capabilities
	1960's–70's	1970's–80's	1980's–90's
Systems Focus	Accounting and control	Operations support	Decision support
Technology	Mainframe	Minicomputer/ Midframe	Desktop workstations/ Personal computers
Primary Users	Central, corporate	Departments and small businesses	End users
Major Projects	Expansion and diversification of accounting functions	Decentralization of systems and new technology investments	New systems to support strategies for market leadership
New System Capabilities	Data collection management reporting	Process support	Data access and analysis
Alignment	Vertical—along management lines		Horizontal—along process lines

Figure 2.1

When computers were first introduced into the workplace in the fifties and sixties, corporate functions such as accounting and financial reporting were the first to be automated.

Minicomputers and midrange machines followed in the 1970's and 1980's. Both were lower cost and able to support the operations of departments and small to medium-sized businesses.

The 1980's also saw the introduction of the personal computer into the business world. In ten years, personal computers became a $50B industry. [Cerutti, 1993] Personal-computers-turned-desktop-workstations were aimed at advancing personal productivity through the likes of spreadsheets and word processing. Through the personal computer, vendors came to realize that the end user was a huge, unserved market for technology products. The end user as a knowledgeable consumer was born.

Another result of the personal computer phenomenon was that the paradigm of the "information technology industry serves IS departments" was smashed. Emerging from the rubble was the information technology and services industry, targeting information needs on many levels from IS to end user.

The Particular Role of the Microprocessor

Despite this evolution, some businesses still have a problem defining the role of technology in their organization. Part of the problem in envisioning this role and managing technology evolution in an organization has been our own biases in what various technologies can and should do. For example, the mainframe has always been connected with "enterprise-level" functions and the microcomputer has been connected with "personal-level" functions. But our concept of a mainframe and a microcomputer were formed thirteen to fifteen years ago, when personal computers were introduced into our business world. Since then, each new generation of microprocessor has doubled the performance of the previous generation—at about the same list price as the previous generation. (The Intel processor is traced as an example in Figure 2.2.) New microprocessor generations have been introduced like clockwork—at eighteen month intervals. At the same time, the conventional mainframe has been experiencing a 20-22 percent compound annual growth rate—resulting in a new generation of mainframes approximately every three-and-a-half years. In the three-and-a-half years it takes to double the capacity of a mainframe, the microprocessor quadruples.

We are at the point now where the raw performance of the microprocessor is on the verge of surpassing the raw performance of a mainframe processor. This is the new microcomputer—or "personal" computer/workstation/server—a startling difference from ten years ago, when we first formed our opinions of what a microcomputer could do and what its role in information systems was.

INTEL PROCESSORS—MIPS

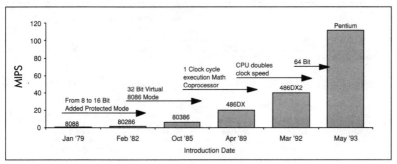

Figure 2.2

As microprocessors have revolutionized computing, parallel architectures are taking the revolution even further, by wiring microprocessors together—harnessing the power and benefiting from the cost efficiencies of mass production. These parallel architectures will become the new generation of "mainframes."

The microprocessor has had a powerful impact on the present and future of technology—that we know. In addition, it is significantly affecting the work habits of individuals. And, it is beginning to have a significant impact on organizational work flow and the location and timing of business activities. *It may be a long time before we fully understand the impact of the microprocessor on our business organizations.*

The Era of Connectivity

The microprocessor has brought us into a new era in computing—the era of connectivity. (See Figure 2.3.)

THE EVOLUTION OF TECHNOLOGY IN BUSINESS

	Centralized Capabilities and Operations →		Distributed Capabilities →	
	1960's–70's	1970's–80's	1980's–90's	1990's–?
Systems Focus	Accounting and control	Operations support	Decision support	Workgroups, information sharing
Technology	Mainframe	Minicomputer/ Midframe	Desktop workstations/ Personal computers	Interconnected networks
Primary Users	Central, corporate	Departments and small businesses	End users	Dynamic workgroups, virtual collectives
Major Projects	Expansion and diversification of accounting functions	Decentralization of systems and new technology investments	New systems to support strategies for market leadership	Facilitate computing "collectives" or communities Support business partnerships
New System Capabilities	Data collection management reporting	Process support	Data access and analysis	Distributed access to common, shared, context-sensitive information
Alignment	◄ Vertical—along management lines ►		◄ Horizontal—along process lines ►	

Figure 2.3

Our focus is shifting from developing and enlarging isolated units of computing to networking, through which we integrate bastions of computing, to *sharing information and computing resources.* The new focus, therefore, is on designing an integrated, distributed information and technology infrastructure.

Characteristics of a Distributed Information and Technology Infrastructure

A distributed computing environment addresses the need to integrate business activities, processes, and information. It does so by distributing, or sharing, *access* to information and computing resources, or by distributing the resources themselves.

Structurally, distributed computing can be organized vertically (centralized) or *horizontally* (decentralized).

- Vertical structures distribute access to a central backbone of computing resources. It's not surprising that companies like IBM, Unisys and Bull, with their heritage of enterprise applications, all offer primarily centralized architectures.

- Horizontal structures distribute the computing resources themselves, linking resources and nodes together as peers. DEC, Sun, and other vendors with departmental computing experience have created decentralized, horizontal structures.

Distributed computing environments may be *homogeneous* or *heterogeneous*.

- Homogeneous environments consist of similar or identical computing platforms supplied by a single vendor.

- Heterogeneous environments contain disparate platforms supplied by multiple vendors.

In a distributed environment, applications design follows the "work flow" or "business process." Data is shared among workgroup members and designed and protected as a corporate asset. An emphasis on networking and integration supports intra- and inter-process information sharing and communication. Patricia Seybold's Office Computing Group provides the following definition:

> *A distributed computing environment is an architecture consisting of a set of protocols, interfaces, and services that provide users and applications with transparent access to data, resources, and other services across a heterogeneous network.*

> —Patricia Seybold's Office Computing Group
> [Interop,1990]

In most organizations, technological heterogeneity is a fact of life. Whether by design, by corporate acquisition, or by chance, enterprise-wide information technology is a collection of products from a multitude of vendors. The real challenge is how to make them all work together.

So What Does All This Have To Do With Open Systems?

It is difficult to separate discussions of distributed computing from discussions of open systems architecture. Distributed computing adds significantly to the complexity of the computing environment, because of added functionality, a larger number of participating nodes, and heterogeneity (products from multiple vendors). Beneath this added complexity, we need a technological framework to make it all work.

What type of framework? One that *identifies the functionality* necessary to support distributed computing. The framework must also provide a *basis for defining* seemingly simple things, such as all of the processors participating in a network having the same concept of time in order to properly time stamp and handle transactions. The framework also needs to support more complex things such as knowing what resources and services are available and how to access them.

And, the technological framework must be both *flexible and stable*. It must be flexible enough to support a wide variety of functions and applications, and stable in order to serve as a base upon which the added functionality associated with distributed computing can be built over time.

One other thing: the technological framework, by necessity, *cannot be vendor-proprietary*. Heterogeneous computing environments are commonplace. The framework must support products from multiple vendors.

Open Systems Are the Only (Realistic) Way to Create Distributed Systems

"Open systems" standards, woven together into an open systems architecture, form the technical framework, the foundation making possible integration of software and hardware products from multiple vendors. While individual vendors may significantly influence, or even drive the technology direction of a portion of the computing environment (e.g., Microsoft and the desktop), no single vendor can set the technology direction for the marketplace as a whole. The computing environment is too complex. The days of a single vendor being able to dominate in everything are gone.

Open systems is the *only* way, realistically, to distribute computing resources.

As such, open systems are the basis for a new computing paradigm. A new model based on sharing information and computing resources in corporate-wide and inter-company networks. And, a model that addresses the need to integrate business activities, processes, and information to help the business become more aware of and responsive to market changes and demands.

Chapter 3

Definitions and Disinformation
—And Then There Was Chaos

I would far rather feel remorse than know how to define it.
—Thomas A. Kempis

> Early concepts of open systems focused on the UNIX operating system—using UNIX as a "standard" operating system platform. Over time, the scope of the open systems vision has expanded from a common operating system platform to encompass a full computing environment—specification of component functionality and standards for interfacing with the component functionality.
>
> Definitions of open systems and descriptions of the attendant properties give us a framework for discussing open systems. The individual definitions of open systems published by various technology vendors and standards organizations highlight the points of concurrence and disagreement between parties setting and following the direction of open systems.
>
> Bottom line: "Openness" is not something that can be acquired, or implemented. The concept is a continuum and as such, "open" can never be fully achieved—there is only "more open" and "less open."

According to William Safire in *Quoth the Maven* [Safire, 1993], the term "disinformation" was first used in the Soviet Union by the predecessor to the K.G.B. to mean the "manipulation of a nation's intelligence system through the injection of credible, but misleading data." Since then, the use of such data has become so prevalent that the word has a more universal definition today—"Incorrect and deliberately misleading information leaked especially by an intelligence agency as a means for negating and discrediting authentic information that an enemy has obtained." [The American Heritage Dictionary]

"Disinformation" is clearly not confined to international intelligence. The term is quite applicable in the technology and information systems arena, and no area is more rife with disinformation than open systems. A quick breeze through articles, periodicals, books, and vendor literature will reveal more opinions on what, where, and how useful open systems are than would be thought possible. The amount of disinformation should not come as a surprise though. The pure concept of open systems challenges the fundamental beliefs (based on their business strategies) of most technology vendors. Defining common terminology, developing consensus, and playing by rules are concepts foreign to the type of innovative minds that create technology. "Cooperation," too, is foreign to minds that benefit from monopolistic-level profits.

Open Systems—What They Are Not!

It is often helpful when defining something, particularly something that is somewhat difficult to define, to begin with what that something is not.

- The term "Open Systems" is not related to a particular hardware platform.

- The term is not a code word for "downsizing" (moving applications from a mainframe to a midrange or microcomputer platform or network).

  P.S. It also does not relate to any other variation on the "sizing" theme (such as "upsizing" or "rightsizing").

- Open systems do not necessarily involve personal computing or some other concept of end user driven computing (although end users have been a significant force in pushing the industry towards open systems).

- Open systems do not require a particular product or operating system. UNIX was the first "open" operating system (because the specifications were freely published and available for nominal charge, and many vendors subsequently made UNIX available on their platforms), and as such, UNIX is often associated with open systems. But, it is disinformation that suggests that by purchasing UNIX or any UNIX variant, one has created an open system. An operating system is but one component of the overall computing environment (an important one, but yet only a single component).

- Open systems cannot be purchased from a particular vendor. Although a given vendor may practice openness within its own set of products, the concept of openness crosses vendors.

With some ideas of what open systems are not, let's look at what they are.

Open Systems Are Based on Standards

Unfortunately, we cannot at this point come up with a definitive statement of what constitutes an open system because the industry has not come to agreement on a definition. To lead up to an understanding of the variety of definitions, however, we can look at various elements, characteristics, and properties of open systems, as well as at their history. At a base level, the industry agrees that open systems consist of computer hardware and software that conform to and are based on *computing standards*.

> Standards play an important role in everyday life. Kilometers and miles, weights and measures, calendars, timepieces, green lights, and black tie events all are examples of standards in our society.
>
> Standards also play an important role in music. The pitch, volume, timbre, and rhythm of sounds are described by notes and notations such as key signature, time signature, accents, accidentals, and other instructions. The method of musical notation allows one to describe a musical thought:
>
> *melodic line, harmonic progression, rhythmic variation, and composer's interpretation...*
>
> ...in a universal vocabulary transcending all language barriers.

Just as musical notation standards allow a collection and variety of musicians and instruments to play a musical composition together, computing standards defining communications and operations allow a collection and variety of computers to communicate, share information, and support the same programs and applications.

Computing standards are specifications or technologies that have widespread acceptance within the computing industry. Standards define the operation of various components in a computing environment to support interaction between those components. Computing *standards* differ from *products* in that standards define functionality expectations at an *interface level* rather than an *execution* level. In other words, standards define what functionality should exist and how it is accessed, rather than how that functionality should execute. A product, on the other hand, embodies the standard and complies with it when executing the prescribed functionality.

Open Systems—Who Needs Them?

There is an old joke about a physician, an engineer, and an IS manager each claiming that his respective profession was the oldest in the world. The physician said that his profession was the oldest because God created Eve using one of Adam's ribs. That was surgery. The engineer objected with the argument that before God brought Adam and Eve to life, he created the universe. That was engineering. The IS manager countered that before God created the universe, there was chaos...and we all know what profession best creates chaos.

Without open systems standards, chaos would rule. Technology development and evolution, spearheaded by individual vendors with no degree of coordination across users would result in a level of haphazardness at a macro, industry level. Haphazardness at an industry level will preclude us from linking technologies into distributed communications and information networks. It is at this industry level, across vendors and between products, that technology users require standards supporting interconnectivity and interoperability to shape, assemble, bridge, and connect technologies. But, open systems are not an easy proposition. Defining standards requires technology vendors to cooperate on a level previously unthinkable—they must not only agree to industry standards, but they also need to share specifications and technology.

Where It All Started...

The genesis of open systems came in the late 1970's. Prior to that time, communication between computers was limited to compatible machines *within* a given vendor's line of computing hardware. Each vendor developed its own set of *proprietary* communication protocols. Such communication protocols are called "proprietary" because they are controlled by a single entity. Some vendors (such as IBM) published their own communication protocols (e.g., 3270, SNA) to allow other machines to connect with theirs. But publishing protocols did not solve the problem of inter-vendor connectivity. Proprietary protocols were modified solely by the vendor and at the vendor's discretion. As with any proprietary product, the vendor was free to change the definitions at whim. It soon became clear that non-proprietary protocols were necessary.

> Two non-proprietary protocol suites were introduced in the late 70's. One, the Internet suite of communication protocols, was sponsored by the U.S. Department of Defense (DoD), a large user of technology. The other, the Open Systems Interconnect (OSI) suite of protocols, was sponsored by International Organization for Standardization (ISO). Although the two protocol suites were started at roughly the same time, the Internet suite has been widely adopted, not only in the defense industry, but also worldwide in both government and private sector, and in virtually all industries from engineering to retail. In contrast with the Internet suite of protocols that was brought to life by the DoD, the OSI suite was planned from the start as an international standard. Ironically, the high goals of the OSI suite have been a barrier to its becoming a reality. OSI standards have been contributed to, commented on, and protracted by experts from every continent. [Rose, 1990]

The Internet communication protocols showed that open systems were indeed possible. But, it was also apparent that standards were needed at more levels than just computer communications. Simply getting two machines to talk to each other was an important, but small step towards sharing information and computing resources. Academic institutions, research institutions, and finally industry standards organizations and consortia set about to define standards at all levels of computing.

Open systems, based on "standards," describe a framework within which vendor cooperation is possible. But defining (definitively) what they are, even in concept, proves elusive. Standards organizations and consortia (in particular, X/Open and OSF) are pioneering definitions of the concepts and content of open systems for government and business users. Each major technology vendor's own definition of open systems has evolved and continues to evolve.

A review of the definitions of open systems published by standards bodies and major technology vendors highlights the points of disagreement between parties setting and following the direction of open systems. The definitions set up discussions in subsequent chapters of the progress standards organizations and vendors have made. In reality, open systems is a continuum of choice, from very open to very closed, across the many products and platforms in a distributed computing environment.

KEY CHARACTERISTICS OF CLOSED VERSUS OPEN SYSTEMS

(Very) Closed		(Very) Open
Proprietary	**Technology**	Standards-based
Primary vendor controls technology direction	**Technology direction**	Industry organizations and alliances direct technology evolution
"*Lockin*"—Choice is limited to products within and supporting the primary vendor's line of products	**Technology selection**	Choice—free among vendors creating competitive products
A vendor is the sole (primary) source for a given customer. Other vendors may provide products that comply with the primary vendor's proprietary protocols under special alliances and agreements	**Vendor participation**	Industry level cooperation and vendor alliances promote that widespread support of common frameworks/models, standards, and source codes
Limited leverage with limited set of vendors	**Purchase leverage**	Open market leads to strong competition on price and feature

Figure 3.1

Clarifying Some Terminology

Many terms are used when identifying and describing open systems. Some of the more common descriptors include:

- Open architecture
- Open systems architecture
- Open systems philosophy
- Open systems environment

- Open computing environment

The terms "open systems," "open architecture," and "open systems architecture" are fairly interchangeable, although the use of "architecture" tends to refer to the *construct* of open systems, as opposed to merely the concept of "openness." The "openness" concept is also referred to in the term "open systems philosophy." An "open systems environment," however, is one which promotes an open systems philosophy.

In referring to the construct of open systems, "architecture" is not limited to *hardware platform*, but instead applies more generally to the concept of *computing platform*. The *computing platform* encompasses all components of the computing architecture, from computer hardware to operating systems, communications software, data repositories, programming environments, graphics interfaces, applications, and user interfaces. To achieve an "open computing environment," open systems concepts must also extend to design paradigms and methods and the resulting data and applications.

Open Systems Properties

Understanding the properties often associated with "openness" can help in understanding the philosophy of open systems. These properties include the following:

> **Scalability**—The ability to use a software product or application on a variety of computers of different size and perhaps architecture within the product line of a single vendor (homogeneous environment).

> **Portability**—The ability to move a software product or application from one computer or software platform to another, perhaps made by different vendors (heterogeneous environment).

> **Interoperability** (or) **Interconnectivity**—The ability to exchange information among software products, applications, and computers from different vendors (heterogeneous environment).

> **Compatibility** or "Backwards" compatibility—The ability of current versions of applications and technology to interact with previous versions.

The addition of compatibility to the list of properties adds a time component to open systems architecture. New releases of operating systems, software products, hardware architectures, and even standards may be compatible with prior versions to retain "openness" as old components evolve and new components are added to the architecture over time.

Figure 3.2 contrasts the properties of very open versus very closed systems.

PROPERTIES OF (VERY) OPEN
VERSUS (VERY) CLOSED SYSTEMS

(Very) **Closed**		(Very) **Open**
Upward and downward scalability limited to models *within* a product line of a given vendor	**Scalability**	Scalable within and across vendor lines supporting similar standards. Translates into the ability to choose platform size according to need and implement environments of multiple sizes
Portability generally limited to the ability to easily move applications upward and downward within a given vendor product family	**Portability**	Ability to run software on multiple platforms and ability to easily move applications from one platform to another (Note: portability may be at a source or binary code level)
Interoperability generally available across product lines from a given vendor. Interoperability between products from differing vendors is non-existent	**Interoperability**	Systems from different vendors can work together
Compatibility generally maintained within a product line until the architecture of that product line is replaced	**Compatibility**	Compatibility generally maintained through standards and architectures until the standards and architectures are replaced

Figure 3.2

The degree to which these properties are present in open systems and how they are supported are topics hotly debated in the industry.

X/Open and OSF

Two major forces that have pioneered open systems and shaped the definition and implementation of open systems are X/Open and the Open Software Foundation (OSF).

X/Open is a consortium formed in 1984 by several European vendors. Today it is an international consortium of vendor and user organizations that is active in setting the open systems direction worldwide. X/Open defines open systems as:

"a vendor-independent computing environment consisting of inter-operable products and technologies that are commonly available, and that have been designed and implemented in accordance with *de jure* and *de facto standards.*"

In X/Open's definition of open systems, several key words illustrate its focus:

- Interoperability

- Commonly available

- *De jure* and *de facto* standards and,

- Vendor independence [X/Open, 1994]

The X/Open consortium does not *create* standards. Instead, it focuses on taking standards and specifications that are already accepted and integrating them into *vendor neutral* guidelines. X/Open has outlined a suite of standards that products must meet to support the goals of portability and interoperation. Those standards are outlined in the XPGn (X/Open Portability Guide version n). X/Open has also created a suite of tests that a product must pass to be "branded"—certified as XPG-compliant. Its trademark license agreement, required for product branding, guarantees the buyer of product conformance to the XPG.

OSF is a consortium formed in 1988 by several prominent technology vendors, primarily American. Today it is an international consortium of over 400 organizations—both vendor and user:

"An open system is one that enables properly engineered applications software to:

- Interact with users in a consistent style

- Be ported across a wide range of platforms from multiple vendors

- Interoperate with other open systems applications." [OSF, December 1993]

OSF's definition also focuses on several key attributes of open systems:

- Consistent user interface

- Portability

- Interoperability

OSF has focused its efforts on creating an open, portable, software environment—also known as "middleware." It defined a technology acquisition process in which Requests for Technology are issued to the industry at large. This acquisition process is used to evaluate the resulting submissions, select the best technologies, then integrate the winning technologies into their open computing environment support software. OSF licenses the source code for the software environment back to technology vendors for implementation on their platforms. In this capacity, OSF acts as a technology integrator. (From inception to mid-1994, OSF also acted as a software developer itself—performing a significant portion of the technology integration. In fact, OSF has been referred to as the world's largest software development house. In early 1994, OSF announced that it would sharply curtail its *development* activities. Prodded by its prominent technology vendor members with concerns about OSF costs, OSF was restructured and the bulk of the technology integration work was turned over to its members.)

Evolution to Standardization is Natural

In computing technology we are pursuing a natural evolution towards standardization that we experience time and again.

> When automobiles were first invented, a standard user interface did not exist. The gas pedal could be anywhere, not always on the floor. The brake was not necessarily in the vicinity of the gas pedal. Doors could be hinged towards the front of the car, or towards the back. Some automobiles had hand clutches for shifting gears. In others, to change gears required stopping the vehicle, getting out, opening the hood, and shifting a lever in the gear box. The internals of the machine were dependent on the inventor or creator. Early versions were cranked by hand to start the engine. Early engines used kerosene or oil

for fuel. Most automobile owners serviced their own vehicles, or went to bike shops for service.

Over time we have standardized both the user interface and the parts of an automobile. The user interface to the automobile is (mostly) standard today: the gas pedal is to the right on the floor and the brake to the left of the gas pedal. And, although we may still be confounded by light switches, wipers, window mechanisms, and trunk latches when renting cars, we generally know how to insert the key, start the engine, and drive off. With respect to the internals of the machines, although not homogeneous, they are sufficiently similar that most vehicles can be serviced at most service garages. And, over time, we have implemented hoards of regulations that define minimum safety and environmental requirements such as acceptable bumper heights, bumper strength, standard safety equipment, and manufacturer fleet gas mileage averages.

One can contrast the approaches of X/Open and OSF to creating open systems using our automobile analogy.

The view of open systems put forth by X/Open and its work in defining computing standards can be equated to *defining the regulations automobiles must comply with to be considered "street legal"*— standards such as size and configuration governing the interaction (so to speak) of vehicles on roads—and certifying that products meet those standards. *Any* vendor's product can be tested and certified as complying with the XPG. As a matter of fact, OSF's products are designed to be certified by X/Open.

On the other hand, OSF's view of open systems and their role in creating support components for a distributed open computing environment can be equated to *defining the various technologies required to build an operational vehicle*—such as fuel-injection system, electronic ignition, anti-lock braking system, etc., then selecting, endorsing and licensing the technologies (or products) that fulfill those requirements.

In other words, X/Open standardizes on specifications—what the product will do. OSF standardizes on the technology or product—how the technology will do whatever it is doing.

Some Vendor Definitions of Open Systems

There is a wide variety of views on how open systems should be implemented, and in particular, how they should be governed. Unfortunately, this divergence of opinions translates into the absence of a single, universally accepted definition of open systems architecture. Instead there are many versions—each reflecting the interpretations, biases, alliances, and intentions of the organization writing the definition. The following definitions represent the variety of opinions and emphases that exist in the vendor community:

HEWLETT PACKARD
[Open systems are:] Computing environments consisting of products and technologies which are designed and implemented in accordance with standards—established and de facto—that are vendor-independent and commonly available. [Hewlett Packard, 1994]

DIGITAL EQUIPMENT CORPORATION
[An open system provides:] Consistent interfaces across multiple architectures, vendors, clients, and servers, based on formal and defacto standards, allowing interoperability, portability and flexibility in meeting users' changing business needs. [DEC, 1994]

IBM
[Open Systems Environment:] The comprehensive set of interfaces, services, and supporting formats, plus user aspects, for interoperability or for portability of applications, data, or people, as specified by information technology standards and profiles. Source: JTC/1 and POSIX 1003.0. [IBM, 1994]

SUN
Open Systems are computing devices that due to their reliance on industry standard technologies and availability from multiple sources, are versatile, compatible, and relatively inexpensive to produce. [SUN, 1994]

BULL
An Open System is a compliant implementation of an evolving set of vendor-neutral specifications for inter-

faces, services, protocols and formats designed to effectively enable the configuration, operation and substitution of the entire system, its applications and/or its components with other equally compliant implementations preferably available from many different vendors. [Bull, 1994]

DATA GENERAL
Open Systems adhere to published hardware and software standards resulting in portability of software and interoperability among systems. [Data General, 1994]

AT&T GLOBAL INFORMATION SOLUTIONS
An open system is characterized by all the interfaces that comprise its connection to the outside world. These include software interfaces (such as user, application, information, and network interfaces) and hardware interfaces (such as bus or peripheral interfaces). [AT&T Global Information Solutions, 1994]

UNISYS
By "Open Systems" we mean multivendor computer and communication systems. In the future—regardless of the operating systems employed—users should be able to take advantage of source-level *portability* of applications across, and *interoperability* (or cooperative processing) between, computers from multiple vendors. [Unisys, 1994]

LOTUS DEVELOPMENT CORPORATION
An open system represents an environment that allows:

• A developer to create a single application that will run without modification on any platform

• An application on any platform to seamlessly interoperate with another application on another platform

• A systems administrator to use a single toolset that provides a unified and consistent view of the entire environment in order to monitor and manage it

MICROSOFT
An open system is one that provides choices to customers. Open systems are those that adhere to avail-

able, market-driven and accepted programmatic interfaces that become de facto standards. These systems allow the incorporation of many de jure and de facto standards from multiple vendors, enabling many different products, running on a wide variety of hardware, to interoperate. Thus, open systems bring a multitude of choices to customers and developers, fostering widespread vendor innovation, competition and hence low prices for customers. Open systems should provide these choices to customers in many areas, including: choices in hardware platforms, add-ons and peripherals, software applications, price/performance, and networking options. These options allow for easy portability of hardware and software systems, and user expertise. Open systems should also provide a foundation for companies' future technological growth, and allow flexible and easy migration to new technologies as they become available. [Microsoft, 1994]

SYBASE
Open Systems used to be synonymous with Unix; then it meant *portability*—the ability to run an application on different platforms. With the advent of client/server computing, we believe a more useful definition of open systems is *interoperability*—the ability for any client to seemlessly interact with any data source or application on any server. [Sybase, 1994]

ORACLE CORPORATION
An open system refers to an operating platform that conforms to respected and mature industry standards and interfaces which enable interoperability with other systems and portability to other platforms. The degree to which a platform may be considered "open" depends upon two factors: 1) implementation: the number of various standards supported and the ease in which applications can meet their interoperability and portability goals with these standards, and, 2) practice: the degree to which open standards on the platform are offered and supported in the market, enabling ISVs, integrators, consultants, and users to build and maintain open software solutions. [Oracle Corporation, 1994]

COMPUTER ASSOCIATES

Open systems are interoperable and portable information systems made possible through the use of commercially-viable standards. [Computer Associates, 1994]

As evidenced by the definitions, there is general agreement that open systems are based on computing standards. However, there is general disagreement on the issue of who should set and control those standards—hence the subtle and very important differences in open systems definitions.[1]

There are Varying Degrees of "Openness"

The properties of open systems (scalability, portability, interoperability, and compatibility) can be achieved at an industry level in several ways:

- By adopting and adhering to *public* or *industry standards*

- Through *vendor alliances* (agreements between a few select vendors)

- By using *published standards* made available by a vendor (generally on a popular technology) to any vendor that wants to use them

Public or *industry standards* are slower to establish and change since the direction of those standards are controlled by independent standards bodies through democratic administration among the body membership. Establishment of standards at an industry level should result in broader participation in standards application. In addition, some public and industry standards bodies are defining *vendor-neutral* standards in an attempt to avoid giving any vendor significant advantage over another. The goal of these efforts is vendor-independent, platform-independent standards. The communications protocol suites TCP/IP and OSI are examples of public standards.

Vendor alliances simply broaden the availability of proprietary technology, making it available to vendors participating in the alliance. However, the direction and ongoing "openness" of any given vendor alliance environment is dependent upon the collective directions of participating vendors *and their commitment to the*

---

[1]Standards and the pros and cons of industry standards versus vendor architectures are discussed further in the chapters on standards organizations and standards.

alliance. In vendor alliances, the goal is interoperability through partnership and shared technology, rather than through published or public standards. Vendor alliances can create more immediate results than public standards because of narrower participation. However, there are several risks to consider. One risk of a vendor alliance is that the technologies will not gain sufficient marketshare to become a *de facto* standard. Another risk is that, as with cartels (another example of a vendor alliance), the temptation to cheat grows along with market share and the partnership will eventually dissolve into the confusion of competing camps. Vendor alliances do not always serve all parties equally. IBM's relationship with Microsoft to build the DOS operating system is a good example of a vendor alliance that worked well for Microsoft, not so well for IBM.

Published standards are another form of vendor alliance. Vendors that innovate technology, particularly those that create "connective" foundation technology, may solicit support for the technology they create and formally publish the interfaces to that technology. By formally publishing standards, *any vendor* can write or build technology that interoperates with the foundation technology. Published standards can lead to open properties when many vendors use the published standards to interface with a popular foundation product or product line. An example of a "published" standard is the Microsoft Windows applications programming interface (WIN32 API). When published standards are widely used, they are known as *de facto standards*, and are often subsequently formalized into public standards.[2]

Open Systems—A Business Definition

At the risk of adding to confusion rather than clarifying, we might build on some of the ideas presented in the vendor definitions to create our own business definition of open systems—one focused on the goals and the whys of open systems rather than on a particular view of technology or standardization.

> Open systems are systems (both hardware and software) that comply with industry standards (*de facto* or *de jure*). Industry standards establish operating parameters for systems functionality allowing vendor products that are built to these industry specifications to work together.

---

[2]As a matter of fact, there is a pretty interesting legal tussle going on right now with several groups trying to move Microsoft's WIN32 API into public domain. Refer to the PWI and WABI entries in the Standards Appendix for more information.

Some of the benefits businesses and users gain from standardized products include:

➤ The ability to link computer systems together (connectivity)

➤ The ability to share data across applications and platforms (interoperability)

➤ The ability to select hardware platforms and software platforms that meet the volume and business needs of the business (portability and scalability)

➤ The ability to assume more direct control over the computing future of the business (compatibility)

The bottom line is that open systems provide businesses and users with greater choice:

➤ Choice in hardware platforms

➤ Choice in add-on hardware and peripherals

➤ Choice in software applications

➤ Choice in operating systems and other systems utilities

➤ Choice in price and service for technology products

➤ Choice in future technology decisions for the business

Summary—"Openness" is a Continuum

While to date no universally accepted definition of open systems architecture exists, it is safe to state that open systems adhere to protocols and industry computing standards that are readily and widely available. It is also safe to state that there are varying degrees of "openness."

One might rate the "openness" of a given technology or product by identifying the source and availability of the *standards* upon which the technology or product is based. Figure 3.3 depicts the spectrum of standard sources as an "Openometer."[3]

---

[3]The name, "Openometer" was coined by John White, of Honeywell and is used here with his very kind permission.

OPENOMETER

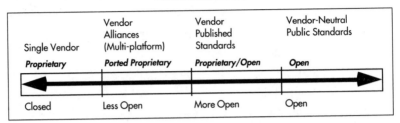

Figure 3.3

As indicated on the Openometer, single vendor, proprietary technology is clearly closed. At the far right of the Openometer, technology based on vendor-neutral, public standards is clearly open. In the middle, technology based on standard interfaces that are openly published and available to anyone (although controlled by the publishing vendor) is considerably more open than technology created through a multi-vendor alliance and available on multiple platforms through agreements between participating vendors.

If we map the differing approaches of X/Open and OSF to open systems architecture against the Openometer, we might arrive at the following. (See Figure 3.4.)

X/OPEN AND OSF ON THE OPENOMETER

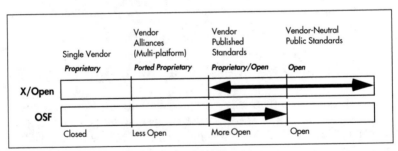

Figure 3.4

The bottom line? "Openness" is not something that can be acquired, or implemented. The concept is a continuum and as such, "totally open," "openness" throughout the computing environment, can never be fully achieved (if it were even desired)—there is only "more open" and "less open."

Chapter 4
Benefits, Opportunities, Costs, Risks AND Barriers—
Here There Be Dragons

Eternal vigilance is the price of liberty.

—Thomas Jefferson

The functional and economic benefits of open systems architecture are significant. All aspects of the organization—the business as a whole, the IS function, and the end user can benefit from open technology. Open systems also open a series of opportunities for both businesses and technology vendors alike. However, open systems are a significant change—in technology, of course, but also in what people do and how they do it. As such, open systems can be a destabilizing force in an organization. While there are some short term cost advantages with open technology, many of the benefits are not recognized in the short term. In the mean time, risks must be managed and barriers cleared. Planning is essential. Organizations are advised to proceed, but proceed with caution.

Within business and government users, "open systems" are an important tool available to IS organizations looking to drive down unit costs of IS products and services—while at the same time meeting the growing computing needs of the organization and the greater demands of the computing end user. Open systems provide great flexibility to the IS organization in selecting, assembling, building, and integrating technology. But, this flexibility is not without cost and risk.

Remember the characteristics of open systems:

* Portable

* Interoperable

* Scalable

* Compatible

Open technology conforms to published standards. Standards may be controlled by an industry body and made available to the industry at large *(open)* or, the "standards" may be specifications published by a controlling vendor *(proprietary/open)*. Open technology that conforms to industry standards may also be vendor neutral. Proprietary/open technology is never vendor neutral.

It is important to re-emphasize that open architecture does not demand *homogeneity* (components that are alike and interchangeable). Instead, it supports *compatible heterogeneity* (components may be specialized but are compatible and connectable). An open environment allows and supports heterogeneity by defining platform and communication standards—expectations of what functionality is supported and how it is invoked. A proprietary component may participate in an open architecture by adopting and adhering to standards for communication and interoperation with open components. An open systems architecture facilitates communication and interoperation among components that would otherwise be impossible without defined standards and protocols. In an open systems architecture, the whole is optimized (clearly sometimes at the expense of individual components).

The effect of open systems and open systems technology on the organization can be short-term and/or strategic, positive and/or negative. Open systems may also present opportunities and risks that are different than in an environment using primarily proprietary technology. In this section, we define:

- Benefits: Direct, positive effects of acquiring, implementing, or operating open systems technology. Benefits may be directly associated with reduced costs, or more indirectly, as advantages to the organization.

- Costs: Direct, negative effects of acquiring, implementing, or operating open systems technology. Costs may be directly equated to dollars, or may be softer disadvantages to the organization.

- Opportunities: Areas of potential advantage to the organization. Opportunities are not as direct as benefits, in that they require the organization to *do something* in order to take advantage of the opportunity. Opportunities also often cannot be as directly linked to economic gains as benefits.

- Risks: Areas of potential disadvantage to the organization. Some risks can be managed by avoidance, others are more dependent upon probabilities and can be planned for or chanced.

Let's explore the effect of open systems in terms of the associated benefits, opportunities, costs, and risks to various parts of the organization and to technology vendors.

Benefits

An open computing environment will benefit technology user and vendor organizations at all levels. (See Figure 4.1.) From a business management perspective, there are powerful business freedom and economic drivers behind standardization. From an IS perspective, an open systems architecture may be the only achievable way of linking diverse computing resources into an integrated whole. From an end user perspective, open systems architecture will facilitate access to information and computing resources, regardless of the platform.

BENEFITS OF OPEN SYSTEMS

TECHNOLOGY USER			TECHNOLOGY VENDOR
Business Management	IS	End User	
• Reduce technology costs • Reduce dependence on single vendor • Reduce technology constraints on business functions • Increase ability to integrate business functions	• Reduce effort building customized interfaces • Protect investment decisions • Increase stability of long-term technical skill needs	• More choices • More "feature-rich" applications	• Interoperability with other vendor products • Larger market for products and services

Figure 4.1

Business Management

- Reduce technology acquisition costs

When acquiring technology, the lower initial costs of open technology are evident. For example, user estimates of the price/performance advantage of UNIX/RISC systems over proprietary counterparts in the midrange systems market range from 4:1 to 10:1. However, elation over this news needs to be tempered by the warning that technology management and support costs are higher with open systems technology due to the increased complexity of the environment and technology. But, most reports and indeed the organizations contributing case studies to this book confirm that overall, organizations feel that open systems technology cost less than proprietary technology.

- Reduce dependence on a single vendor

Being able to sidestep non-competitive pricing and limited product offerings, or poor service/support are obvious benefits of reducing dependence on a single technology vendor. But beyond these obvious advantages, the turmoil in the technology marketplace makes vendor independence even more important to the technology user organization.

- Reduce technology constraints on business functions

Technology interoperation and integration facilitates process integration. But today, all too often, integration of business processes is hampered or stumped by the difficulty of getting technology components to work together. An open computing platform reduces the constraints placed on business functions by technology.

- Increase ability to integrate business functions

Open systems provide a workable, cost-effective means of linking disparate technology and distribute technology resources. Open systems is the only (realistic) way to create large distributed systems and integrate the business units of very large, multi-national and global organizations.

IS Function

- Reduce effort building customized interfaces

Efforts required to migrate and port applications and system functions between vendor platforms are minimized through standard application and hardware/firmware interfaces. The time and effort required to build customized interfaces between platforms is minimized through support of standard interfaces. This is a significant benefit to both IS and the business, because time spent by IS building custom interfaces adds no value to the organization.

- Protect investment decisions

The ability to migrate, port, and swap technology products protects investment in the computing architecture as a whole and decreases the risk of any given technology decision.

- Increase stability of long-term technical skill needs

  The technology skills required to support the technology environment are more predictable and less variant due to the predictability and longevity of public standards.

End Users

- More choices

  The widest possible choice of hardware, software, and applications is available because of open systems. Standardization increases the potential for substitution (choice) as well as competition.

- More "feature rich" applications

  Because of more intense competition, vendors are forced to compete based on the features of *each of their products* rather than rely on the strength of an overall product line. A larger pool of vendors with the opportunity to serve (and sell) stimulates competition based on features. And, the prospect of portability to multiple platforms encourages vendors to invest in "base" packages.

Technology Vendor

- Interoperability with other vendor products

  Interoperability with products from other vendors allows a vendor to specialize, focus on features, and position their products relative to others in the marketplace.

- Larger market for products and services

  Overall, standardization opens the marketplace, particularly for smaller vendors that were shut out of the computing platforms and customers of larger vendors.

Costs

Transition costs, however, are a deterrence for the market as a whole, for individual organizations attempting to implement open architectures, and for technology vendors. (See Figure 4.2.) The investment required to learn and implement standards is large, as is the continuing investment in ensuring and enforcing compliance. Inertia also is a factor. Vendors and organizations have tremendous investments in proprietary systems environments, the software that runs in those environments, and the people, methods, and tools that keep the environment running. Inertia caused by existing investment, practices, and knowledge will slow the evolution toward open architectures.

COSTS OF OPEN SYSTEMS

TECHNOLOGY USER			TECHNOLOGY VENDOR
Business Management	IS	End User	
• Early retirement of existing proprietary technology • Product overpricing • "Branding" • Transition costs	• Standards/architecture management • Technology integration • Investment in knowledge and skills • Technology and network operation and support • Technology administration • Loss of one-stop shopping • Investment in standards	• Learning curve	• Investment in standards • Early retirement of existing proprietary technology • Investment in knowledge and skills • Transition costs

Figure 4.2

Business Management

- Early retirement of existing proprietary technology

  Introduction of open systems technology may bring about or require early replacement of existing systems technology. The magnitude of the existing investment will contribute to inertia slowing progress towards a new computing architecture.

- Product overpricing

  Although open systems technology is *generally* less costly than proprietary alternatives, that is not always the case. Just like proprietary counterparts, open systems products may be more costly as they are first introduced into the market, or in technology areas where there is little competition.

- Branding

  The cost of industry specifications and "branding" (independent testing) adds to the price of open systems technology.

Branding is hotly debated in the open systems industry right now. Users like the added safety and security of industry product testing for standards compliance, but they don't want to pay extra for it. [Dataquest, 1993]

- Transition costs

The computing industry, technology vendors and users alike, will need to maintain current proprietary environments while creating an open computing environment.

IS Function

- Standards/architecture management

Defining and managing the standards framework and overall technology architecture of the computing environment is a cost to IS that was previously borne by the major technology supplier. This is not a cost that should be minimized. Establishing and maintaining standards is an important part of creating an open system environment. And, depending on the business, users may want to and need to be actively involved in the standards and architecture definition process.

- Technology integration

As the mix of technology and technology sources broadens in an organization, the burden of testing and integrating the technologies shifts from the primary vendor to IS or the technology user. New technology products need to be "shaken out" in production environments to identify and overcome functional and performance deficiencies. Testing is another cost that should not be minimized. It is impossible, today (and will remain impossible in the near future), to rely on industry "branding" or vendor claims of standards compliance and interoperability.

- Investment in knowledge and skills

The staff and staff skills required to design, create, and support an open computing environment are not the same as the skills required to support a proprietary architecture. Organizations, both technology vendor and technology user, need to invest in developing and acquiring new technology skills.

- Technology and network operation and support

   There is a support cost associated with distributing technology, either in the form of remote management (if the tools are available) or on-site support. This cost is associated with both the increased complexity of open systems technology and the increased complexity of the distributed computing environment.

- Technology administration

   There is also a cost associated with asset management and licensing of products in a distributed environment. In reality, the increased costs incurred in technology administration are not as directly attributable to "openness" as they are to the more widespread use of products (particularly desktop products) by end users in a distributed environment.

- Loss of one-stop shopping

   Associated with the ability to choose products from a multitude of sources comes the cost of evaluating, selecting, and purchasing products from a multitude of sources. In the past, technology acquisition was rather easy and the direct cost attributed to "shopping" was minimized when the selection was limited to the products of one or just a few supplying vendors.

- Investment in standards

   IS bears a cost in understanding the "state of standards and technology" in order to develop the technology direction and framework for the organization as well as an ongoing effort to follow the progress of standards. Organizations that choose to participate in industry standards efforts bear the additional cost of time spent in those efforts (but benefit from the participation in the ability to influence the direction of standards efforts and knowledge).

End User

- Learning curve

   There is no doubt that there is a direct cost to the end user in terms of time spent understanding and navigating the added complexity of open systems technology. Just understanding the realm of available choices makes product selection more complex, much less the challenge of selecting products that work together and learning to use them.

Technology Vendor

- Investment in standards

  The industry must *invest* in agreeing upon, developing, integrating, and managing technology standards. The technology vendor bears the cost of participating in setting the industry direction as part of the standards definition process, or dealing with the aftermath of a direction that they didn't participate in setting.

- Early retirement of existing proprietary technology

  Just as technology users face early replacement of existing technology, technology vendors face the costs involved with cannibalizing existing proprietary technologies. The value of the proprietary marketplace heavily influences the speed at which technology vendors are adopting open systems concepts and introducing open systems technologies. The inability or unwillingness to replace existing technology is a barrier to introducing open systems.

- Investment in knowledge and skills

  Like technology user organizations, vendors too must invest in retraining and updating the skills of their staffs from older proprietary products to newer open technologies.

Opportunities

Open systems offer many opportunities to the business, IS, the end user, and the technology vendor alike. (See Figure 4.3.)

OPEN SYSTEMS OPPORTUNITIES

TECHNOLOGY USER			TECHNOLOGY VENDOR
Business Management	**IS**	**End User**	
• Investments tied to business changes rather than technology changes • Focus on integrating business processes • Computing platform flexibility • Ability to continually "renew" technology capabilities	• Freedom in setting technology direction • Ability to manage technology infrastructure • Reduce development time (for comparable functionality)	• Access to information • Ease-of-use	• Computing architecture investment protection • Consistent paradigm for distributed applications • Reduce time to market • Cost savings

Figure 4.3

Business Management

- Investments tied to business changes rather than technology changes

Because of the inherent componentization and scalability of open systems, once the initial transition investment is made, subsequent investments should constitute additions to, rather than wholesale replacement of major portions of the technology base. Technology investments can then be more directly related to changes in the business (e.g., an organization may purchase incremental capacity tied with business volume increases or new functionality, rather than having to swap out large machines for larger machines once a capacity limitation is reached). Emphasis on standard components will smooth the IS investment stream and facilitate a longer term perspective on investment return.

- Focus on integrating business processes

In an open systems environment, the means to share data and interface platforms, perhaps even integrate applications and data, supports the business focus on integrating business processes.

- Increased computing platform flexibility

The open computing platform offers more choices and with choice, more flexibility in selecting and assembling technology. Components can be added to the overall computing environment creating a customized, more flexible information infrastructure that can change with the business.

- Ability to continually "renew" technology capabilities

The flexibility of the open computing platform makes it easier to add technology into the mix of existing technologies. This will enable organizations to add new technology to the mix as the new technology proves promising rather than having to continually swap out significant portions of the technology base in order to add new technology.

IS Function

- Freedom in setting technology direction

The availability of industry standards gives the IS function more freedom in setting the technology direction for the organization. IS can make the explicit choice to follow public standards initiatives or select unique vendor products, rather than being limited to tactical (product) decisions while technology vendors set strategic priorities.

- Ability to manage technology infrastructure

Specification of the technology *standards* adopted by an organization rather than specification of the products may improve the ability of IS to manage the technology infrastructure, while still allowing users the freedom to choose individual products and vendors.

- Reduce development time (for comparable functionality)

Once the initial investment in learning the standards has been made, subsequent learning curves for developers and end users are reduced through common user and programmer interfaces. Overall development times should decrease.

End User

- Access to information

Open systems provide better information access by making connectivity and interoperability more achievable.

- Ease-of-use

With a standard user interface, the end user will no longer have to learn how to navigate the network to find information.

Technology Vendor

- Computing architecture investment protection

  From a technology vendor and integrator perspective, open systems architecture will widen the market for products and services as well as protect technology and knowledge investments made in standard environments. By easing the burden of migrating and porting products, open systems decrease the risk of technology investments.

- Consistent paradigm for distributed applications

  When an industry model for distributed computing is agreed to, vendors will have a consistent paradigm for distributed applications supported on a broad range of open platforms. Common models should simplify the design and creation of distributed applications, improve productivity through code reuse, and broaden the market for products.

- Reduce time to market

  Consistent models and a stable framework of standards will reduce the development time of vendors and ultimately the time to market for new products.

- Cost savings

  As standards and technology mature, open systems concepts (such as joint R&D, industry developed and managed models, industry collected requirements, etc.) should offer tremendous cost savings, at a macro-economic level, to the industry as a whole.

Risks

The major risks attributed to open systems stem primarily from the magnitude of the change, from lack of technology maturity, and from the shift in roles and responsibilities from technology vendors to technology users and from individual technology vendors to the industry. (See Figure 4.4.)

OPEN SYSTEMS RISKS

TECHNOLOGY USER			TECHNOLOGY VENDOR
Business Management	IS	End User	
• Business disruption due to technology immaturity • Technology investment risk due to market immaturity • Inability of organization to change or absorb change • Technology lag • Vendor misbehavior • Information and system security	• Shift in roles and responsibilities • Standards direction • Standards compliance • Product availability	• User frustration	• Shift in roles and responsibilities • Loss of customer "commitment"

Figure 4.4

Management

- Business disruption due to technology immaturity

  There is the risk of business interruption due to performance problems when bringing up very large transaction processing and real time processing systems. Open systems technologies are generally less mature in these areas than some proprietary technologies.

- Technology investment risk due to market immaturity

  Selection of open products may be riskier than might be expected. While the market is in transition from proprietary to open, *standards* and "open" *products* are being developed simultaneously. A full set of accepted standards that cover all layers of a computing architecture has not been agreed upon and adopted by a single standards body, much less the industry. Quite to the contrary, there are several reigning "industry frameworks" and many approaches to developing standards. It is sometimes difficult to predict who and what will ultimately win. In this market, it is relatively easy to make an investment decision that ends up at a ninety degree angle from the industry direction.

- Inability of organization to change or absorb change

  Open systems are a big change, for the IS function and users alike. As with any program that fundamentally challenges the way people work—what they do, and how they do it, there is the risk that change will be resisted or that the change will happen too quickly (or too slowly).

- Technology lag

   Standards-based technology generally (not always) lags market state-of-the-art proprietary products in terms of features. Organizations may find it difficult to find open technology if they have state-of-the-art functionality needs. Or, they may incur additional costs in acquiring additional products to meet their needs.

- Vendor misbehavior

   Let's just say, some vendors are more committed to open systems than others.

- Information and system security

   Information and system security may be at risk. The concepts of share/open and protect/secure are in direct conflict. As the keys to logical access within the computing environment are handed out, protection from misuse and abuse must be addressed. Yet, unfortunately, information protection is a topic that is often overlooked—until it is too late. At that point, either something happens, or it is infeasible to protect against something that might happen.[1]

IS Function

- Shift in roles and responsibilities

   Open systems architecture offers the technology user the opportunity to set and manage the strategic technology direction of the organization. If the organization chooses, the technology planning burden shifts from the primary vendor to the technology user. And, if the organization chooses to set its own strategic technology direction, the following become important steps in assuming the new role:

   – Management and IS will be required to plan the business and technology support of the business together.

---

[1]Note: We describe information protection concern in an open environment in chapters 8 and 9.

- IS needs to confirm or elicit support from supplying vendors for the technology direction of the organization.

- Standards direction

  The future state and support for a given standard is not always
  as clear as we would like it to be. There are many competing
  standards, and winners are not always easy to pick. There is
  the risk, when selecting standards, that the standard will fall
  behind the market, languish without vendor support, be over-
  thrown by a competing standard or product, or be extin-
  guished altogether.

- Standards compliance

  An efficient, accepted mechanism for testing vendor product
  compliance with industry standards does not yet exist. Some
  industry level "branding" (independent testing) is being done,
  but somewhat sporadically. Branding tests are available only
  for certain standards. The tests are costly to develop and costly to administer. And, testing for standards compliance within
  IS is impractical for all but the largest of organizations. So,
  proof of standards "compliance" remains elusive and the subject of elaborate contractual agreements between technology
  purchasers and the vendors supplying products.

- Product availability

  Current and expected future product availability needs to be
  considered when setting an open systems direction and selecting standards. The development of open vendor products is
  dependent upon:

  - Standards definition and industry adoption

  - Vendor acceptance and compliance with those standards

  - Perceived demand for the products

End User

- User frustration

  User frustration with the magnitude of change and the information overload associated with a wide selection of technology
  and technology standards is a very real risk. Before it becomes
  necessary to cart people away in rubber wagons, it is helpful
  to clarify the role they are expected to play and provide lots of
  readily available support.

Technology Vendors

- Shift in roles and responsibilities

  The technology vendor experiences a shift in roles and responsibilities in two directions. Control over the industry direction of technology is passing from a few very large technology vendors to the industry as a whole and a few dominant technology vendors (some of whom are very new to the market leadership role). Control over the technology direction of a given business is passing from the primary supplier to the business itself.

- Loss of customer "commitment"

  As technology and the marketplace open up, vendors face losing "locked-in" customer "commitment" to their technology direction and products.

Barriers

It would be unfair to leave a discussion of the effect of open systems on organizations without mentioning some of the barriers to implementing open systems today. These barriers really exist at the industry level, there is little an individual organization can do to remove the barriers except "take up arms and join the battle!" Some of today's challenges include:

- There are several incompatible versions of open systems

  As we have mentioned several times, there are competing groups promoting competing notions of open systems and competing frameworks. Until the industry settles on one model, incompatible versions will remain a barrier to widespread implementation of open systems.

- There are too many competing standards

  At a level below the industry frameworks, competition between standards is also a barrier. Competition exists at many levels:

  - Between proprietary/open technology and technology governed by industry standards (e.g., between Microsoft Windows NT and UNIX)

- Between versions of proprietary/open technology (e.g., between ODBC and IDAPI)

- Between industry standards (e.g., between TCP/IP and OSI)

- Converting from proprietary to open is costly

  The costs associated with conversion to open systems are high. "Bridging" products that clean up and reestablish data structures and code are arriving on the scene and will help. But today, conversion is a very costly proposition.

- Converting from proprietary to open is difficult

  Beyond the cost associated with conversion, it is also difficult to convert from a proprietary environment and from a proprietary mindset. This holds true for user organizations and technology vendors alike.

- The standards process is too slow

  There is no question that the standards process is too slow. Users are complaining about it. Industry standards bodies know it and are scrambling to try to streamline processes to shorten the cycle time to standards. Technology vendors are often working both sides of the issue—benefiting from the slow standards process in that higher margin proprietary and proprietary/open technologies are more attractive to the marketplace in a slow standards process environment—and, working within the standards body to respond to market demands to speed up the processes. Although progress is being made, this barrier will not be removed in the near term or foreseeable future.

Summary

The business benefits of interoperability and integration will drive the transition to open systems. In the short run, open systems offer the attractive benefits of price, feature, and investment protection. In the long run, the economics of an open environment are less of an issue. Open systems are the only realistic and cost-effective way to build large distributed systems. Multi-national and global organizations are some of the largest implementors of open systems and are pushing the open systems industry forward.

However, it must be recognized that the concepts behind open systems may be a destabilizing force in the computing architecture and information systems infrastructure of an organization. While they support the business direction of process integration, they require a level of planning, integration, and ongoing cooperation between management and IS, and between IS and technology vendors that is unprecedented in most organizations.

Open systems offer attractive cost advantages in technology acquisition, but many of the benefits are not realized in the short term. Planning and management are key to benefiting from open systems over the longer haul. The speed and fervor with which a business should embrace open systems is dependent upon business needs and the stability, serviceability and investment in existing proprietary systems.

Organizations are urged to proceed, but proceed with caution. Benefits tend to come slowly to those with the foresight and patience to extract them. Costs and risks, on the other hand, materialize quickly.

Chapter 5

Standards Organizations and Vendor Alliances—New Rules and Who Rules?

Liberty, too, must be limited in order to be possessed.

—Edmond Burke

Users are driving for standardization to achieve connectivity and share information across their organizations, as well as to drive down their computing costs. Vendors are driving for standardization to respond to market pressures, level the playing field, and differentiate themselves. The market is such that no single user or vendor can significantly influence standardization (except through invention and widespread acceptance). Accordingly, the marketplace is aligning itself into camps.

This section begins with some background on standardization and standards bodies. We present an overview of the standards market—defining who is promoting standardization and why. We introduce the concepts of standards creators, standards adopters/integrators, and standards influencers, to help the reader understand the different roles of various organizations. Additionally, we provide brief summaries of some of the major organizations and players involved in establishing a forum and process for defining, implementing, and managing standards.

We also discuss the process of creating standards and some of the limitations of the process as it exists and introduce some of the major criteria influencing the speed of standards development and adoption.

One measure of the importance of standards to the computing industry today is the number of standards and standards setting bodies created in the past few years. "The good thing about standards is that there are so many to choose from" is a common joke. The same can be said of the organizations that set them.

As in other industries, innovations in computing have been brought to market by proud inventors and marketers who developed solutions and products they thought were the best. These innovations are absorbed into the mainstream of corporate operations. Users, looking for best products at the best price, select the innovations that suit their purposes, regardless of the vendor offering them. This "shopping among vendors" raises the need for integration of innovations with other functions and innovations, often competing ones. Public and industry standards bodies are a mechanism for determining the requirements and specifications for standardized interfaces, interoperation, and management of the components of an integrated computing architecture. (See Figure 5.1.)

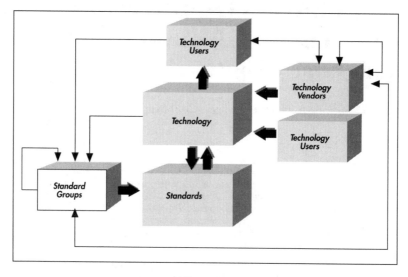

Figure 5.1

One of the oldest and best known standards bodies is ANSI, the American National Standards Institute, founded in 1918. ANSI is a private, nonprofit membership organization that coordinates the U.S. voluntary consensus standards and approves American National Standards. Many countries also have national standards bodies, such as the British Standards Institution (BSI), the Deutsches Institut für Normung e. V. (DIN), the Instituto Portugues de Qualidade (IPQ), Schweizerische Normen-Vereinigung (SNV), and the Japanese Standards Association (JSA).

The first standards for computing languages were developed in the sixties. Since then, hundreds of standards, covering most imaginable aspects of computing, and dozens of standards organizations, have emerged.

Standards: A Definition

Let's start with defining a standard. A standard can be a specification or a specific product that has become widely accepted, either

STANDARDS ORGANIZATIONS AND VENDOR ALLIANCES—New Rules and Who Rules?

63

formally or informally, and used as a preferable interface or method.

There are two types of standards: *de jure* and *de facto*. (See Figure 5.2.) These Latin phrases mean, respectively, "according to law" and "as a matter of fact."

TYPES OF STANDARDS

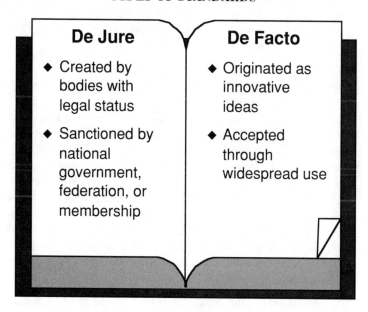

Figure 5.2

The major difference between de facto and de jure standards is governance—who sets and controls the direction of the standard.

- *De jure* standards are produced by a body with legal status, and sanctioned by a national government, federation, or membership. These bodies use a formal procedure, or an *open process*, in which any person, company, or country with an interest must be allowed to comment on drafts of the standard. Comments must be addressed by the working group responsible for the standard creation. This is a public process. Consequently *de jure* standards are generally known as *public* or *industry* standards, established by public bodies.

  User input into the process of defining requirements for *de jure* standards is increasing. Vendors participate in defining detailed standards specifications, and vote on approval and acceptance of standards. The independent body may also develop test suites to verify compliance with the *de jure* specifications, then "brand" products that pass the test suites as a warranty of sorts.

De jure standards may also be *vendor neutral*. This means that in defining a standard, all portions of the specification that would give a vendor a competitive advantage are either avoided or pulled out of the specification.

- *De facto* standards are developed by a single vendor. In contrast, to *de jure* standards, *de facto* standards may or may not be the result of a conscious effort to create a standard. The term *de facto* describes a standard which exists in fact, whether or not its originators had intended to create it. *De facto* standards generally arise from innovative products with high sales or a very specific niche. The innovating vendor publishes the interface to the product and solicits support from other vendors to grow sales. With *de facto* standards, the vendor controls the direction of the standard. There is generally no compliance testing or branding. A *de facto* standard, when published by a vendor for the purpose of gaining support for that vendor's product, can also be called an *API* (applications programming interface).

When *de facto* standards are widely used and fill a market need, they are often formalized into *de jure* standards.

For any specification to be considered a standard, it must be viewed as such by the consensus of the marketplace. Because of the inevitable combination of interests involved in reaching consensus, *de jure* standards invariably take longer to come into use than their *de facto* counterparts.

Overview of the Industry Standards Market

There are several, quite logical, steps to establishing standards:

- Define the requirements
- Define the standards
- Integrate the standards with other standards
- Accept and use the standards
- Update and enhance the standards

There is some structure to the collection of seemingly diverse and numerous groups publishing and adopting standards, although that structure is difficult to discern because many of the groups have competing missions, goals, and membership. It is helpful to look at the plethora of standards organizations by sorting them according to what they do—their primary role in the standards process:

- Standards Creators—organizations defining and approving standards

- Standards Adopters/Integrators—organizations endorsing and integrating standards

- Standards Influencers—organizations defining requirements for standards

This structure is diagrammed in Figure 5.3.

INDUSTRY STANDARDS GROUPS

Standards Creators	Standards Adopters/ Integrators	Standards Influencers	
ISO	X/Open	X/Open	"Group of 10"
IEEE	OSF	COS	SOS
ANSI	Uniforum	ECMA	OURS
BSI	OMG	Open Systems Interconnect Management Forum	Government
CCITT			Industry Groups
		Individual Vendors	
Standard Bodies	**Technology Manufacturers/ Suppliers**	**Technology Users**	

Figure 5.3

Let's examine the role of each of these types of standards organizations.

Creators

Standards creators are sanctioned bodies—public standards groups—charged with defining, specifying, or approving the standards themselves, and integrating, managing, and maintaining the standards. Membership in public standards bodies is generally open to any organization or individual with the time and money to invest in the process. Much of the work in public standards bodies is done by volunteers—often donated by parties with a vested interest in the outcome.

Three of the best known standards creators are ANSI, ISO and IEEE.

ANSI—American National Standards Institute.

ANSI is a nonprofit, privately funded membership organization. ANSI coordinates the development of U.S. Voluntary National Standards in the private sector for a diverse array of things from film products to bicycle helmets to programming languages. Standards are not developed by ANSI. Instead they are submitted for approval by ANSI by technical and professional societies, trade associations, and other groups accredited by ANSI. ANSI is the U.S. member body to ISO and IEC. [ANSI, 1993]

ISO—International Organization for Standardization. ("ISO" comes from the Greek prefix *iso*, meaning "same.")

ISO is a worldwide federation of national standards bodies, founded in 1947, with a Central Secretariat in Geneva. A non-governmental organization, it develops international standards for voluntary implementation, covering virtually all technical fields except electrical and electrotechnical standardization. With regard to information processing standards, ISO and IEC (International Electrotechnical Commission) in 1987 set up the JTC1, Joint Technical Committee, Information Technology.

ISO is made up of 96 national standards bodies, one from each country. These standards bodies are the most representative of standardization in their respective countries. More than 70 percent are governmental institutions or organizations incorporated by public law. The remainder have close links to the public administration in their own countries. [ISO, 1993]

STANDARDS ORGANIZATIONS AND VENDOR ALLIANCES—New Rules and Who Rules?

67

IEEE—Institute of Electrical and Electronic Engineers.

IEEE is a membership organization that includes engineers, scientists, and students in electronics and allied fields.

> Founded in 1963, it has more than 320,000 members and is the world's largest technical professional organization, with members in 150 countries. The institute is a leading authority in areas ranging from computers, aerospace and telecommunications to electric power, consumer electronics and biomedical technology. [IEEE, 1993]

The work of IEEE is well known. IEEE originally defined the CSMA/CD (Carrier Sense Multiple Access/Collision Detect) protocol. This protocol is used in Ethernet™, token ring, and token bus communication standards in support of the OSI (Open Systems Interconnect) communications model. That model was also originally defined by IEEE. IEEE has hundreds of standards development committees, including a committee chartered in 1985 to develop a portable operating system/applications interface, the P1003 Committee, also known as the "POSIX" Committee.

Adopters/Integrators

Standards adopters/integrators are involved in adopting, endorsing, and commissioning standards. Their goal is to integrate standards required to define aspects of a computing environment. Standards adopters/integrators are generally vendor consortia, banded together to pool R&D efforts and create a market alliance to a technology direction or set of technologies.

Standards adopters/integrators also support the efforts of technology vendors in creating and delivering compliant technologies and products. They do so by integrating standards, supporting *de facto* standards to fill in where industry standards do not exist, and developing test suites to confirm standards compliance.

Membership in these bodies is generally open to any organization or individual, but many types of membership exist. Often there are "sponsors" who have more say in the direction of the activities of the organization and participating members who work on the specific initiatives.

Well-known organizations involved in adopting and integrating standards include X/Open, OSF, and UniForum. OSF plays a unique role in this category as an *integrator* and *provider* of open systems technology, as well as an integrator of standards.

X/Open Co. Ltd.

X/Open's mission is to bring greater value to information technology users through the practical implementation of open systems. Founded in 1984, X/Open is a worldwide, independent company dedicated to bringing the benefits of open systems to market. The company markets products and services to computer system buyers, system suppliers, software developers and standards organizations. By integrating prioritized requirements and expertise from each of these groups, X/Open is able to evolve and manage a comprehensive set of publicly available open systems specifications, including de facto and international standards, called the Common Applications Environment (CAE). X/Open operates a test and verification process for products developed in line with its specifications, and awards its brand as the mark of compliance.

In September, 1993, the UNIX contingency of the open systems market (consisting of more than 70 IT suppliers) appointed X/Open to manage the evolution of a set of common application programming interfaces (APIs) that will directly encourage the increased availability of open systems in the market (Spec 1170). [X/Open, 1994]

OSF—Open Software Foundation.

The Open Software Foundation (OSF™) is an open systems technology delivery organization with the objective of enabling users of information technology to exploit that technology to fundamentally improve the way they do business. OSF supplies software to make information technology easier to learn and easier to use, while enabling products of various vendors to work together, sharing applications and information across distributed, open computing environments.

OSF is a not-for-profit R&D organization, founded in 1988 by major computer vendors to help accelerate the adoption of open systems. Today OSF is an international coalition of 400 organizations—vendors and

STANDARDS ORGANIZATIONS AND VENDOR ALLIANCES—New Rules
and Who Rules?

69

users—working together to identify, acquire, enhance, and implement open systems technologies. Headquartered in Cambridge, MA, OSF has more than 200 employees worldwide.

OSF's hardware-independent software offerings are the OSF/Motif® graphical user interface and the OSF/1® operating system, the OSF Distributed Computing Environment (DCE), and the OSF Distributed Management Environment (DME). [OSF, 1993]

UniForum—The International Association of Open Systems Professionals.

Formerly called \user\group, UniForum is a nonprofit, vendor-independent association of UNIX and open systems professionals dedicated to the standardization, education and implementation of open systems. The association serves as a forum to exchange information about open systems, the UNIX operating system, software, and applications.

Membership includes software developers, systems analysts, engineers, MIS directors, technical executives, VARS, end users, systems integrators, and software vendors. There are over 80 corporate sponsors and over 30 affiliate members from around the world. Overall, UniForum has more than 6,500 members worldwide. [UniForum, 1993]

OMG—The Object Management Group.

OMG is a nonprofit international organization of more than 330+ members representing vendors, software developers, systems integrators and end users. OMG was founded in 1989. It is dedicated to maximizing the portability, reusability and interoperability of computer software and has become the industry focal point for standardization of distributed systems. The members are creating a framework and supporting specifications for commercially available object-oriented environments. The group has adopted the Object Request Broker, a standard for sending messages across client/server networks for application integration and development. [OMG, 1993]

Influencers

Standards influencers are organizations consisting of users and/or vendors who have banded together to influence and set requirements for standards bodies and integrators, as well as to expand the market for standards-based open systems products and services. These organizations are not actively involved in defining or integrating standards at a detail level. Instead, they are involved in defining the *requirements* for standards, endorsing standards body and integrator activities, influencing the direction and emphasis of those activities, and marketing standards-based products and services.

COS—Corporation for Open Systems International.

COS was formed in 1986. It is an international not-for-profit consortium dedicated to the successful introduction of interoperable open systems networking products and services for the computer communications and telecommunications industries. COS has many initiatives for many interrelated technologies including ISDN, TCP/IP, open systems transition and deployment strategies, electronic messaging, multiprotocol routers, and video teleconferencing.

The mission of COS is to accelerate the implementation, deployment, and usage of standards-based, interoperable, open systems networking products and services. [COS, 1994]

SOS—Standards and Open Systems Group.

SOS is an open systems user group that was formed in 1991. The aim of SOS is to force systems and software vendors to create products that allow interoperability between legacy and open systems. The SOS group has called on the major system vendors to work with the Open System Environment Implementors Workshop (OIW) to develop profiles based on available standards and publicly available specifications. [Heffernan, 1992]

OURS—Open User Recommended Systems.

Formed in September 1991, OURS is an end user oriented group formed to do task-force investigations into interoperability, specifically in the areas of software licensing, security, multi-vendor education, and information exchange. [McMullen, 1993]

There are many more organizations involved in standards integration activities. Additional detail on the organizations mentioned, and on other organizations, can be found in the *Standards Groups* appendix of this book.

Creating Standards

The process of creating standards is a well defined one—with very specific procedures and rules about who can participate, when, and how. In general, the process strives for consensus among the participants by drafting specifications, voting on them, then redrafting them until a majority or full consensus (depending on the rules) is achieved. Throughout the process, compromises are common in order to get to agreement on a standard that is acceptable to a majority.

Creating a standard takes time. The process can be expedited in 12-18 months, but it is not unusual for standards to be under development for several years before being approved and adopted by the sponsoring body.

Dr. Pamela Gray, President of UniForum, has described three broad classes of standards. These definitions help explain the process of creating standards:

- *Minimal standard*—A minimal standard embodies only those features about which the participants can easily agree and avoids areas known to be controversial. When a standard is drafted from competing products, the minimal outcome is the intersection of the product definitions—features common to all the competing products.

  Minimal standards are the easiest path for achieving consensus. Existing products usually do not need to be modified to comply with minimal standards. However, since they are usually only marginally functional, these are the worst possible standards in the marketplace and generally only useful as the first step in the standards process.

- *Compromise standard*—A compromise standard also stems from competing products, but adds a few new features to the existing implementations—features that are judged to be valuable in all implementations. Completely new features are usually avoided.

Compromise standards generally require modification to existing products to produce compliance.

- *Maximal standard*—A maximal standard takes one or several existing implementations and builds on them, resulting in a more comprehensive specification than any existing or single implementation.

  Maximal standards require substantial modifications to existing implementations to bring them into compliance. [Gray, 1991]

Open Systems and "Open" Politics

The creation of standards is a long, imperfect process. Power and politics inevitably play a part in the process. Ask a vendor about its support of open systems, and the answer will invariably include a litany of standards organizations to which it belongs. This is to be expected (and even desired), because the standards organizations are defining the future of the vendors' technology. On the other hand, vendors have a vested interest in championing their own technologies—so the process is rife with politics and special interest lobbying, and sometimes falls short of otherwise noble goals.

Some of the political and logistical problems in creating consensus include:

- Avoiding strengthening the position of a single vendor

  In defining standards, the goal is to define them in such a way as to be comprehensible, complete, reliable, and implementable. This works relatively well in cases where a *de facto* standard exists—the process essentially does no more than formalize existing technology. The drawback is that formalizing standards from existing technology gives particular technology vendors significant market advantages.

- Achieving consensus while retaining the value of the standard

  The goal of a vendor-neutral standards process is to define the standards in a way that gives no vendor a significant advantage over another. The process is particularly difficult when *de facto* standards exist, or where there are several competing technologies. In these cases, the standards committee needs to

avoid the appearance of favoritism and takes great pains to
remove any semblance of partiality from the standards. In
order to reach agreement on standards among participants
with competitive and opposing interests, standards committees
are often forced to produce a minimal definition of the standard or include several interface options thereby jeopardizing
or restricting the value. As a result, vendor-neutral standards
are sometimes referred to jokingly as implementation-neutral.[1]

Marshall Rose, in his book on OSI wrote a tongue-in-cheek
criticism of the standards process: "Democracy might be a fine
way to run a government, but it is no way to produce rational
technology." [Rose, 1991]

- Getting the specifications details worked out and achieving a
  quality end-product

The composition of the standards committee at various points
in the standard definition lifecycle is another issue. When a
technology enters the standards process, vendors are motivated to send their best and brightest to represent and safeguard
their proprietary interests. Once the direction is set, however,
the best may be called back to the office to perform more productive tasks, while more "expendable" persons may be sent
to finish the specifications and integrate them into a coherent
set of standards. [Rose, 1991]

Criteria Influencing Standards Development and Adoption

We discussed the focus and work of X/Open and OSF in the
Definitions and Disinformation chapter as examples of differing
approaches to defining and implementing open systems architecture. These approaches reflect the tensions in establishing a consensus forum for defining and managing standards. The tensions in
turn reflect differing perspectives on the benefits and costs of open
systems architecture to the various types of organizations involved:
standards bodies, technology manufacturers and suppliers, and
technology users.

---

[1]This comment was overheard, muttered by a vendor technician responsible for
creating his company's version of a compliant product.

Figure 5.4 introduces some criteria that may be useful in understanding the differing perspectives of organizations involved in defining and adopting open systems standards.

DIFFERING PERSPECTIVES ON OPEN SYSTEMS STANDARDS

Criteria	Standards Creators	Standards Adopters/Integrators	Standards Influencers	
Commitment to Open Systems	high	moderate	low	high
Sense of urgency	low	moderate	high	high
Inertia due to existing investment	low	high	high	moderate
Vendor independence	high	low	low	moderate
Technology independence	high	moderate	low	moderate
Knowledge of specific business requirements	low	moderate	moderate	high
Understanding of technology	moderate	high	high	low
	Standards Bodies	Technology Manufacturers and Suppliers	Technology Users	

Figure 5.4

On one end, the standards bodies are committed to defining standards and are generally vendor-and product-neutral in their allegiance. But these bodies have a low sense of urgency, perhaps because they are rather far away from the technology users and have little understanding of user requirements.

On the other end are technology users who express a high commitment to open systems and have a high sense of urgency to get them implemented. But users also must deal with existing business crises, the inertia caused by their existing investment in proprietary technology, and the technical knowledge that they must infuse in their organizations to implement and manage open technology.

Squarely in the middle, and often on the fence in the market, sit technology vendors. They are the ones that ultimately hold responsibility for translating standards into technology that works—bringing the standards to life at a price users are willing to pay. They also have the most to lose in a fully specified, open environment. They lose the security of their proprietary hold on existing customers as cost barriers are lowered—both the cost of entry into a customer organization by another technology vendor and the cost to the customer of switching vendors and technologies.

Another line might be added to the table (Figure 5.5); the Fear, Uncertainty and Doubt (FUD) factor.

ADDING THE FUD FACTOR

Criteria	Standards Creators	Standards Adopters/Integrators	Standards Influencers	
Commitment to Open Systems	high	moderate	low	high
Sense of urgency	low	moderate	high	high
Inertia due to existing investment	low	high	high	moderate
Vendor independence	high	low	low	moderate
Technology independence	high	moderate	low	moderate
Knowledge of specific business requirements	low	moderate	moderate	high
Understanding of technology	moderate	high	high	low
FUD	**low**	**moderate**	**high**	**low**
	Standards Bodies	Technology Manufacturers and Suppliers	Technology Users	

Figure 5.5

Summary

The market is exerting tremendous pressure to have standards produced as soon as possible. Some vendors, quite naturally, are resisting—looking to protect their market interests. Other vendors are enticed by the prospect of a "level playing field" on which they can develop standard-compliant products and make inroads into clients formerly locked in by proprietary technologies of prominent vendors.

What began as a number of standards organizations, all with their own and sometimes competing agendas in setting the direction of open systems, is now evolving into a network of groups—each playing a more defined, refined role in the overall process of creating workable, usable technology. Standards creators define and integrate base technology standards. They operate on industry, national, and international levels. Standards adopters/integrators provide more support to technology vendors, both hardware and software vendors, in setting the direction for technology and supporting the development of standards compliant technology. Standards influencers provide a voice to the end users of technology in the form of participation in standards requirements processes and combining purchasing power to influence the direction of open systems activities and vendor products. Standards influencers also support end user implementations through training and education on open systems, purchase specifications (X/Open) and branding (e.g., X/Open and COS).

Standards bodies are making progress in specifying computing standards. However, the higher sense of urgency on the part of users often causes users and technology vendors to preempt the work of the standards bodies. The result is a constant battle to resolve inconsistencies between the standards and the implementation of the standards.

Some very impressive work has been accomplished to date. While the mechanisms for defining standards requirements and specifying and implementing standards are imperfect, they are working. The recent and continued reorganizing of various bodies participating in the standards process will further clarify the goals and roles in standardization.

Today, the market is still struggling to establish a formal, accepted, and timely forum and process for creating and maintaining computing standards.

Chapter 6

Standards and Architecture
—The New Game: Who Controls the API?

They are ill discoverers that think that there is no land, when they can see nothing but sea.

—*Sir Francis Bacon*

A little monograph on the ashes of one hundred and forty different varieties of pipe, cigar, and cigarette tobacco.

—*Sir Arthur Conan Doyle*

In this section, we discuss architecture and its role in managing complexity in a heterogeneous, distributed computing environment. We introduce the concepts of open versus proprietary/open technologies and discuss the differences between de jure and de facto standards. Both points of contrast are related to battles for architectural dominance being waged in the marketplace. We introduce the concept of a technology stack, then use the technology stack to format brief discussions of some of the major de jure and de facto standards in the market today.

Standards play a part in every day life. Light bulbs and batteries come in standard sizes. We buy milk and other groceries in standard weights and measures. We are forever arguing about labeling and advertising standards. Standards are forged to facilitate interaction. But some of the most interesting standards and lack of standards show up in human communications.

> *Genesis suggests that at one time "the whole earth used the same language and the same words," and that when Mankind—in overweening pride—began to build a tower (Babel) to reach into Heaven, God confused their language and scattered the people about the Earth.*
> [Genesis 11; Shenker]

Today, there are conservatively 3,000 to 4,000 languages in the world, of which slightly more than 200 are used widely enough to be classified as languages of international importance. More than 95 percent of the world's population uses fewer than 100 languages. You would need just two dozen languages to communicate with about three-quarters of all people living today. Chinese is spoken by

77

20 percent of the world's population. Add English, Spanish, Russian, and Hindi and you can communicate with 45 percent of the world population. Obviously, international travel and communications are rapidly leveling the earth's language barriers. [Katzner, 1975]

From religion to science fiction, we dream of a universal language. The Pentecost refers to followers speaking in tongues to communicate with their listeners from many lands. In Star Trek—The Next Generation, the crew of the starship Enterprise has the benefit of a "Universal Translator," a technology tool that translates the many languages of the inhabitants of the universe into the language of the user.

In today's world, many believe that foreign language barriers can be surmounted through the use of an "artificial" language—a language which has been specially invented to facilitate international communication. Esperanto is the most widely used artificial international language.

> Esperanto, created in 1887, is the dream child of a Polish oculist, L. L. Zamenhof. Esperanto has a simple, uniform structure with simple, regular grammar. Adjectives end in "a," adverbs end in "e," and nouns end in "o." This uniformity contrasts with the inconsistencies of English, which boasts 728 separate endings for irregular verbs alone. Esperanto has only 16 rules of grammar. Its orthography is phonetic, meaning all words are spelled as they are pronounced. The accent of a word always falls on the next-to-last syllable, and each letter has only one sound, unlike, for example, the soft and hard "c" of English. In Esperanto, word derivations are simple. There is one basic root word for every meaning—and each root word can be changed from noun to adjective to adverb to verb simply by affixing the proper suffix. In one edition of an Esperanto-English dictionary, there are only 9,000 Esperanto entries, compared with 19,500 in English. John Wells, a phonetics scholar at the University College in London, called the language "a work of genius." Joseph Stalin once described it as "the language of spies." Estimates of the number of speakers worldwide range from fewer than 1 million to more than 15 million. [Crystal, 1987; Lee, 1987]

The main obstacle to widespread acceptance of Esperanto (a de jure standard) is competition from existing languages, (de facto standards). When Zamenhof invented Esperanto, there were three truly international tongues: English for commerce, French for diplomacy, and German for science. Since then, English has outdistanced the other two in international parlance, and is becoming the *de facto* standard. [Lee, 1987]

In human communications, Esperanto is seeing all the problems of de jure standard acceptance. Although Esperanto is widely considered simpler than English in construction, and robust in the vocabulary of science, diplomacy, commerce, and even poetry, English is a formidable de facto contender.

One of the biggest reasons for non-acceptance of a de jure language standard is the investment we have all made in our native languages and the investment required to learn another.

But when we look closely at the economics, we might reconsider the investment. There is an added cost to international organizations working in multiple languages. Several years ago, the *Economist* pointed to the EEC (European Economic Community) in Brussels as an example of an organization that would benefit from adoption of Esperanto. The EEC translates proceedings into its nine official languages at an estimated cost of $15 per word. Language translation accounts for about a third of the European Commission's total administrative budget.[Economist, 1987] In fact, the EEC undertook a large, multi-year project to develop a prototype automated language translator, using Esperanto as a "bridge" language. The project eventually lost funding and the EEC continues to translate its proceedings by hand.

An Industry View of Computing Architecture— the First Step

Standards for computing *should be* easier to develop than standards governing human communication.

The taxonomy of human communications and interaction is far, far more complex than that of computer operations and communication. However, we see many of the same problems in the definition, acceptance, and use of computing standards as we have witnessed in the development of artificial human languages.[1]

The first step in being able to communicate and interact is agreeing to the taxonomy, or the domain of the interaction and the required classes of interaction. The computing equivalent of this taxonomy is the computing architecture.

COMPUTING ARCHITECTURE

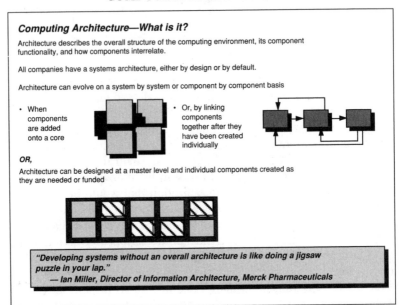

Computing Architecture—What is it?

Architecture describes the overall structure of the computing environment, its component functionality, and how components interrelate.

All companies have a systems architecture, either by design or by default.

Architecture can evolve on a system by system or component by component basis

- When components are added onto a core

- Or, by linking components together after they have been created individually

OR,

Architecture can be designed at a master level and individual components created as they are needed or funded

"Developing systems without an overall architecture is like doing a jigsaw puzzle in your lap."
— Ian Miller, Director of Information Architecture, Merck Pharmaceuticals

Figure 6.1

A computing architecture is the overall structure of the computing environment, its component functionality, and how they interrelate. All computing environments have an architecture, whether it evolved by design or haphazardly. (See Figure 6.1.) Vendor products are generally created in support of the vendor's overall computing architecture. The computing environments in businesses and

---

[1]It seems only logical that conditions would point to somewhat easier going in establishing computing standards than developing a standard human language. However, we are innovating technology at an increasing rate. We cannot possibly establish standards for things that we do not yet know. And, like writers, poets, artists, politicians, and teenagers who continuously renew our languages by creating new words and giving old words new meanings, we will be innovating technology for the foreseeable future. Continuous innovation will require continuous rewriting of standards.

government may contain products from multiple vendors, thereby adding a layer of complexity that make it more difficult to figure out where all the products fit and work together. These heterogeneous environments raised the need for an industry view of architecture—throwing us into what many have referred to as an "architectural crisis."

A Very Simple Logical Computing Model

A model of the computing environment is a useful tool for discussing the various functions involved in a computing environment and how these functions interrelate. At a very high level it is easy to think about a computing architecture in terms of just a few layers. (See Figure 6.2.)

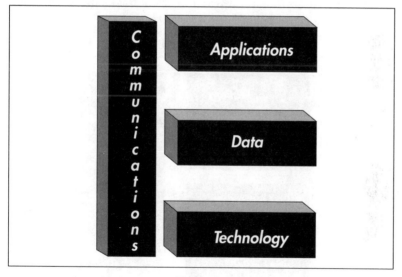

Figure 6.2

- *The applications layer* contains user applications

- *The data layer* contains user data. Data may be physically stored in a variety of formats, including flat files and various databases.

- *The technology layer* contains all the technology necessary to support the data and applications. This layer includes computing hardware, operating system, repositories, management utilities, development languages and tools, etc.

- *The communications layer* contains the technology (network connections, hardware, and communications software) necessary to exchange data between computers.

In these few layers, we can position the functionality and technology of most computing environments.

A Slightly More Complex Logical Computing Model

But, to look at the components of an open environment and the dynamics of the marketplace, we really need to decompose the technology components (technology and communications) into a slightly more complex architectural framework or *technology stack*. (See Figure 6.3.)

TECHNOLOGY STACK

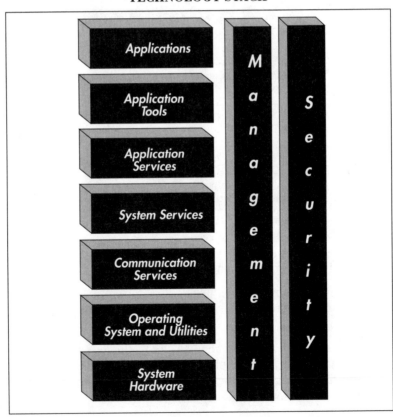

Figure 6.3

The technology stack is a useful model for representing the elements of a complete computing environment from hardware to applications. Here is a brief definition of each element:

- *The applications layer* contains user applications. Logically distinct from the other layers, applications are supported by the services in all of the other components.

- *The applications tools layer* contains a variety of tools and services required by the developer to design, develop, and maintain applications. Among these tools and services are programming languages, CASE tools, code generators, debug facilities, and so on.

- *The applications services layer* consists of services that "enable" applications, by processing, sharing, displaying, or printing data. Examples of applications services include data repository, data access language, data management facilities, transaction processing monitor. A portion of the graphical user interface may also be represented in this layer.

- *The systems services layer* provides the facilities common to all distributed services. Included are the processing model (the distributed object model), the naming model (federated naming), the management framework, and the time service. In a distributed world, even seemingly simple things, such as all nodes in the network having a common concept of time, become very complex.

- *The communications services layer* provides communication between applications on the nodes in the network. Communication services provide support for inter-networking protocol suites and the basic framework for client/server computing independent of the underlying RPC mechanism.

- *The operating system and utilities layer* provides basic operating system and graphics services at each node in the network. Core operating system services provide a consistent approach to fundamental services such as memory management, I/O, and process scheduling.

- *The system hardware layer* contains the physical technology. Included are processors, memory, disk, terminal/workstations, system clock, network links, etc.

- *The management layer* contains system and network management functions to monitor and tune performance throughout the computing environment. Management services are drawn as a vertical box since they monitor and affect every level of the architecture.

- *The security layer* contains security functions to monitor and control access to the computing environment. Security services are drawn as a vertical box since they affect every level of the architecture.

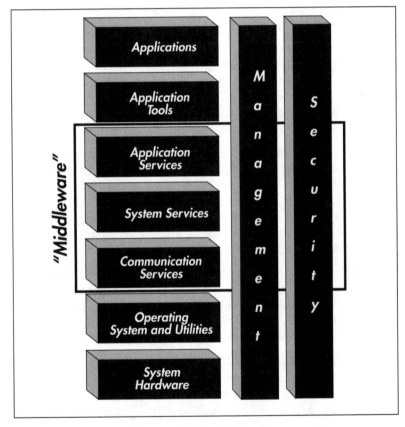

Figure 6.4

"Middleware" is a term often heard in technology discussions today. "Middleware" refers to products that package services at the middle layers of the technology stack required for distributed systems. (See Figure 6.4.) Through discrete segmentation, the technology stack provides a coherent set of architectural building blocks that together constitute a complete computing environment. Each component provides uniquely specific functions, and each layer retains logical independence from the others. **The model can be considered "open" if interfaces are made available for each of the component services and tools within the layers, and the interfaces are well documented and based on *de jure* or *de facto* standards.**

Architecture—the Battlefield

Architectural strategies have become of paramount importance because of the rapid rate of technology innovation. No single vendor is able to lead today's market in everything, and technology users have insisted upon mixing together products from a variety of vendors into a computing environment of their own design. Architectures have become critical because they impose order on the computing environment and make the characteristics of open systems: portability, scalability, interoperability, and compatibility possible.

Competing on architecture is nothing new. Companies have been competing on architecture for years. Before "open systems"— before heterogeneous environments, the users of technology bought the architecture of the technology provider. For example, IBM mainframe users bought the IBM 370 architecture. They benefited from IBM's innovation and improvement of the technology. Because IBM published standards for the architecture, they could choose products from droves of vendors supplying products that worked with the 370 architecture. Because IBM licensed the MVS operating system to Amdahl, they could even buy competing, clone mainframes from a few companies such as Fujitsu. Once they bought into the IBM 370 architecture, mainframe users were, however, "locked into" the architectural framework. They couldn't, for example, buy a package designed to run on a DEC VAX and pop it onto the mainframe (without a *lot of effort*). IBM benefited from this "lockin." Proprietary architectures help ensure continued customer loyalty.

In light of the competition on architecture, standards organizations have invested a great deal in defining industry views of computing architectures (e.g., X/Open and CAE, Unix International and Atlas, OSF and its framework for DCE and DME). These non-proprietary architectures are necessary to create order out of the somewhat chaotic juxtaposition of technology products and guide the standards and technology creation, integration, and evolution efforts of standards organizations. These architectures also provide a macro view to technology evolution and integration—a view that is independent of the direction of any given vendor.

The New Game: Who Controls the API?

When considering architecture and open systems, keep in mind these axioms:

> **Axiom #1: Standardization at any layer in the technology stack makes the layer directly below exchangeable. The question then becomes: "Who controls the standard/API: an industry body or a dominant vendor?"**

A pretty big discussion is going on over *how* to implement open systems. The majority of the commotion focuses on the question of whether or not open systems properties can be achieved with proprietary technologies. And that question centers on who should define and control the direction of and interfaces to technology in the various layers of the technology stack.

In the heterogeneous "open systems" era, technology vendors have worked hard to strengthen the connectivity and thereby the market appeal of their proprietary architectures. Most vendors have given up on the thought of controlling the overall technology stack—those days are gone. Instead, they are focusing on controlling one or more layers (or key components) of the technology stack by attempting to dominate the layer with a *de facto* standard. They can then establish control of the direction of that layer at an industry level by publishing and managing the interface to their product—the set of APIs (application programming interfaces).

> **Axiom #2: Products are valuable at a point in time, but proprietary architectures are valuable over time.**

Proprietary architectures are profitable. If a vendor controls the interfaces to a layer of the technology stack, that vendor has an advantage over other vendors. Since the controlling vendor sets the direction for and maintains the APIs (interface standards), the controlling vendor is in a better position to develop products that maximize the capabilities of the technology layer. And, by modifying the

APIs, the controlling vendor can discipline vendors of competing products.

Microsoft, for instance, is ingenious at the "who controls the API?" game. The Microsoft Windows operating system was positioned as a user interface/operating system. In fact, it was an architecture, based on the rich suite of Win32 APIs for applications development, applications interconnectivity and interoperability, and user navigation, all based on the "look and feel" of the MS Windows environment. Upon this architecture, Microsoft very successfully launched its suite of office products: MS Word, Excel, PowerPoint, Access, and so on. IBM's OS2 operating system was the incumbent in this category with a several year head start, a mature product, and an installed base. But IBM was not as successful as Microsoft in packaging and selling the OS2 architecture. Microsoft handily dominated the desktop operating system and office products markets.

Axiom #3: Technology leads, standards follow.

Proprietary architectures are also valuable to the technology user. Because proprietary architectures are constantly under attack in the open market, they are vigorously defended and are the source of significant technological innovation. With few exceptions, technology leads standardization. (See Figure 6.5.) Great products become *de facto* standards because they fill a need, are better than competitor offerings, and achieve a wide following. Similarly, great products and innovative technologies are formalized into *de jure* standards because they address a need or achieve a wide following (and the vendor or R&D institute agrees to release the technology to the industry).

TECHNOLOGY LEADS, STANDARDS FOLLOW

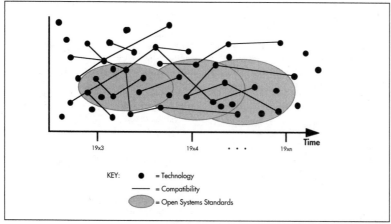

Figure 6.5

Open Versus "Proprietary/Open" Versus Proprietary

We are at the point now where we can add a few more details to our chart depicting *Key Characteristics of Closed versus Open Systems* introduced in the Definitions chapter (Figure 3.1). There are trade-offs between open and proprietary technology. With open technology, there is a level of consistency and predictability when the direction is set and managed at an industry level. With proprietary technology, on the other hand, the speed-to-market of products can be significantly faster given that proprietary technology avoids the whole consensus and support-building process. There are those that argue that there is a subsequent higher rate of innovation with proprietary technology. Therefore, the delicate balance of "proprietary/open" offers some of the benefits and ills of both ends of the spectrum. (See Figure 6.6.)

KEY CHARACTERISTICS OF PROPRIETARY VERSUS OPEN SYSTEMS

	Proprietary	Proprietary/Open	Open
Technology Direction	Direction established by a single vendor	Direction established and managed by the dominant vendor	Direction established by an industry standards body or consortium
Rate of Technology Innovation	High	High	Perhaps somewhat lower. Slower speed-to-market
Technology Selection	"Lockin"—Choice is limited to products within and supporting the primary vendor's line of products	"Lockin"—Choice is limited to vendors supplying compatible, complementary products	Choice free among vendors creating competitive products
Vendor Participation	The vendor is the sole (primary) source for a given customer. Other vendors may provide products that comply with the primary vendor's proprietary protocols under special alliances and agreements	Vendor supplying architecture encourages support for the architecture from other vendors. Generally widespread participation for dominant products	Industry level cooperation and vendor alliances promote widespread support of common frameworks/ models, standards, and source code
Purchase Leverage	Limited leverage with limited set of participating vendors	Limited leverage with vendor supplying the architecture. Strong competition on price and feature among other participating vendors	Open market leads to strong competition on price and feature

Figure 6.6

Choosing Standards and Proprietary/Open APIs

When selecting open standards and proprietary/open APIs, it is important to understand where they came from, who is promoting and supporting them, and why. In particular it is helpful to know:

- *Where did it come from?*

   This question is important in understanding the "baggage" the standard/API may be carrying and the associated politics.

   In the case of proprietary/open API's, the answer to this question may be obvious. But, in the case of standards, the answer may be more obscure. The standard may have been derived from a product as an abstraction of several products, or it might have been written "on spec"—to satisfy a need where no technology products currently exist. The fact that the standard is derived from a product is not necessarily bad, and is often good because of the assurance that the technology worked at one time.

   Knowing where a standard came from can also give some clue as to what it can be used for and the environments in which the standard can be useful. For example, there is a very specialized human language called "Police Motu," spoken by New Guinea constabulary. Given the derivation and use of Police Motu, we can surmise that it is highly unlikely it would be a great language in which to write poetry.

- *How mature is the standard or API?*

   Standards come in all degrees of maturity. They may be just a gleam in an organization's eye, or be proven and well supported. Because of the length of time to consensus, early standards are often little more than a "good start" toward a common approach, and they are valuable only in anticipating the direction of things to come. If the standard is trying to blend several technologies, it may be a minimal version, specifying only the lowest common denominator. As such, it may not really be usable. Immature standards may change directions several times before settling down. Mature standards, however, are usable and reasonably stable.

- *Who supports the standard/API? Who is in control of its direction?*

Who supported or voted on the standard? Was it really open to the "industry" or to just a few "big buck" players?

APIs generally have competitor APIs, with support split along the lines of vendor alliances. It is important to understand what competing APIs exist and which vendors are in the competing camps.

Support for a standard or API can be a good indicator of its potential direction and life span. Just as there are still several hundred languages spoken by only 50,000 Australian aborigines—there are thousands of standards and APIs dying a slow death of disuse and lost support.

- *Standards: What proprietary extensions are contemplated?*

Standards are constantly evolving—often lagging in functionality behind the products that are compliant with them. In selecting standards, it is helpful to understand the direction of standardization efforts—specifically, what extensions or additions are planned for the standard?

Just as a hard cover version of the *American Heritage Dictionary* is of only marginal use when attempting to translate the banter of teenagers in a high school locker room, standards are never as up-to-date as the proprietary products in which they are embedded.

- *What compliant and supporting products are available now?*

To totally ruin a good quote: "Standards for standards' sake makes no more sense than gin for gin's sake." It is important to investigate the products that support the standard, and go beyond "intent to deliver" to "up and running in these environments."

- *Standards: What compliance testing/branding is available?*

Testing for compliance is a difficult issue and a big expense to the technology buyer. To reduce or eliminate this expense, buyers can rest on several levels of assurance:

- Independent verification by an industry organization that creates test suites and "brands" compliant products.

- Verification by user organizations that the product works in certain mainstream environments.

- Vendor warranty—this may be one of the riskier approaches as there is often wide room for interpretation of what constitutes "compliance."

- In-house testing—this is generally the safest approach as the technology buyer can test the product's interaction with specific other products. But, it is also the most costly.

Some Key Standards and Proprietary/Open APIs

It is difficult to keep up with the standards that are being created, adopted, and promoted in the industry today. However, some major standards are often discussed in organizations, vendor materials, and industry press. A few of the major standards are listed here, using the layers of the computing architecture as a guide. Some of the proprietary/open technologies that have become *de facto* standards are also included in this list because of their frequent reference in standards organization and vendor material. The sponsoring group is listed along with each standard/proprietary/open API.

Application Tools

At the application tools level, some common elements include ANSI standard COBOL, ANSI standard C, and specifications that facilitate use of the development tools and debug facilities commonly found in UNIX environments.

Application Services

Several standards organizations concentrate their attention at the application services level in data standards and GUI standards. Other application services are covered by standards integrators.

Examples:

SQL—Structured Query Language.

Pronounced "see kwill" (ANSI, NIST, FIPS). SQL is used to interrogate and process data in a relational database. SQL was originally developed by IBM for its mainframes. It now has many implementations, created for mainframe, mini, and micro database applications. [Electronic Computer Glossary, 1994]

ODBC—Open Database Connectivity specification (Microsoft).

Provides an application programming interface (API) that gives ODBC-enabled front-end applications equal access to most databases. [Windows, 1993]

IDAPI—Independent Database API (Borland, IBM, Novell, WordPerfect).

IDAPI is a programming interface that provides a common language for applications to access the many types of databases that may exist on a network. It includes support for non-SQL and non-relational databases. [Electronic Computer Glossary, 1994]

DAL—Data Access Language (Apple).

DAL is a database interface that allows a Macintosh to access DAL-supported databases on Macintoshes or non-Apple computers. It is a superset of SQL. Database vendors license the specifications for DAL and translate DAL calls to their database engines. [Electronic Computer Glossary, 1994]

DRDA—Distributed Relational Database Architecture (IBM).

DRDA is an SAA-compliant enhancement that allows data to be distributed among DB2 and other SQL/DS databases. Users or programs can access data from SAA or non-SAA systems that implement DRDA. [Electronic Computer Glossary, 1994]

Note: ODBC, IDAPI, DAL, and DRDA are competitive proprietary/open APIs.

NFS—Network File System.

A distributed file system from Sun Microsystems, Inc., that allows data to be shared with many users in a network. NFS allows users to share data regardless of processor type, operating system, network architecture or protocol. NFS implements a subset of UNIX file system semantics, and has been ported to a variety of UNIX and non-UNIX systems. [DG/UX, 1991]

FTAM—File Transfer Access and Management (OSI, GOSIP).

FTAM is an OSI protocol and international standard

that provides access to files stored on dissimilar systems. [Newton, 1993]

OLE—Object Linking and Embedding (Microsoft).

Object Linking and Embedding is an approach for tying information in one document to information in another document (that may be of a different form). The pieces of information are linked so that changes made to the information in one document will be reflected in the other. [Newton, 1993]

VIM—Vendor Independent Messaging Interface (Lotus, Novell, IBM, Apple, Borland, MCI, WordPerfect, and Oracle).

VIM is a programming interface that enables an application to send and receive mail over a VIM-compliant message system such as CC:Mail. [Electronic Computer Glossary, 1994]

MAPI—Microsoft's Windows Messaging Application Programming Interface (Microsoft).

MAPI is Microsoft's Windows Messaging API that is part of WOSA (Windows Open Services Architecture). When Microsoft announced its At Work architecture on June 9, 1993, it said one of At Work's benefits was its integration with Windows messaging. Microsoft said the At Work message protocol interfaces with the Windows Messaging API (MAPI). Users will be able to send and receive messages to and from Microsoft At Work-based devices through any MAPI-enabled e-mail software. [Newton, 1993]

OSF Motif.

Motif is a graphical user interface, the result of the first Request for Technology (RFT) issued by OSF. Motif provides a three-dimensional environment based on the X/Window System™ standard developed by MIT. [OSF, 1991]

OPENLOOK™—Graphical user interface (SUN Microsystems).

OPENLOOK is implemented in two tool kits, one based on X Windows, the other based on NeWS. [DG/UX, 1991]

System Services

Standards creators, integrators, and some special interest groups are working to establish standards at the system services level.

Example:

X.400—(ITU).

X.400 is an international standard that enables disparate electronic mail systems to exchange messages even though each e-mail system may operate internally with its own, proprietary set of protocols. The X.400 protocol acts as a translating software between electronic mail systems allowing users to reach beyond their own e-mail system to the universe of interconnected systems. [Newton, 1993]

X.500—(ITU) Directory Services.

Recommendation X.500, together with other recommendations in this series, was produced to facilitate the interconnection of information processing systems to provide directory services. The set of all such systems, together with the directory information they hold, can be viewed as an integrated whole, called the "Directory." The information held by the Directory, collectively known as the Directory Information Base (DIB), is typically used to facilitate communication between, with, or about objects such as application entities, people, terminals, and distribution lists.

The Directory plays a significant role in the Open Systems Interconnection. It provides the directory capabilities required by OSI applications, management processes, other OSI layers, and telecommunications services. [88Open, 1991]

Communication Services

Significant progress has been made in standardizing communications and achieving widespread adoption of a limited number of communications protocols.

Examples:

OSI—Open Systems Interconnection (ISO).

OSI is a suite of communication protocols and the only internationally accepted framework of standards for communication between different systems made by different vendors. The OSI model organizes the communications process into seven different categories and places these categories in a layered sequence based on their relation to the user. [Newton, 1993]

TCP/IP—Transmission Control Protocol/ Internet Program (DARPA).

TCP/IP is a set of protocols that was developed in the 1970s by the U.S. Department of Defense's Advanced Research Projects Agency (DARPA) as a military standard. It was developed by the military as a means of connecting dissimilar computers across many types of networks. Its multi-vendor connectivity is attractive to commercial users as well. Many organizations have adopted TCP/IP as an interim step, while awaiting the availability of OSI products. Consequently, TCP/IP now is supported by a wide array of vendors on virtually all platforms from super computers to minicomputers, personal computers, mainframes, technical workstations and data communications equipment. It is also the protocol commonly used over Ethernet (as well as X.25) networks and is the communications protocol on the Internet. [Newton, 1993]

Operating System and Utilities

Significant attention has been devoted to standardizing interfaces of operating system and utilities to facilitate portability of applications across computing platforms.

Examples:

POSIX—Portable Operating System Interface (IEEE).

POSIX is formally known as the IEEE 1003.1 standard defining the language interface between application programs and operating systems. Adherence to

POSIX enables source code compatibility when moving programs from one operating system to another POSIX-compliant operating system. POSIX specifications were originally compiled from features of UNIX System V and BSD UNIX but in recent years has been modified to define interface specifications for non-UNIX operating systems. [Electronic Computer Glossary, 1994]

SVID—System V Interface Definition (AT&T).

SVID is the AT&T specification defining the UNIX System V operating system. SVID Release 3 specifies the interface for UNIX System V Release 4. [Electronic Computer Glossary, 1994]

SPEC 1170—(X/Open).

Spec 1170 defines a common set of APIs across multiple flavors of Unix. All Spec 1170-compliant Unix versions will interoperate, and any application written to the spec will run on any compliant Unix flavor without modification. Incompatibility at the binary level will remain. [Digital News & Review, 1994; Datamation, 1994]

System Management

Progress in standardizing interfaces at the system management level is not as far along.

Examples:

SNMP—Simple Network Management Protocol (DoD).

The Department of Defense and commercial TCP/IP implementors collaborated in 1988 to design a network management architecture for the needs of the average internet (a collection of disparate networks joined together with bridges or routers). SNMP was originally designed as the TCP's stack network management protocol. It can now manage virtually any network type and has been extended to include non-TCP devices such as 802.1 Ethernet bridges. SNMP is widely deployed in TCP/IP (Transmission Control

Protocol/Internet Protocol) network. However, through transport independence, it has been implemented over Ethernet as well as OSI transports. SNMP became a TCP/IP standard protocol in May 1990. It operates on top of the Internet Protocol, and is similar in concept to IBM's NetView and ISO's CMIP. [Newton, 1993]

CMIP—Common Management Information Protocol (ISO).

CMIP is used for exchanging network management information. Typically, this information is exchanged between two management stations. Through CMIP, information can be exchanged between an application and a management station. CMIP has been designed for OSI networks, but it is transport independent. Theoretically, it could run across a variety of transports, including, for example, IBM's Systems Network Architecture. [Newton, 1993]

System Hardware

Interfaces at the system hardware level are addressed by alliances of vendors with similar technology platforms and by industry standards organizations.

Examples:

ABI—Application Binary Interface (UI).

A specification that defines interfaces to make applications portable across different architectures at the binary level. [Datapro, 1994]

ANDF—Architecture Neutral software Distribution Format (OSF).

Architecture Neutral Distribution Format (ANDF) supports binary compatibility of applications across platforms. The developer generates the applications in an intermediate ANDF language. The ANDF language is then compiled into machine language at the time it is installed on the target machine. The goal of ANDF is to facilitate economic development and distribution of shrink-wrapped packages. [OSF, 1991]

FDDI—Fiber Optic Data Distribution Interface (ANSI, GOSIP, ISO).

Fiber Distributed Data Interface. FDDI is a 100 Mbps fiber optic LAN ANSI standard. It uses a "counter-rotating" token ring topology and is compatible with the standards for the physical layer of the OSI model. An FDDI LAN is typically known as a "backbone" LAN, used for joining file servers together and for joining other LANs together. The theoretical limit of Ethernet, measured in 64 byte packets, is 14,800 packets per second. By comparison, Token Ring is 30,000 and FDDI is 170,000 pps. FDDI LANs also work on twisted copper pairs. [Newton, 1993]

System Security

System security requirements are often generated by government work, although some standards organizations are also addressing security standards.

Example:

DES—Data Encryption Standard (NIST, FIPS).

DES is an algorithm for encrypting (coding) data designed by the National Bureau of Standards. DES is designed to make it impossible for anyone without the decryption key to get the data back in unscrambled form. The DES standard enciphers and deciphers data using a 64-bit key specified in the Federal Information Processing Standard Publication 46, dated January 15, 1977. [Newton, 1993]

Integrated Environments

A number of organizations are specifying the components required to support a complete computing environment and endorsing various standards and products to create the environment. These specifications are used to develop and integrate technologies and products, as well as for spelling out purchasing requirements. On the following pages some of the better-known frameworks are listed.

Examples:

CAE—Common Applications Environment (X/Open).

CAE is a broad conceptual framework for implementing open systems. The CAE identifies those areas X/Open sees as critical for portability and interoperability. They include: systems management, object management, workstation data access, on-line transaction processing, mainframe data access, programming languages, data management, data interchange, security, and internationalization. This comprehensive environment covers all the standards, above the hardware level, that are needed to support open systems. XPG defines detailed specifications and interfaces for communicating within this framework. [X/Open, 1994]

XPG—X/Open Portability Guide.

X/Open designed the XPG as the vehicle for implementing open systems in the field. XPG is an evolving portfolio of applications programming interfaces (API), protocols, and other specifications that are supported with an extensive set of conformance tests and a distinct trademark carried only on products that comply with the X/Open definitions. There have been many releases of the XPG, beginning with XPG1 in 1985 that specified a core set of interfaces and services. The most recent release, XPG4, has expanded dramatically into the area of communications and networking. By using the XPG, vendors can build products that conform to the most complete and practical set of open systems definitions available. [X/Open, 1994]

DCE—Distributed Computing Environment (OSF).

The Open Software Foundation Distributed Computing Environment (DCE) allows programmers to build distributed applications that put standard protocols and services to work. DCE is a collection of tools and services that ease the development of distributed applications, which in turn, make information available throughout a network. This technology allows users to retrieve information easily—regardless of where it is stored—and distribute it to wherever it is needed. DCE includes security, directory naming, time synchronization, file sharing, RPCs and multithreading services. [OSF, 1994]

DME—Distributed Management Environment (OSF).

The OSF Distributed Management Environment (DME) provides a unified approach for managing systems, networks, and user applications in heterogeneous environments. Its purpose is to make system and network more efficient and cost effective. OSF is integrating several technologies to form a DME framework that supports the management of systems resources as well as the development of applications for distributed systems management. [OSF, 1994]

GOSIP—Government Open Systems Interconnect Profile.

GOSIP is the U.S. government's version of the OSI protocols, and is used typically as a compliance requirement in government networking purchases. GOSIP addresses communication and interoperation among end systems and intermediate systems. It defines specific peer-level, process-to-process and terminal access functionality required within and across government agencies. [Newton, 1994]

CORBA—Common Object Request Broker Architecture.

The Object Management Group sponsors standard-setting for the systems-software mechanism required to realize distributed object computing. This mechanism is called an Object Request Broker (ORB). OMG's first cut at open ORB standards, the Common Object Request Broker Architecture (CORBA) version 1.1, was released October 1991. [Shelton, 1993]

Summary

De jure and *de facto* standards, open and proprietary technologies—they all have a role. They all have their pros and cons. It is important to be able to put the various standards and technologies into perspective—to understand their relative contributions to the overall computing architecture.

While the number of standards and published APIs may seem bewildering at first, the quantity correlates to the complexity of the computing environment. Remarkable progress has been made, particularly in the efforts of defining interface standards (the communications level) and in defining complete computing environments. Communications standards, particularly TCP/IP (*de facto*) and OSI (*de jure*) have gained widespread support. OSF's integrated computing environment, DCE, has been released to technology vendors and is beginning to show up in some business environments.

We are seeing significant progress toward the goal of a standard operating environment. While we still have a long way to go, it does seem that we are making more progress in the development of a standard or set of standard computing environments than we are making in developing and accepting a standard human language.

Perhaps logic prevails, after all...

Chapter 7

Vendor Directions—
Looking Beyond "OpenSpeak"

But four young Oysters hurried up, All eager for the treat: Their coats were brushed, their faces washed, Their shoes were clean and neat— And this was odd, because, you know, They hadn't any feet.

—Lewis Carroll

My interest is in the future because I am going to spend the rest of my life there.

—Charles F. Kettering

Major technology vendors are actively committed to open systems, but in individualized ways, depending upon their desire to protect proprietary product lines or their allegiance to particular standards organizations. To go beyond generic OpenSpeak and pin down the specific direction of a given vendor and the compliance of that vendors products with specific standards, potential buyers must conduct a careful, detailed analysis of "open" products and technologies. In this section, we begin with an overview of the open systems technology marketplace and a view of the various goals and motivations of major players in that marketplace. We then propose a framework for evaluating the open direction and intent of technology vendors, as well as the actual 'openness' of their products. We close this chapter with a discussion of the open direction and products of several major technology vendors: HP, Sun, Dec, IBM, and Microsoft.

"Then you should say what you mean," the March Hare went on. "I do," Alice hastily replied; "at least—at least I mean what I say—that's the same thing, you know." "Not the same thing a bit!" said the Hatter. "Why, you might just as well say that 'I see what I eat' is the same thing as 'I eat what I see!'"

"You might just as well say," added the March Hare, "that 'I like what I get' is the same thing as 'I get what I like!'" "You might just as well say," added the Dormouse, which seemed to be talking in its sleep, "that 'I breathe when I sleep' is the same thing as 'I sleep when I breathe!'"

—Lewis Carroll, Alice's Adventures in Wonderland

This conversation at the Mad Hatter's tea party is no more confusing to Alice than the marketing banter surrounding open systems to organizations wanting to buy open products and implement open systems. We refer to the vendors' mantra-like repetition of open intentions, directions, support of standards, and membership in standards organizations as *OpenSpeak*. But behind the seemingly mandatory *OpenSpeak*, real miscommunication exists—some unintentional, some intentional. It is a confusing time for everyone. Vendors are attempting to decipher customer needs while reckoning just exactly how far and how fast they want to and need to conform to industry standards to placate current customers and woo new ones. Users are struggling to derive, determine, and communicate their needs. Standards organizations and vendor alliances often sit in the middle, sometimes helping communication, sometimes muddying it. Even with the best of intentions, all parties have their own agendas. And between the parties, the many interpretations of words and intentions contribute to an air of confusion, for everyone.

Because of the prolific development of new products, when selecting products and establishing vendor relationships, you must ask some key questions: How do we make sense of the marketplace? How do we go beyond the generic *OpenSpeak* that seems to be a marketing requirement today and truly understand where a vendor stands on open systems?

Overview of the Technology Marketplace

The technology marketplace exists to serve those who use the technology, so let's back up and briefly review the needs of the business—the ultimate technology customer.

Business computing needs exist on several levels. That is, businesses need:

- The ability to implement computing technology that will enhance the competitive position of the business

- The ability to implement functionality-rich technology that meets the needs of the organization and the user and is palatable to and usable by both

- The ability to continuously assimilate new technology into the computing environment as new technology promises to deliver business benefit

- The ability to manage technology costs (or, alternatively, the ability to protect significant technology investments)

Basically, businesses need the flexibility and freedom to choose and "knit together," or *integrate*, technologies into a computing environment customized to their own business situation. Each business must be able to constantly renew the computing environment by incorporating new technologies. But, the business also needs a degree of stability in its computing environment—no business can afford, either from a cost or a business disruption standpoint, to constantly throw out technologies and replace them with new.

Open Systems are Changing the Approach to Systems Integration

To understand the technology marketplace today, one must realize that open systems have radically changed that marketplace. As a result, they have also changed the approach of IS functions to systems integration.

In the past, major technology vendors assumed architectural leadership in the marketplace by defining the architecture of their products. Large vendors led, smaller vendors followed. By and large, the marketplace view of technology architecture (the technology stack view) was defined in terms of the architectures of just a few major vendors (e.g., IBM, DEC). In the wake of open systems efforts to standardize technology definition and the interfaces into technology components, no single vendor owns the definition of the full technology stack within the marketplace. And today, within large technology user organizations, no single vendor owns the full implementation of the technology stack. The concept of a computing architecture has become larger than a single vendor's implementation.

Historically, when integrating systems technologies—selecting and assembling the components of the computing environment, IS as the technology representative of the business, was limited to the architecture of the primary technology vendor servicing the organization. Today, by defining and managing the implementation of the technology stack, the IS function is able to define a computing architecture customized to the business needs—knitting together industry standards and technology from multiple vendors. The resulting framework gives the organization greater control in managing the evolution of its own collection of technology. By using standardized interfaces between technologies and gaining independence in the process, organizations have greater freedom to substitute technologies at each layer independently of the other layers. Those substitutions can be made on a schedule and in a manner driven by the organization, not the vendor.

Benefits of this independence include:

- Flexibility in integrating new technology at one level of the technology stack without seriously disturbing technology at another level

- Greater flexibility in scaling technology components to meet changing business needs

- Flexibility in choosing technologies and switching between vendors

Openness offers choice to the technology consumer. The key is defining the architecture—the framework of standards, technologies, and interfaces that will give the organization the needed flexibility to support its computing needs as well as the strength to manage its vendor relationships. The challenge to the IS organization is to become more adept at systems integration and assume technology leadership within the organization, roles previously provided by the vendors.

Openness is a Delicate Balance for Technology Vendors

Complicating the technology marketplace today is the fact that technology customer and vendor objectives, at times, are in direct conflict. While the market is demanding vendor-independent definitions of the levels and component technology of the technology stack, vendors are faced with the harsh reality of building and sustaining profitable entities in a tumultuous technology marketplace. Developing a practical, commercial approach to open systems means delving into untested, unknown areas. Successful market strategies in the past have been based on proprietary product lines with strong competition between product lines, not necessarily always between individual products. Most vendors are clinging to the known, profitable business model ("as proprietary as possible") while embarking on a marketing strategy singing the praises of open systems ("as open as possible"). With the advent of open systems, vendors are forced to reevaluate their own business strategies against the demands of the market as a whole and their customers in particular.

From a vendor's viewpoint, the balance between open and proprietary is a delicate one. The dilemma is one of control, competition, customer demands, distribution channels, and organizational structure. Proprietary technologies offer more control and less competition, narrower distribution but more specialized channels, higher profit margins with admittedly dwindling long term market appeal. On the other hand, open technologies offer broader market appeal, less control and more competition, broader distribution and lower margins. Open systems require a more flexible vendor organization geared toward high competition while still maintaining a level of customer service.

Today's vendors span the full spectrum of business models, from very proprietary to very open. For example, IBM is faced with the difficult challenge of protecting its proprietary product lines and the associated captive customer base, while answering user demands for open systems. In response, IBM promotes a "user-centric" view of open systems that highlights the need for a common user interface, while downplaying the importance of openness in other layers of the technology stack. This posture allows IBM to argue that its proprietary product lines offer the benefits of open systems.

Vendors with proprietary product lines will continue developing strategies to satisfy market demands for open systems while avoiding the risks of writing off their proprietary product lines.

Microsoft's marketing strategy has been to position open systems as the effective management of the application programming interface (API). The company proposes that technology users standardize on APIs between each layer of the technology stack, allowing for the smooth transition of technology components. Microsoft's business strategy is *to own but publish* the APIs at several layers of the technology stack—a clearly proprietary/open move.

Personal computers (PCs) are a classic example of the power of a proprietary/open strategy. Publishing interface standards allows other vendors to play, both in direct competition and as supporting cast, at a layer in the technology stack, while at the same time avoiding the inertia and delays created by the more formal definition of industry interface standards. PC technology has expanded rapidly because of published interfaces to component technology, while allowing the owners of the technology (e.g., Intel processors, Microsoft operating systems, and Apple's published technologies) to establish strong proprietary positions in the PC technology marketplace.

Our experience in the PC marketplace illustrates both the up- and down-side commercial risks of introducing broad-scale open information technology.

- On the positive side, a multibillion dollar industry was created de novo within a few years. Many old and new firms profited, and this technology continues to advance and be actively demanded by the marketplace.

- On the downside, many technology vendors struggled and continue to struggle with both the rapid pace of change and the new market rules of standardization and openness. Today, of all the giant mainframe vendors, only IBM remains to play a dominant role in the PC marketplace.

Open systems vendors are striving to capture the benefits of broader market appeal and distribution (grabbing the open systems tiger by the tail), while avoiding the risks of losing the competition for the most "popular open products" and/or support for profitable proprietary product lines (being eaten in the fruckus).

Technology Vendors Wear Multiple Hats

In monitoring today's technology marketplace, it is fascinating to observe technology vendors in the open systems game because they concurrently play many different (and at times, conflicting) roles: (See Figure 7.1.)

- As members of standards-integrating bodies

- As standards influencers

- As technology creators

- As technology market leaders and visionaries with and without pure R&D alliances

- As manufacturers of final products

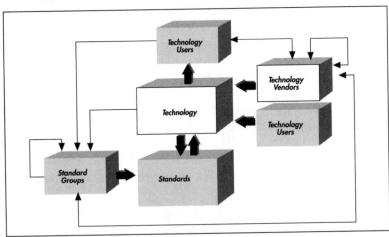

Figure 7.1

To succeed in all these roles, vendors pursue multiple strategies simultaneously. For example:

- Microsoft chooses to own APIs while publishing the architecture of its products so that other vendors can use and connect with Microsoft technology

- Sun is an innovator that creates *de facto* standards by licensing its technology specifications to other vendors who can then create technology that works with and competes with Sun's technology

- IBM is pursuing both "open" and proprietary product lines—both have strong markets

- Most major technology vendors participate in standards-setting and standards-integrating bodies in one capacity or another (and often in multiple capacities)

Spectators are naturally confused because the vendors themselves are genuinely laboring to create a cohesive vision from conflicting product strategies, conflicting customer needs, and disparate tactical responses. Therefore, the prudent open systems buyer must research facts carefully and challenge public statements which may overstate vendors' total commitment to open systems.

Transitional Market Behaviors are Conflicting

The marketplace, like the technology, is in transition. Throughout this book, we have emphasized the contrast between the traditional, homogeneous computing environment and the distributed, open systems environment.

The industry is not squarely in either corner today: it is in transition between these two very different worlds. It may be comforting to consider that perhaps this book is being written during the "adolescence" of open systems computing. (At least we are past the "terrible twos"!) We concurrently observe vendor behaviors appropriate to both traditional and open realms, which can be very confusing:

- Vendors join standards-setting groups, ostensibly to promote neutral standards—BUT—they exert great pressure within the standards groups to adopt their own proprietary technologies and products or to slow the standards process until their own technology catches up

- Vendors support the need to produce standards-compliant products—BUT—they add *features* to the products to differentiate them, often in the process negating the open intentions of the product

If the open systems movement defines the equivalent of "3-pronged electrical plugs," we will be able in the future to distinguish without difficulty among all the various appliances that use those standard plugs. However, while we are still in the standards-defining process, the marketplace is extremely complex to understand. The wide variety of vendor open systems *definitions* is only the tip of the iceberg. The variety of open systems strategies and real products is even more boggling. Navigating the marketplace is not easy.

Assessing the Openness of Vendor Strategies and Technologies

The complexity of the open systems world today, with its multiplicity of standards and vendor claims, makes a valid, objective assessment of vendor direction difficult. For a company changing technology platforms today, there are no easy, clear choices leading to one direction or another (proprietary or open, this vendor or that). We offer a framework that can assist in understanding the relative commitment of technology vendors to open systems.

This framework, however, is limited to assessing the "openness" of particular vendor strategies and technologies, not the functionality or performance of the technology or its applicability to any given business environment. A particular company or "user group" should use this framework and the subsequent vendor reviews only in conjunction with its own strategic business goals, computing capability needs, strategic systems direction, and assessment of the functionality and fit of given technologies.

Vendor Assessment Framework

In looking at vendor commitment to open systems, it is helpful to first understand the vendor's strategic direction and competitive strategies, then look at the vendor's specific technologies. (See Figure 7.2.)

VENDOR AND TECHNOLOGY EVALUATION FRAMEWORK

Vendor strategic direction and strategies

- Business situation and financial condition

- Stated approach to open systems

- Business competitive strategies—e.g., technology innovator and de facto standards leader versus adoptor of industry standards

- Commitment to and participation in industry standards bodies

- Rate of standards adoption

- Research and development direction(s)

"Openness" of various technologies

- Standards supported

- Technology direction

- Visibility of 'extensions'

Figure 7.2

This framework is useful in understanding both the current and probable future openness of a particular product given the open commitment and support of the vendor. In this chapter, we illustrate an approach to understanding vendor support of open systems and the "openness" of products using this framework. In discussing the approach towards open systems of our selected vendors, we will use the following format:

- Historical perspective

- Recent financial performance

- Definition of open systems

- Open systems strategy

- Observed strategy (product level evidence)

- Summary

Open Systems Technology Trends

Before we move into the discussion of specific vendor strategies, we would like to point out some trends or rough directions in open systems technology to keep in mind when reviewing vendor strategies:

Trend #1: As layers within the technology stack are standardized, the competition for market differentiation is pushed to the next higher layer.

What we mean is that as the standardization of each technology stack layer occurs, the products within that layer acquire "commodity-like" characteristics. The competition for differentiation between vendors is then logically pushed to the next higher layer in the technology stack. For example, the industry is solidifying its support for TCP/IP and OSI as the open communication standards and has moved its attention to the operating system layer of the technology stack—the topic of current heated debate. However, the industry is beginning to come to terms at the operating system layer as well. Soon, attention will be forced upwards to middleware, databases, and other applications services.

What will be the final frontier? Ultimately, if hardware, operating systems, application tools and services become "commodities," the only possible differentiator may be applications. The continued packaging of application software, along with bundling of best practices in the software packages, will be a trend limiting differentiation even within the applications layer. And even this layer offers some standardization, suggesting that the final differentiation may lie in how businesses apply applications to their own business processes in the quest for competitive advantage. However, at least in the short term (5-to-7 years) expect to see the competition move from the operating system/utilities and communication services layers to the "middleware" layers (systems services and applications services).

Trend #2: Open systems technologies will influence the client/server movement.

Open systems will impact network services (interoperability between clients and servers, servers and servers, etc.) through middleware products like DCE, which has the potential to become a force in this arena. Middleware products address the connectivity issues of systems distribution and the integration of products from multiple vendors.

While vendors support this facet of open systems (interoperability) because it will reduce bridging costs across vendor platforms, they will continue to insert "non-standard" features to differentiate their products from the competition and to maximize the computing efficiency and power within their product lines.

Trend #3: Distributed object computing is coming.

Almost all vendors discussed in this chapter are planning to implement distributed object computing strategies on top of DCE in the 2-to-4 year timeframe. CORBA 2.0, the object management group's (OMG) standard, is positioned to be a key enabler for interoperability, and perhaps portability, in a distributed object environment.

Trend #4: Vendors are fighting for survival in the open systems world.

Hardware vendor revenues and profit levels have been hit as never before. Restructuring will remain a key factor over the transition years. An important vendor evaluation criterion (for both hardware and software vendors) in the near term should be, "What are the chances of the particular vendor surviving the restructuring?" For example, many players, including the large database vendors, are entering the race to provide front-end client/server development tools. As the market matures and is saturated with products, the weaker vendors' competitive advantages will erode and they will lose their footing in an impending market shakeout within the next few years.

Trend #5: Vendors will continue to pool R&D resources via consortia and alliances.

The industry is currently realigning the respective roles of standards organizations, various consortia, and participating vendors. Although the industry is withdrawing from pooling development and marketing resources, the trend of sharing R&D costs through vendor consortia and alliances will continue in the near term.

The Open Systems Strategies of Several Technology Vendors

The material in this section was compiled from vendor-published materials.[1] We will use the assessment framework described above, as well as the technology stack introduced in the *Standards* chapter to describe and contrast the open systems strategies of five major technology vendors:

- Digital Equipment Corporation (DEC)

- Hewlett-Packard (HP)

- International Business Machines (IBM)

- Microsoft Corporation

- Sun Microsystems (Sun)

    These discussions should suggest to the reader (among other things) the level of detail to which one must (unfortunately) descend to comprehend the nuances of open systems product offerings.

Digital Equipment Corporation (DEC)

During the '60s and '70s Digital established itself as a leading computer vendor with the PDP line of computers. These were so successful that Digital introduced new PDP models even after launching the VAX product line in the later 1970s. The VAX gained popularity by providing scalable products from workstation to midrange server. VAXes formed the backbone of Digital throughout the 1980s and into the 1990s, inventing and popularizing distributed computing. For years Digital was the only alternative to the IBM glass house.

    But as the open systems movement gathered steam, Digital found itself in a situation similar to IBM's—torn between a highly profitable, proprietary product line and market forces demanding open systems, interoperability, and reduced dependence on individual vendors. Initially, Digital leaned toward the higher margins of proprietary hardware and software, and in the process lost market share in the workstation segment to Sun and HP. By 1990, Digital

---

[1]We also confirmed the compilation with the vendors themselves—passing through several cycles of review.

recognized the market shift toward open systems and responded with a corporate thrust into Open Systems, and the Alpha product line—a scalable, high speed RISC platform, announced in 1992. And while it took a full 5 years for the VAX to reach 50% of DEC's hardware system revenues, Alpha reached the 50% mark in only 18 months.

DIGITAL RECENT FINANCIAL PERFORMANCE

Year	Revenue (000s)	Income (Loss) (000s)
1993	$14,371,000	($251,000)
1992	$13,931,000	($2,796,000)
1991	$13,911,000	($617,000)
1990	$12,943,000	$74,000
1989	$12,742,000	$1,073,000

Definition of Open Systems

In Digital's view, users want openness to accomplish several basic business objectives: design flexibility, adaptability to change, optimum use of assets, and productivity. As a result, Digital has coupled Openness with Client/Server as the prime corporate directive. In designing products, Digital uses the IEEE P1003.0 Working Group definition of open systems:

> "A system that implements sufficient open specifications for interfaces, services and supporting formats to enable properly engineered applications software:
>
> • To be ported with minimal changes across a wide range of systems
>
> • To interoperate with other applications on local and remote systems
>
> • To interact with users in a style that facilitates user portability"

Stated Open Systems Strategy

The Digital strategy for Open Systems is "to provide the silicon, software, networking and services customers need to implement Open Systems using the Client/Server model." In silicon, Digital continues in its Alpha product line the scalable component philosophy that it began with the VAX, expanding to mainframes and supercomputers. In software, Digital provides middleware products to address users' needs to join products from different vendors into one corporate architecture. Digital is a long-standing supporter of open systems architecture, delivered through a set of products that are based on X/Open, OSF, ISO, ANSI, and IEEE standards, and delivered on many other vendor platforms as well. Digital continues to incorporate standards into its products, providing, for example, products that meet X/Open XPG4 specifications.

Digital's UNIX implementation is DEC OSF/1, which runs on Alpha platforms. Digital still ships and maintains its ULTRIX implementation, compatible with DEC OSF/1, for VAX and MIPS-based systems. DEC OSF/1 carries a commitment to standards conformance. DEC OSF/1 and OpenVMS have both achieved XPG3 branding. DEC OSF/1 is XPG4 branded as well. All three of Digital's current operating system products—DEC OSF/1, OpenVMS, and Windows NT—conform to the POSIX 1003.1 standard and have been certified according to the US government's FIPS (Federal Information Processing Standard) 151-2. DEC OSF/1 also conforms to the POSIX 1003.2 standard for shell and utilities and to the final draft of the 1003.1b (formerly 1003.4) real-time extensions standard.

Digital maintains active membership in 150 standards committees, including IEEE POSIX, X/Open, the Open Software Foundation, the Object Management Group, and other formal standards and consortia activities. Digital participated in founding OSF, X/Open, and X Consortium and has been active in developing standards through various recent means such as:

- Contributions to OSF/Motif technology: Digital's XUI Toolkit Application Programming Interface (API) and the User Interface Language (UIL)

- Contributing technology to the OSF DCE (Distributed Computing Environment)

- Contribution of the TxRPC transaction processing specification to X/Open

- Contribution of the CORBA specification to OMG

SPEC 1170 has emerged as a widely accepted definition of what a common UNIX specification should provide. Announced September 1, 1993, it is a multi-vendor agreement on a set of Application Programming Interfaces (APIs) that define the UNIX operating environment. Formally endorsed by over 75 companies,

SPEC 1170 will become an X/Open specification. X/Open will implement a branding and certification program, in which Digital intends to participate.

Observed Strategy

Digital's current hardware line consists of three classes of processors:

- VAX CPUs

- Alpha AXP RISC CPUs, ranging from PC-class to mainframe-class machines

- Intel-based PC processors

The VAXes are DEC's very successful, proprietary minicomputer platforms. They still account for the majority of Digital's sales volume. DEC says it intends to continue to produce the VAX line for the foreseeable future.

Digital's RISC technology is Alpha, an enhanced-performance chip used in everything from high performance workstations to supercomputers. Alpha was the first true 64 bit chip, and is listed in the *Guinness Book of Records* as the fastest chip in the world. Digital developed and licenses the Alpha chip.

Digital supports the OpenVMS, DEC/OSF/1, and Windows NT operating systems (and MS/DOS on its Intel line).

- VMS is Digital's long-standing, extremely successful, proprietary operating system (non-UNIX). Now called OpenVMS, it runs on the VAX and Alpha product lines. OpenVMS supports major industry standards, including those for networking, data management, system, language, and user interface services. Examples of OpenVMS support include OSF/DCE, POSIX 1003.1, and OSF/Motif.

- DEC OSF/1 is Digital's UNIX operating system for the Alpha platform, designed to handle both commercial and technical computing. DEC OSF/1 brings the System V and Berkeley Software Distribution (BSD) UNIX variants together on the Mach kernel of OSF/1. Digital also offers the System V Environment for DEC OSF/1 V2.0, which provides a UNIX System V Release 4, (SVR4), user environment for general users, application programmers and system administrators by providing SVR4 commands, libraries and tools as an extension to the DEC OSF/1 operating system.

• Windows NT is Digital's implementation of the Microsoft operating system on Alpha, and in the future on Intel machines.

Digital spans its operating systems across the line of hardware
platforms, as well as implementing third-party operating systems on
its Intel products. Digital hardware platform-operating system combinations are illustrated in Figure 7.3 (current capabilities are
marked "Y" for "yes" and future plans are marked "ITD" for "Intend
to Deliver"). DEC OSF/1 is engineered by Digital, based on operating system technology components from the Open Software
Foundation; OpenVMS is engineered by Digital, but incorporates
more third party components over time; and Windows NT is engineered by Microsoft and implemented by Digital on its platforms. In
addition, Digital emphasizes that engineering is increasingly done
by one central group (especially the open systems components such
as DCE and objects) and then implemented by product line, so questions of portability should be reduced over time.

DEC OPERATING SYSTEMS

Hardware	OpenVMS	ULTRIX	OSF/1	Windows NT	SCO UNIX	DOS,OS2, Windows
VAX	Y	Y				
Alpha	Y		Y	Y		
Intel				ITD	Y	Y

Figure 7.3

The major standards and proprietary/open technologies supported by Digital are depicted using our technology stack for each
of Digital's major platforms in Figure 7.4.

In summary, Digital's operating system and hardware strategies are broad. Digital maintains that the broad focus is required to
help users with issues of connectivity and interoperability. The company is managing the broadness of its strategies by leveraging outside resources (Microsoft, OSF, etc.) and using central engineering
to increase commonality between operating environments and
reduce cost. Digital has repeatedly stressed its commitment to openness, and its success with open systems-based products is rising as
the focus on open systems has shifted from "hot boxes" to multi-vendor interoperability, an area of traditional strength for Digital. Digital
feels that it has met the challenge of retaining the profitability of its

VAX product line while making the transition to open systems, by providing users with a choice in how they implement Open Systems. In this light, the open features and connectivity strength of Digital's data communications and middleware products are typically perceived as very strong.

DIGITAL PLATFORMS

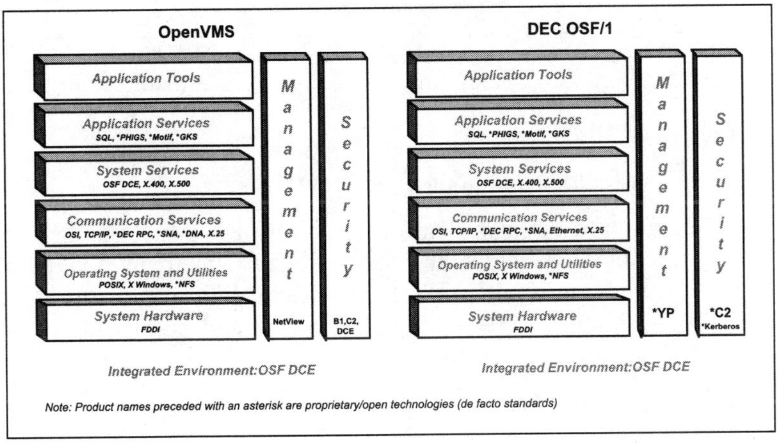

Figure 7.4

Hewlett-Packard (HP)

Hewlett-Packard (HP) is one of the foremost computer vendors in the world today. The company has positioned itself as the premier open systems solutions vendor in the marketplace. HP has taken a leadership role in defining industry standards such as X/Open's XPG4, IEEE POSIX, OMG's CORBA, and more. The company is a committed supporter of OSF, X/Open, OMG, COS, and other groups. Its rate of investment in open systems standards has been high, and early. In 1991-92 HP was the first vendor to ship a system that was compliant with X/Open XPG3, ISO/OSI, and SVVS2 (System V Verification Suite 2)—the HP9000 series computers (with HP-UX as its UNIX-based operating system).

HP RECENT FINANCIAL PERFORMANCE

Year	Revenue (000s)	Income (Loss) (000s)
1993	$20,317,000	$1,177,000
1992	$16,410,000	$549,000
1991	$14,676,000	$755,000
1990	$13,485,000	$739,000
1989	$12,160,000	$829,000

Definition of Open Systems

HP uses the X/Open definition of open systems:

> Software environments consisting of products and technologies which are designed and implemented in accordance with standards—established and de facto—that are vendor-independent and commonly available.

Open Systems Strategy

As mentioned above, HP has a long-standing reputation as a supporter of open systems. HP is one of the founding members of both the Open Software Foundation (OSF) and the Object Management Group (OMG), serves on the board for X/Open, and is also a member of the MIT X consortium and of IEEE/POSIX and ISO/OSI standards committees. HP has engaged in selective strategic vendor alliances with IBM, Sun Microsystems, DEC, Hitachi, Convex, Transarc and Stratus to advance open systems technology development. Several HP products have been adopted by OSF as *de facto* product standards:

- Apollo's Network Computing System (NCS) was adopted by the OSF as a key component of Distributed Computing Environment (DCE)

- HP's dimensional user interface tools were selected by OSF as part of the OSF/Motif user interface

- Three products were contributed to the OSF/DME standards selection process: the HP OpenView Network Management Server, Software Distribution Utilities, and HP Network License System (NetLS)

Strategically, HP has shown strong commitment to integrating systems and application software from multiple vendors. HP's commitment to quality in products and services underlies its strategy for the 1990s, which includes a scalable family of fast machines, networking, open systems architecture, acceptance of industry standards, PC integration, and active use of third party software developers, consultative staff and an effective sales/support staff.

Observed Strategy

HP has clearly demonstrated its commitment to open systems through its *participation* in standards organizations (as opposed to just *membership*). HP has also demonstrated its commitment to industry standards through adherence to standards and rapid standards adoption. However, the competitive threat to UNIX-based systems, positioned mainly by Microsoft (Windows NT and Chicago), has caused HP to reevaluate its primarily UNIX approach. Recently, HP caved in and pledged support for NT on its platforms. This "hedging" of the UNIX bet could soften HP's leadership vision and lead to a dilution of research and development funds over the next few years. HP, however, continues to receive high marks in their evaluation, investment and implementation of emerging technologies, both *de jure* and *de facto* standards, at rates appropriate with the market's acceptance.

HP has three major hardware product lines and has made a major effort to integrate them with one another, although full application portability between all models is not assured.

- The HP 9000 Series 800 super minicomputers ("Corporate Business Servers") utilize HP's second generation Precision Architecture (PA) RISC-based technology.

- The HP 9000 Series 700 workstations are single user workstations that also run second generation PA-RISC and are reported to be fully compatible with the 9000/800s.

- The HP 3000 models specialize in On-Line Transaction Processing (OLTP) performance and functionality. The 3000s are reported to utilize RISC and non-RISC architectures.

Over the next few years, HP plans to invest heavily in the HP9000 series—HP's platform of the future. The 9000 series is highly scalable and portable, with SMP (symmetrical multi-processing) at the high end of the product line. Its strengths include the support of major *de facto* and industry standards, and an open network computing strategy and/or philosophy.

The HP3000 series, although still a proprietary system, has also received considerable investment and supports POSIX, X-Windows, OSF/Motif, and Microsoft Windows standards. The HP3000 is highly scalable and portable. Limitations include: no C++ or Ada support, and the 'internal' details of the proprietary MPE/ix operating system are not available to customers.

HP has articulated clear, standards-based directions for the operating systems in its product lines:

- Today the HP 9000 series runs HP-UX, which is based on AT&T's UNIX System V Release 3.0 with selected Berkeley Software Distribution (BSD) 4.3 and proprietary enhancements. HP-UX complies extensively with open systems tests and standards. HP plans to evolve HP-UX to comply with Spec/1170 and X/Open's XPG4+. In addition, the OSF standards of DCE and the emerging DME (distributed computing and management environments) are supported by HP-UX.

- Today the Series 3000 runs MPE, a proprietary non-UNIX operating system. The company intends to make the 3000s open through selective compliance with POSIX and XPG standards and through adopting other OSF products and frameworks such as Motif, DCE and DME.

The major standards and proprietary/open technologies supported by HP are depicted in Figure 7.5 using our technology stack for each of HP's major platforms.

In summary, Hewlett-Packard is viewed as a vendor with a strong demonstrated commitment to multi-vendor published standards within and across its hardware and operating system product lines. In a recent ranking of the openness of vendor technologies by Gartner Group, HP scored second highest in the interoperability category among all major computer vendors, and first in the portability category. [MCS, 1993] HP appears to be solidifying its position as a leading, world-wide open systems vendor.

HEWLETT-PACKARD PLATFORMS

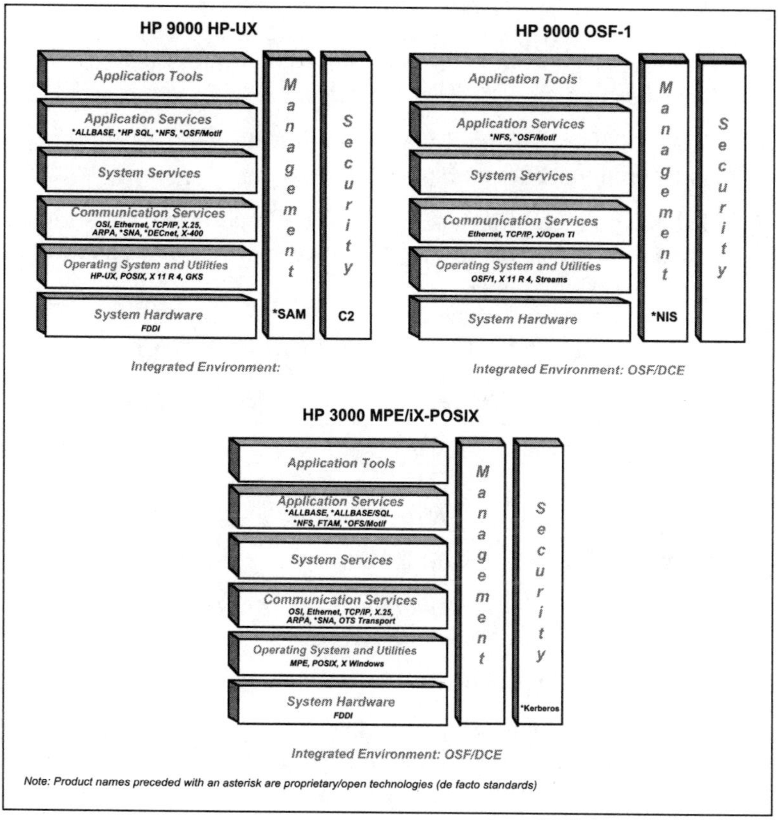

Figure 7.5

International Business Machines (IBM)

From 1964, when the System/360 mainframe was introduced, until the late 1980s, IBM was clearly the dominant force in the computer industry. IBM developed a culture and organization built around the mainframe computing environment. As technology developments produced smaller and faster systems, inertia within IBM would not allow the organization to respond quickly to market demands. Additionally, the marketing strategy of building competitive barriers and "locking in" customers was totally contrary to the IS organization's desire for open systems. As a result, IBM has suffered tremendously in the early 1990s.

IBM began responding to the market changes with several initiatives:

- The RS/6000 product line was introduced with scalable, UNIX-based systems ranging from the desktop to server

- IBM itself was divided into a number of business units with individual marketing responsibilities

- IBM announced its "Open Enterprise" open systems strategy in an effort to provide a single, "open systems" direction for its multiple product lines

IBM RECENT FINANCIAL PERFORMANCE

Year	Revenue (000s)	Income (Loss) (000s)
1993	$62,716,000	($8,148,000)
1992	$64,523,000	($4,965,000)
1991	$64,792,000	($2,827,000)
1990	$69,018,000	$6,020,000
1989	$62,710,000	$3,758,000

Definition of Open Systems

IBM's philosophy is that every customer will have a different definition of open systems depending on their technology architecture. Formally, IBM chooses the following IEEE definition of open systems:

> *"Open Systems Environment: the comprehensive set of interfaces, services, and supporting formats, plus user aspects, for interoperability or for portability of applications, data, or people, as specified by information technology standards and profiles."*
>
> —IEEE Joint Technical Committee on Operating
> Systems, December, 1993

Throughout IBM publications describing the company's view of "Open Client/Server Computing," IBM frequently refers to open systems as being "user-centric," where all users are presented with a consistent interface to all of the information that they are required to access, independent of the underlying technology.

Stated Open Systems Strategy

While initially slow to adopt the notion of open systems and UNIX as an operating system, IBM has integrated open systems into its stated business strategy and incorporated open systems philosophies across its diverse product lines. Since the introduction of the RS/6000 product line in 1990, IBM has become a major player in the open systems market. In 1991, IBM released its open systems strategy, called "Open Enterprise," containing the following components:

- Support for industry hardware and software standards

- Implementation of innovative technology

- Recognized need for architectures and products that facilitate interoperability

- Recognized need for services and support to facilitate heterogeneous systems implementation

For the last several years, IBM has internally been addressing interoperability issues through their "Open Distributed Computing Structure." In April, 1994, IBM formalized (to the marketplace) this approach towards system architecture with: "Open Blueprint," a framework to organize and think about how systems are put together. This approach views the whole network as if it is a single system, treating each individual computing system as a component within the overall network. "Open Blueprint" serves as the framework in designing and evolving a distributed system by identifying the interfaces required within any computing environment and defining the interfaces based on industry standards. IBM intends to support the company's "Open Blueprint" and make the definition available to both developers and IS users as a guide for building systems and applications in a distributed computing environment.

Starting in the 1980's, IBM began participating in standards organizations and vendor alliances. IBM realized that it must concentrate on products for the future, and has become very active in alliances and standards bodies.

During the late 1980s, IBM had up to 1700 people working with standards organizations. The company was a founding member of X/Open, OSF, and OMG and is currently an executive sponsor of the OSF.

IBM has been active in multivendor alliances as well. The IBM, Apple, Motorola alliance has produced the PowerPC RISC chip. IBM and Apple (and just recently HP) have joined forces in the development of Taligent, an object-oriented operating system and to develop industry standards for multimedia.

The IBM alliance with Apple and Motorola is developing several new technologies including the PowerPC RISC chip, an object-oriented operating system, and industry standards for multimedia.

Observed Strategy

IBM has four distinct product lines, with each having a strategy to move toward an "Open Client/Server Computing" model. IBM has concurrently enhanced existing products to be more open and developed products to provide interoperability within their family of products.

- The ES/9000 series is the mainframe product line. This architecture was announced in 1990 and new models have been introduced since that time. The MVS operating system has been extended with a POSIX-compliant version. Based on these activities, it is clear that IBM plans on marketing and supporting its mainframe line for years to come.

- The AS/400 series is the proprietary midrange product line. Introduced in 1988 as an easy-to-use system designed for small business commercial use, it has been extremely popular. Recently, IBM has developed a POSIX-compliant version of OS/400 in an effort towards standardization.

- The RS/6000 series is the UNIX-based workstation and server product line. The first workstations were available in 1990 and additional products have been introduced continually since that time. This RISC architecture has been designed to be scalable and to address technical and commercial applications.

- The PC products are comprised of several different lines aimed at different market segments. Ambra, PS/1, PS/VP, and PS/2 target mass distribution channel, the home user, the low-end business user, and the premium business user, respectively. The Thinkpad, IBM's line of notebook computers, has been very successful.

- The PowerPC RISC processor is an important technology for IBM's future. This chip will be incorporated into the PC, RS/6000, and the AS/400 product lines.

IBM has focused on a client/server model to integrate each of its product lines and to move towards an open systems environment. The issue is the speed at which this movement will happen. The company is still motivated to maintain its more profitable proprietary lines. Yet at the same time, it must react to the market pressure and the future direction of open systems standards.

The major standards and proprietary/open technologies supported by IBM are depicted in Figure 7.6 using our technology stack for IBM's Open Blueprint.

IBM OPEN BLUEPRINT

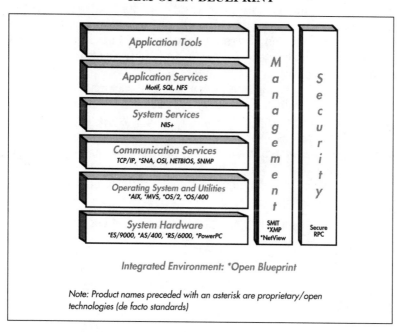

Figure 7.6

In summary, IBM understands that its strategy must contain the element of open systems. The company is clearly moving in that direction by adopting standards and licensing technology. However, IBM will continue to face the cultural hurdle of making the transition to open systems from its flagship, proprietary product lines. IBM's participation in multiple vendor alliances indicates that the company will continue to pursue development of technologies that will give it a competitive advantage—even if it means partnering with other vendors.

Microsoft

Compared with the hardware-dominant vendors discussed in this chapter, Microsoft has had a shorter track record in developing and marketing products in the computing industry. However, Microsoft's impact on the computing industry has been quite profound and arguably more significant than its hardware-oriented competitors. The company's MS-DOS and Windows operating systems for personal computers have become *de facto* standards and are the most widely used systems incorporating many *de jure* and *de facto* standards from multiple vendors.

Microsoft has long been a controversial, albeit active, player in the computing industry. Although, Microsoft's focus has been on the personal computing platform, the company has not shied away from influencing the formation of innovative technologies and standards in the transitioning computing industry. In pushing its vision called *Information at Your Fingertips*, Microsoft appears committed to the continued development and deployment of open systems— but on its own terms.

MICROSOFT RECENT FINANCIAL PERFORMANCE

Year	Revenue (000s)	Income (Loss) (000s)
1993	$3,753,000	$953,000
1992	$2,759,000	$708,000
1991	$1,843,000	$463,000
1990	$1,183,000	$279,000
1989	$804,000	$171,000

Definition of Open Systems

Microsoft feels that there is no generally accepted definition of open systems, but rather a consistent set of themes that reoccur. Microsoft has defined a strategy to help achieve the goals and benefits of open systems computing which includes four elements structured to focus on the benefits of openness such as:

- Choice in hardware platforms (essentially addressing portability and scalability)
- Choice in add-on hardware and peripherals
- Choice in software applications

- Choice in price

- Choice for the future (ensuring flexibility, compatibility and protection of investment)

Microsoft defines the four elements of its open systems strategy as follows:

- Foster broad industry participation and innovation

- Provide the best connectivity, compatibility and interoperability across multiple platforms

- Incorporate industry and customer-driven standards in a pragmatic, customer-focused manner

- Ensure smooth transitions to new technologies

Through a forum called the *Open Process*, Microsoft executes its open systems strategy by seeking participation from the industry and its customers in developing new technology. By providing preliminary specifications for application programming interfaces (APIs) to independent hardware and software vendors, software architects, OEMs, corporate developers and others, Microsoft is not only able to refine its products but also ensure customer acceptance. Additionally, Microsoft has aggressively used its marketing muscle to create demand for its newer technology. The *Open Process* forum, along with active participation in industry groups, is the method Microsoft uses to address the four elements of their open systems strategy.

Stated Open Systems Strategy

Since Microsoft's role in the open systems arena has been focused on the development and deployment of products in the operating systems layer, an examination of Microsoft's open systems strategy in relation to the company's software products indicates that Microsoft has and will continue to strengthen its influence on the middle layers between applications and hardware.

- Fostering broad industry participation and innovation

Although not *de jure* standards, Microsoft's MS-DOS and Windows products have achieved unprecedented success. Microsoft has licensed more than 100 million copies of MS-DOS and approximately 50 million copies of Windows. These systems run on a broad range of personal computers from more than 500 manufacturers. By achieving broad industry participation, Microsoft has been able to bring the benefits of openness to the marketplace.

- Provide the best connectivity, compatibility and interoperability across multiple platforms

From a network connectivity standpoint, the Microsoft Windows family of operating systems supports multiple levels of *de facto* and *de jure* standards. For instance, Windows NT has built-in support for major network topologies (Ethernet, Token Ring and Arcnet) and network protocols (TCP/IP, IPX/SPX, NETBEUI, DECNet, OSI, Appletalk and others). Additionally, through a specific API (Windows Sockets), it is possible to integrate Windows-based and UNIX-based applications across a network.

Microsoft has been able to ensure application software compatibility and interoperability within the Windows platform by developing a single API (Win32) for the entire Windows family. To broaden Windows-based software interoperability, Microsoft is planning on making Win32 API available on the Macintosh and UNIX platforms as well. Microsoft has addressed hardware compatibility for Win32-based (32-bit) applications by deploying this API on CISC-based (Intel X86 and Pentium) and RISC-based (DEC Alpha AXP, MIPS Rx400 and PowerPC) computers.

- Incorporating industry and customer-driven standards

Microsoft is fairly active in participating on various standards setting bodies and user organizations. The following is a listing of some of the major organizations Microsoft interacts with and some of the *de jure* and *de facto* standards it supports:

- ANSI (ANSI SQL)
- DCE-compatible remote call procedure (RPC)
- IEEE (POSIX)
- ISO
- National Information Infrastructure Advisory Council
- OSF

- SQL Access Group
- Unicode Consortium
- X.400 Application Program Interface Association
- X/Open

Microsoft has also developed the Windows Open Services Architecture (WOSA) to promote the integration of Windows-based applications within heterogeneous enterprise-wide computing environments. WOSA provides common application services (Open Database Connectivity, Messaging API and Windows Telephony) and communication services (Windows SNA API, Windows Sockets API and Remote Call Procedure).

- Ensuring smooth transitions to new technologies

Microsoft has focused on providing upward compatibility to ensure a smoother migration path to newer technology as it evolves its Windows platform. Also, through WOSA, Microsoft wants to facilitate the integration of Windows-based applications with legacy systems.

Observed Strategy

As Microsoft attempts to enhance its position as a leader and a key player in the middle layers of the technology stack, it is evident that Microsoft is focusing on establishing itself as the creator and seller of architecture and not just software products. Figure 7.7 shows how Microsoft is targeting the middle layers with key products.

Microsoft has done a masterful job at marketing and evolving its Windows platform, creating products that become almost *de facto* standards at both the client and server levels.

- Windows 3.1: Clearly the dominant client-based GUI interface in the marketplace today with a vast number of applications. By adding OLE 2.0 capability, Microsoft has extended the advantages of OLE 1.0 to make application integration a reality with a growing object class library.

- Windows NT: By being a part of the Windows family, NT has a significant advantage in the marketplace. It has the same OLE 2.0 interface as Windows 3.1 and NT-based application development is easier and more portable across architectures (Intel, Alpha, MIPS, etc.) due to WOSA and its drivers. NT provides multi-tasking, multi-threading, symmetric multi-programming and C2 level security. It also offers compatible or easy ports for Windows 3.1, UNIX, OS/2 and MS DOS applications. It achieves full source code compatibility across Intel and RISC processors (with DEC Alpha, MIPS, and PowerPC to follow).

- Chicago: Also referred to as Windows 4.0, Chicago is being projected by industry experts to be Microsoft's next best seller. It will have many of the features of NT including built-in peer networking and a Netware redirector that works in protected mode (which will be available in an upcoming release of Windows NT).

MICROSOFT

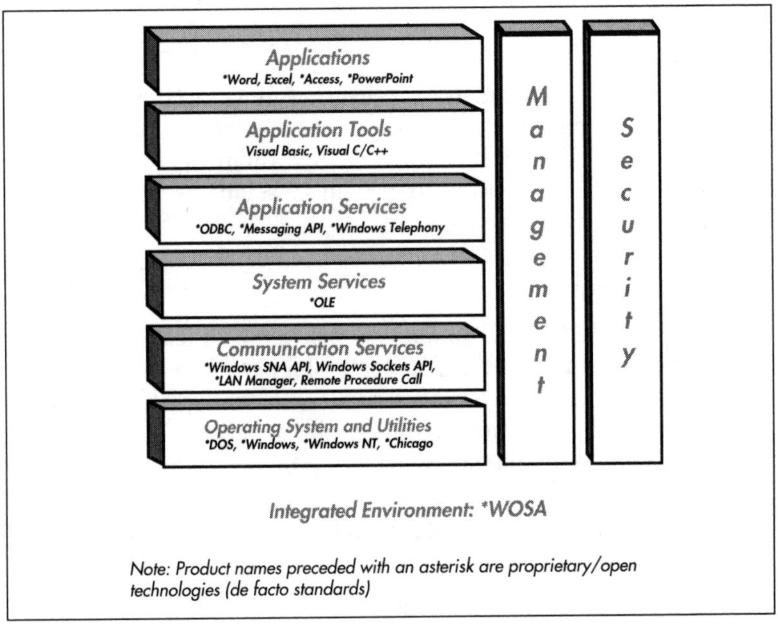

Applications
*Word, Excel, *Access, *PowerPoint

Application Tools
Visual Basic, Visual C/C++

Application Services
*ODBC, *Messaging API, *Windows Telephony

System Services
*OLE

Communication Services
*Windows SNA API, Windows Sockets API,
*LAN Manager, Remote Procedure Call

Operating System and Utilities
*DOS, *Windows, *Windows NT, *Chicago

Management

Security

Integrated Environment: *WOSA

Note: Product names preceded with an asterisk are proprietary/open technologies (de facto standards)

Figure 7.7

In summary, Microsoft has developed an open systems strategy that is focused on delivering the benefits of open systems. Microsoft's Windows family of products has been very successful and it is expected to be a dominant platform in the distributed computing environment of the '90s. Microsoft is clearly a force to reckon with in the computing industry and should continue to significantly influence the open systems arena.

Sun Microsystems and SunSoft

Sun is the largest RISC-based UNIX workstation vendor in the market, with approximately 39% of the market share [SunSoft, 1994]. In addition, Sun has long been an innovator in the open systems arena. The company has aggressively pioneered technologies and flooded the market-place with them, hoping to create—and in many cases succeeding in creating—*de facto* standards long before the 'slow-moving' standards setting bodies gained consensus on these same standards.

SUN RECENT FINANCIAL PERFORMANCE

Year	Revenue (000s)	Income (Loss) (000s)
1993	$4,308,606	$156,726
1992	$3,588,885	$173,313
1991	$3,221,000	$190,000
1990	$2,466,000	$111,000
1989	$1,765,000	$61,000

Definition of Open Systems

Sun has its own definition of open systems:

> [Open systems are] computing devices that due to their reliance on industry standard technologies and availability from multiple sources, are versatile, compatible, and relatively inexpensive to produce.
>
> —SunSoft

Open Systems Strategy

Sun has been very active in the open systems standards process. Sun participated in founding several industry groups including UNIX International (UI), SPARC International, the Object Management Group (OMG), the CASE Interoperability Alliance, and the Transaction Processing Performance Council (TPC). Sun is a member of many other open systems organizations and committees, including X/Open, ISO, CCITT, and recently, OSF. The launch of SunSoft (the system software subsidiary of Sun Microsystems) and strategic partnerships with AT&T, Xerox, and Hewlett-Packard have resulted in the creation or promotion of many successful products. Sun also partnered with Intel and delivered Solaris, its version of the

System V UNIX operating system, on the Intel chip-based platform (micro-computers and networks) in mid-1993. In addition, Intergraph intends to port the Windows NT operating system to run on Sun's SPARC RISC chip-based workstations/servers.

The Sun Microsystems approach to open systems differs greatly from those of HP, DEC, and IBM, and is probably most similar to Microsoft's. Sun's general approach is to invent technologies and license products to anyone in the industry. By taking this approach, Sun feels that they will become the open systems leader by sheer volume.

SunSoft's philosophy as a software company is to be an inventor of technology; and therefore the company does not license strategic technologies from other vendors. This is the primary reason for their historic disdain for OSF. OSF's recent change in charter to defining specifications rather than developing products, opened the door for Sun to join OSF as an executive sponsor (at the same level of participation as DEC, HP and IBM). Regardless, Sun will continue to conform to a different suite of standards, including many of its own. Sun openly licenses its software interfaces. It also licenses its SPARC RISC chip, making the SPARC RISC a proprietary/open technology.

Sun's strength as an inventor of technologies also casts a different light on its commitment to openness. The general perspective reported by critics is, "Sure they're today's UNIX workstation market leader, but will they continue to be on top tomorrow?"

Observed Strategy

Sun has demonstrated its commitment to open systems through a high level of participation in standards organizations. Sun also has a reputation for adhering to standards and a high rate of standards adoption. However, Sun's speed and aggressive growth has left it with various "chinks" in its armor. Sun's continued success will depend on how well it is able to consolidate its successful products/strategies and at the same time, bolster its weaknesses—which it is trying to do by forging various alliances with third parties. The marketplace, even the Sun workstation-worshipping hoards, will however need to see a consolidated strategy from Sun, rather than a 'piece-meal' enterprise-wide open systems strategy implied by the third party alliances mentioned above.

Sun's strength in hardware platforms is widely acknowledged: Sun has been the leading supplier of UNIX workstations for years. In 1990, the company eliminated its existing Motorola- and Intel-processor-based systems so that today's product line consists entirely of workstations and servers powered by the RISC-based SPARC (Scalable Processor ARChitecture) microprocessor.

Although Sun itself developed SPARC in the mid-1980s, SPARC stations are considered "proprietary/open" because Sun openly licenses SPARC worldwide to semiconductor and system manufacturers. Sun also promotes SPARC as an open RISC standard through the work of SPARC International. Sun's workstations are generally considered open and inter-compatible. There are more than 20 vendors who supply SPARC-based computers.

Regarding operating systems, SunSoft has a reputation as an aggressive, pace-setting UNIX developer. Understanding Sun's UNIX strategy involves examining three products: SunOS, Solaris, and Interactive UNIX.

- SunOS was one of the four operating systems incorporated by USL into industry-standard SVR4. SunOS 5.0, based on SVR4, represents a departure for Sun from its utilization of BSD-based UNIX in earlier SunOS products and, although 5.0 is reported to be backwardly compatible with the previous BSD OS's, migration to 5.0 is not trivial. SunOS 5.0's standards support is very strong and it also supports symmetric multiprocessing, multithreading, real-time extensions, increased security, simplified system administration, and advanced internationalization capabilities.

- The Solaris products are shrink-wrapped distributed computing solutions. Solaris 2.0, commercially available since June 1992, bundled together SunOS 5.0, Open Windows V3, Open Look and DeskSet V3, and adds distributed computing support of Sun's Open Network Computing (ONC) products. Solaris is available on SPARC, Intel x86/Pentium, and IBM/Apple Power PC platforms.

  However, perhaps the biggest news about Solaris 2.0 is its support for application source code compatibility between Intel 80X86 platforms and SPARC-compliant hardware platforms. This multi-platform capability would be achieved by integrating features of the Interactive UNIX product (described next). Solaris 2.0 would position Sun to compete against the products purportedly being developed by Microsoft and the IBM/Apple alliance (i.e., 32-bit multitasking operating systems designed to run on multiple platforms).

- Interactive UNIX is a popular implementation of UNIX for PCs. It was acquired by SunSoft from Interactive Systems

Corporation in January 1992. Interactive is based on UNIX System V Release 3.2 and also is reported to be binary compatible with Xenix. Along with Interactive UNIX, SunSoft also acquired other UNIX products from Interactive Systems which specifically integrate DOS and UNIX on a single platform and provide the Intel/SPARC integration features of Solaris 2.0. If Sun successfully engineers this integration, Solaris 2.0 would be an extremely innovative and powerful product.

Sun's strong and widespread investment in inventing technologies that form the basis for standards is evident in Figure 7.8.

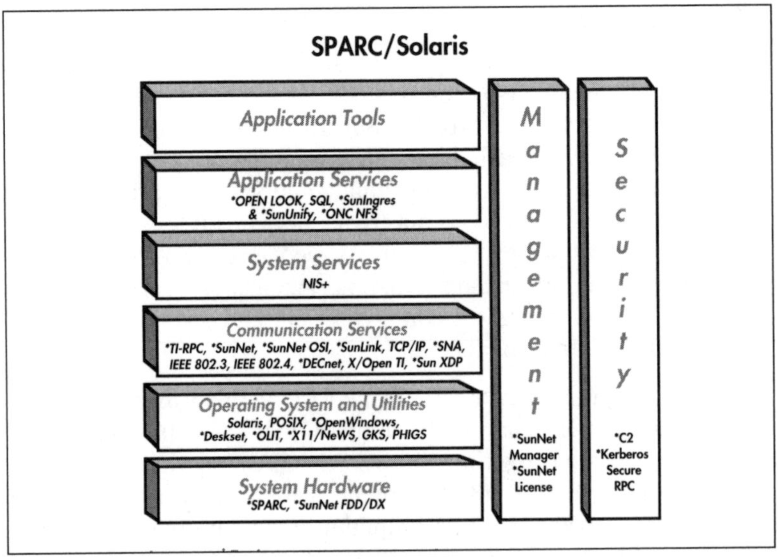

Figure 7.8

In summary, Sun is viewed as a creative technological leader whose products are offered and available as potential standards. Critics assume Sun's strategy of "leader of the pack" succeeds by building better mousetraps and having those products adopted as standards. Recent studies have rated Sun's products as somewhat poor in interoperability, but good/very good in almost all other categories, including user interface, personal productivity and mission critical applications, groupware/graphics/multimedia applications, and inter-application communications. In a recent Gartner Group comparative study on interoperability and portability, Sun tied for fifth in interoperability, and tied for tenth in portability. [MCS, 1993]

Stay Tuned for the Latest Developments From Open Systems Vendors

Are technology vendors genuinely embracing openness? The answer is definitely "yes"—with a curious mixture of both protectionism and open systems zeal. When depicted on our Openometer, the strategies of the five vendors discussed here span different ranges of openness. (See Figure 7.9.)

OPENOMETER

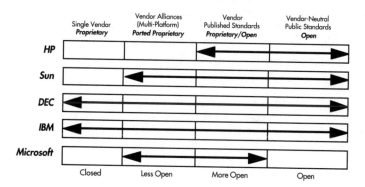

Figure 7.9

Hewlett Packard's open systems portfolio relies more on published, public standards than the other vendors. Sun, because of its strength as a technology inventor, is perceived to be comparatively less open because of its use of alliances to license its otherwise proprietary products. DEC's representation on the Openometer tells two stories: first, because of its VAX product line, it is the least open of the vendors. Second, because of its public statements and participation in open systems groups, DEC is "all over the board:" both proprietary and open. Similarly, IBM appears within each range of the Openometer because of its proprietary product lines (ES9000 and AS/400), and its propensity to establish alliances while also supporting standards bodies. IBM supports so many initiatives and currently has such a sketchy plan for implementing open systems, that it will likely remain within each category in the short-term. Microsoft is more focused towards the development and deployment of operating systems (Windows family of products). Because of this, the company does not compare directly with the other vendors discussed in this chapter. However, by "owning" APIs, Microsoft is expected to reinforce its dominance of the middle layers of the computing model.

When vendors articulate a strong commitment to open technologies, this reassures corporate management that past investments were wise and future investments are safe. It is difficult even for the well-intentioned consumer to sort out true commitments from *OpenSpeak*. A truer assessment of commitment requires probing product features and vendor intentions scrupulously, remaining cautious of the word "open" merely being grafted onto old product features and watching for lax commitment to the goals and intent of open systems on the part of vendors.

Caveat emptor.

(Would you like some more tea?)

Chapter 8

Information Protection—
Exploring the Basics *By Harry B. DeMaio*

"We have met the enemy and he is us"
—*Pogo Possum (Walt Kelly)*

"Something there is that doesn't love a wall that wants it down...
Before I built a wall, I'd ask to know
What I was walling in or walling out."
—*Robert Frost*

> This is the first of two chapters on Information Protection in an Open Distributed Environment. In this chapter, we'll begin with a high-level examination of the meaning and implications of protecting information resources. We'll look at the topic from a business process viewpoint and then within the particular context of distributed computing environments, with major emphasis on open systems implementations. In the next chapter, we'll survey some of the available protection models and discuss the nature, advantages and disadvantages of some of the alternatives available in Open Systems. For comparative purposes, we will use the single-image mainframe which is by no means dead and which still appears not only in "pure play" form but as one component in hybrid implementations.

In 1914, when Robert Frost wrote his poem *Mending Wall* (quoted above), he might have unwittingly been anticipating the problems faced by Information Protection designers and implementers in the 1990's. Some walls are necessary in Open Systems environments but indiscriminate placement or overkill for the sake of playing it safe is inefficient, ineffective and even from a security standpoint, often counterproductive. So, in a real sense, the information protection quandary in distributed environments is an extension of the overall Open Systems quandary—choices, choices, choices.

As more enterprises entrust their success and very existence to information systems, the issue of information protection (IP) becomes more vital. The "information empowerment" of massive numbers of people through workstation-based distributed systems creates two key information processing characteristics, both with significant IP implications.

Over time these empowered individuals will develop:

- Increasingly Widespread Access—to information, processing power, tools, facilities, other nodes, other users and, through global networks, the world.

- Increasingly Widespread Knowledge—about the structure, mechanisms, contents, paths and vulnerabilities of the distributed information processing universe.

Access and knowledge, of course, can enhance the power of the individual to the benefit of the enterprise. Conversely, "need to know" and "controlled privilege" (or equivalent restrictions) have been in the management vocabulary for centuries. There is an ongoing debate as to who is more potentially dangerous to a system—knowledgeable insiders (with an attitude?) or uninformed outsiders (who always do the unexpected). To the IP specialist, the only appropriate answer is—both.

So, let's get the bad news up front. For the moment, the organization faced with trying to develop an integrated distributed information protection program has a lot of discovering, deciding and implementing to do when it comes to protecting its information resources. As we've seen, choice and decision are endemic to the Open Systems environment.

Over the longer haul, standards will certainly help to guide that decision process. Oddly, the standards groups working on IP are in some ways, well ahead of the market. In other cases, they are woefully behind. At this moment, as we will see in this and the next chapter, these standards are just beginning to appear in actual product offerings. Only a few products and vendors even come close to offering a complete (!) suite of IP tools and methods to deal with the issues that connectivity, scalability, portability and interoperability bring with them. So the user must make choices based on current realities.

However, doing nothing about IP until the ideal IP technology surfaces is a much worse alternative. Inaction could literally destroy your systems and (hopefully not) your organization. The good news is that some design and implementation choices are there to be made.

Today's environment is only a hint of things to come. The relatively small population of information processing specialists who dominated the computing scene only a few short years ago is being joined by an overwhelmingly large influx of computer literate (or at least process literate) knowledge workers and users. (If you don't believe that, just ask the next eight-year-old you meet.)

This democratization of information processing cannot (and should not) be reversed. However, there are many IP specialists and an increasing number of other observers who wish the empowerment process had happened somewhat differently. In the rush to provide large numbers of high-powered, interconnected (and often interoperable) information systems and workstations to departments and individuals, the question of fundamental protection has all too frequently been left at the starting gate.

Unfortunately, as we will see, protection is not a function that is easily retrofitted into distributed environments. If it's not designed in from the start, it may not be there at all. This situation is quite different from the traditional experience of many information protection specialists for whom retrofit is the norm. It is also different from the mainframe model where system-based retrofit of security is common. Is the fact that information protection is often behind the power curve something to be concerned about? Well, let's see what business management thinks.

A number of executive surveys conducted in the last several years (including several by Deloitte & Touche) indicate that IP is something senior management is increasingly worried about, even if their investment in action programs isn't always commensurate with their stated concerns. For example, in a market survey conducted for D&T by G2 Research Inc. in the Spring of 1993, we asked these senior managers why their interest in information protection was greater in 1993 than, say, in 1985. We got three answers:

- Their increased reliance on information and information systems for compiling mission critical, financial material and conducting content-sensitive business processes.

- The sharp increase in the number of "enabled" people inside *and outside* the enterprise who are equipped with a full complement of powerful information processing tools and have access to critical business data and processes. One important aspect of distribution is the *extended enterprise*. The physical and institutional walls of an organization no longer define the sphere of information processing activity. Most organizations share access to information and supporting processes with a large number of business partners—vendors, suppliers, customers, regulators, research facilities and countless others, including the public. There may still be walls but they are becoming increasingly porous.

- The current and future volatility of information processing hardware and software. This volatility refers to both stability and life expectancy. The executives we talked to didn't see this situation changing anytime soon. Frankly, neither do we. For the rest of the 90's, rapid obsolescence, fragility and incomplete or incompatible process will probably be a way of distributed life in spite of (or perhaps because of) efforts on standardization.

The bottom line is that management has an itch about information protection and isn't quite sure where or how strongly to scratch. This discussion won't answer all the questions but we hope it provides some relief.

As we progress through these two chapters, we'll discover that information protection in the distributed environment, has become highly situational. Unlike the more traditional single image mainframe-based systems that some of us have become accustomed to, one protection model no longer fits all business requirements. Interestingly enough, the converse is also true: a number of different approaches to protection may fit the same technology and processing environment. The difference is that the design of information protection is now driven by the business needs, not specific platforms or technologies.

What is Information Protection?

Information protection (IP) is the establishment and preservation of the continuity, integrity and confidentiality of information resources. *(Information Protection is not the same as Information Security and we'll explain why in a few moments.)*

Notice that the definition is a positive statement. Information Protection must be an ongoing program of process enhancement which contributes to the bottom line of the organization. Properly designed and implemented, it should link with business process "quality," "reliability," "stability," "effectiveness," and "efficiency." The purpose of information protection is to enable, not inhibit. By strengthening the systems and applications that support the enterprise, the enterprise itself is strengthened.

Nevertheless, it would be naive to imply that protection doesn't have a prohibitive and inhibitive side. After all, you are protecting *against* some unwanted thing or things. However, simply preventing undesired events is only one dimension of a well-structured protection program. Let's illustrate. Throughout this book, the automobile appears and reappears as a source of examples. So, one more time!

Yet Another Automotive Analogy

Some specialists have compared information protection to enforcing seat belt use, requiring mandatory airbags, having a spare tire or being able to call roadside assistance if something goes wrong. These are reactive processes and are very welcome if you have a flat tire or a breakdown. However, to illustrate the positive approach, we'd like to use a proactive automotive example—anti-lock brakes and traction control. These functions are there not only to ensure a safer ride but to improve the driving experience. With these features, you can drive when others can't. You can go places where others won't venture. You can continue to operate under difficult conditions without shattering your nerve ends or parts of your body. The driving process is enhanced and strengthened.

Similarly with IP, the business process is enhanced and strengthened. That's our view of information protection—*making it easier to keep your business operating efficiently and effectively.*

Unless we can clearly understand and can make explicit senior management's IP expectations for the business, we may be designing a process that is overly inhibitive, insufficiently robust or simply inappropriate for the organization's need. Of course, senior management may have difficulty articulating its protective desires without a little help.

IP = Continuity, Integrity and Confidentiality

Let's define each of those terms and then consider why we've linked them together under the umbrella of IP. In the process, we'll differentiate Information Protection from Information Security.

- **Business Continuity:** This concept refers to the uninterrupted availability of all the resources necessary to operate an enterprise or business process at a level acceptable to senior management. That may not mean full capacity or even normal capacity. What is acceptable in the face of disruption is uniquely decided by each company's senior management, generally by business process or function, and measured against the associated costs. One of the major objectives of business continuity planning is to provide management with the appropriate data and metrics to make that decision. We use a technique called Business Impact Analysis which puts threats, risk and vulnerability in a context of business priority. Not all threats are equally important. Not all vulnerabilities require the same level of attention. The analysis enables management to weigh these against one another in making decisions.

- **Information Resource Continuity** is a subset of Business Continuity and refers to the uninterrupted availability of all the information resources necessary to operate an enterprise or business process at a level acceptable to senior management.

- **Integrity:** In a narrow information protection context, the preferred definition of integrity is "freedom from unauthorized modification" or "freedom from corruption." Integrity answers the question: Can I trust this data, process or path? Achieving integrity normally involves controlling the privileges of individuals and processes to "create, modify, transmit, store, reproduce and dispose of" information resources.

  Integrity may also refer to a wider set of quality- and reliability-related concerns about the validity, accuracy, completeness, consistency, timeliness, pertinence and presentation of the information resources.

- **Confidentiality:** In the strict sense, confidentiality involves the "read" privilege. There are two sub-components to confidentiality:

  - Protection of intellectual property (trade secrets, business data, etc.) from unauthorized exposure

  - Protection of personal information (information privacy) from unauthorized exposure

  Confidentiality has been getting most of the public's attention, especially in fiction and sensational news reports about industrial and military espionage and privacy invasion. These threats are very real but they do not describe the entire or even the dominant aspects of the IP universe. In the minds of many individuals, confidentiality and security are interchangeable terms. They are not.

What's Important?

In today's business environment, most executives will identify continuity and/or integrity as their first concerns. Unless the enterprise operates in a defense-related, regulated or mandated fiduciary environment, or deals with intellectual property or private personal information as its primary product or service, management concern for confidentiality is usually restricted to a relatively small proportion of its information assets—customer files, proprietary information, business strategies, human resource or medical records, as examples. However, and unfortunately, information protection theory and practice has for quite a while been confined to confidentiality—"need to know." In fact, control of integrity- and continuity-related privilege is actually the more appropriate road to business-justified protective measures. Privilege control subsumes "need to know." In most circumstances, what you can *do* has a greater impact than what you can *see*.

The definition of Information Protection offered above differs from Information Security. IP combines continuity with integrity and confidentiality. Many organizations and specialists regard *information security* strictly as confidentiality and integrity concerns. They sever continuity from the definition and consider it to be an operations or business process issue.

What's Different Now?

This compartmentalization of IP related activities may have been appropriate for the past. But, the combination of integrity, continuity and confidentiality reflects a new interdependence brought about by networking and distribution and more fundamentally, by the new ways in which the information process is integrated into the business process. Think about the impact that viruses, or unauthorized access or modification of data and software can have on a system's continuity. Increasingly, systems, applications and networks go down for "logical" (non-physical) causes as well as for the traditional "physical" causes such as fire, power loss or flood. Conversely, there a number of integrity and confidentiality questions which should be addressed in continuity and business resumption planning (e.g., protecting backup files and continuity plans.) Many organizations are finding the somewhat artificial separation of continuity from integrity and confidentiality to impede their ability to design and implement comprehensive programs.

A SHORT DIGRESSION—THE CONTINUITY DILEMMA IN DISTRIBUTED SYSTEMS

Distribution of business and information processing creates an interesting continuity dilemma. At first glance, decentralizing your information processing from a single data center into diverse localities would seem to greatly reduce the "all your eggs in one basket" problem. It often does. By distributing your hardware and processing activities around a variety of sites, you can normally reduce the impact of a localized physical outage. However, by using distributed design, you may now become reliant on a complex network to interconnect these different sites and to support interdependent processes. The network can become a major point of failure itself and can also serve as a vehicle for propagating local logical (nonphysical) failures to other sites and processors. The point is, the act of *distributing information resources is continuity-neutral (at best!)*. The level of interconnection, interoperability and interdependence required by your distribution plan and the robustness of your network will give you a better index of whether, in your situation, distribution has made a positive or negative contribution to your business continuity risk.

Some Basic IP Concepts and Constructs

Before examining IP in distributed environments, we should examine some of the fundamental concepts and constructs of IP that are key to our considerations—regardless of the nature of the processing environment. This examination won't hurt and it will help to contrast the single image mainframe model from the distributed model. We'll only touch on the highlights.

Regardless of the business process or supporting technologies, certain basic protection functions are required.

- **Classification**: Determining what protective steps are necessary based on the value of the specific information resources to the enterprise. During the mainframe era, very few organizations classified their information; if they did, they used levels of required confidentiality as the only metric. Yet those same institutions used access control facilities to protect their information. How can you control access without classification of the resource? It's easy when the transaction, not the information, is the object of control. If I can prevent unauthorized users from invoking the transaction suite that updates customer files, theoretically, I can thus preserve the integrity and confidentiality of those files. *That's true, provided that transaction suite is the only user path to the data and there is only one copy of the information extant.* Both of these conditions are far less likely in a distributed environment. The exclusive, one-to-one, tightly coupled relationship between transactions and data is fading. In fact, distribution, by definition, implies exactly the opposite. Which brings us to the next concept...

- **Object of Control**: As the name suggests, the object of control is the resource and/or process we are seeking to protect. In the mainframe world, we generally could control the object (usually data) by controlling access to the transaction(s) that used the data. As long as there was a tightly coupled relationship between the two, by controlling one, you controlled the other. However, as we expand the number of potential paths to a resource and the number of "clients" traversing those paths, controlling the traffic to control the data object may not always be sufficient or even possible. Thus by default, the process *object itself*, not the process, often becomes the appropriate focus of our control efforts.

  We may have to encrypt the object to achieve the desired control level. If the data is encrypted, then only an authorized cryptographic keyholder should be able to use the data meaningfully. Maybe you can access the information, but unless you have an appropriate key you can't do anything useful with it. You could, of course, still maliciously corrupt or destroy the data, but most encryption systems are built to *detect and report* modification. Fraudulent changes or browsing for content are inhibited. *Prevention* of indiscriminate corruption or malicious destruction will still require access control. We'll cover encryption in a little more detail later.

- **Authorization**: Establishing the rights and privileges of individuals and processes seeking access to information resources. What are you allowed to do? There are business management and technology aspects to this process and we'll discuss a few authorization management mechanisms in a few moments.

- **Identification:** Determining who or what the user or process is that is seeking access.

- **Authentication:** (verification) Confirming, to the degree necessary, the identity of the user or process. (See Figure 8.1.)

THE BASIC MODES OF IDENTIFICATION
AND AUTHENTICATION

(Used singly or in combination based on the level of confirmation required)

- **What do you know?**—password, PIN, personal facts

- **What do you have?**—token, smartcard, one-time password devices

- **What are you like?**—biometrics such as palm or fingerprint, voiceprint, signature dynamics (the movements of signing your name, not the form of the signature)

- **Where/When/How are you seeking access?**—supplementary environmental information like date, time, place, device, or application path that can assist in identification and verification

- **Who or What is your sponsor?**—additional corroboration of your identity. A trusted person or process vouches for you or a process working for you

In open systems it is important not only to validate WHO you are but WHERE you are and WHAT facilities you are using to gain access and WHEN you are trying to gain access. For example, you may be granted access to certain data from a trusted workstation over a trusted path but not on an unprotected dial-up connection. Your personal rights are conditioned by the potential hostility of the environment in which you are operating.

Figure 8.1

- **Access Management:** The actual granting or monitoring of access, including path control, logging, journaling, alarms and protective responses in case of attempted or actual violation.

- **Level of Privilege:** A more accurate and useful authorization term than "need to know." It can be subdivided into areas affecting confidentiality, integrity and continuity. For example, while everyone in the organization may have "read" privilege to certain public files, only a small number of individuals may have any or all of the "update, copy, backup, transmit, create, append or destroy" privileges.

- **Domains of Trust:** This is a key concept in the open environment. When terminals were hard-wired or locally connected to a mainframe, the terminal could trust the identity of the mainframe and the mainframe could trust the identity of the terminal (but, not necessarily the users who still had to identify and verify themselves through IDs and passwords). Technologically, local, physical connections were the only game in town. In an open environment, we cannot rely as heavily on physical access as a level of protection and must enhance our means of logical authentication. (See Figure 8.2.) One of the critical questions that each user and process (client or server; peer among peers) must ask is: "Can I trust the identity and authorization of the nodes and paths to which I am connecting or who are attempting to connect to me?" This problem is not restricted to large processors or servers. It is equally important that the end user at the workstation be able to trust the paths and processes to which he or she is connecting. Incoming as well as outgoing traffic is equally at risk or risky. Thus, active, session-by session, (sometimes transaction-by-transaction) authentication becomes a necessity in every environment in which proof cannot be given that a sufficient level of trust is warranted to omit such authentication.

In the interest of efficiency and ease of use, many enterprises create "trusted-domains" to cut down on the need for constant authentication. By definition, trusted domains restrict connection and interoperation to already known and trusted processes, nodes and paths, and keep all other traffic and attempts to connect out. Obviously, this structure won't suit every business or personal need. The alternative is the use of such authentication techniques as outlined in the Open Software Foundation/Distributed Computing Environment (OSF/DCE) security model (based on Kerberos) and in MIT's third party authentication process, Kerberos. We discuss these in more detail in the next chapter.

MOVING FROM PHYSICAL PROTECTION
TO LOGICAL AUTHENTICATION

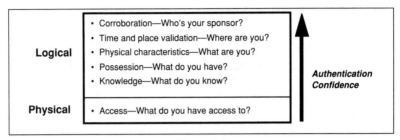

Figure 8.2

- **Auditability**: The capability of reconstructing an information process and identifying the individuals and processes involved. What happened?

- **Accountability**: The ability to assign responsibility for the processes involved and the results of those processes. Who is responsible?

Human Nature—The IP Wild Card

Several years ago, Harry DeMaio published a book entitled: *Information Protection and Other Unnatural Acts*. While the title may have enhanced sales in X-rated bookstores, it has a basis in fact. *Information Protection* is not only unnatural to human beings, it strongly conflicts with many of our basic drives. Protection, however, is an innate behavior. Consider: humans and most animals are extremely territorial and possessive about tangible objects and turf. One of the first words a child utters is "Mine." Try taking a bone from a dog. Acquire, keep and protect are very fundamental human and animal objectives for tangible possessions.

Change the scenario to information and knowledge and our innate behaviors and associated priorities change. We are certainly information acquisitive. But what we call greed and possessiveness in describing overactive accumulation of goods and chattels is converted to a more neutral characteristic called curiosity (or ennobled as intellectual curiosity) when the target is information. In other words, our values are ambivalent. When does healthy curiosity become nosiness? What's more important, your right to know or my right to privacy? Don't answer too fast.

Unlike the transfer of tangibles, we don't lose possession of information when we transfer it. So, we can give it away freely, we trade and barter with it and we establish our own credentials and prestige on the basis of it. Sporting an advanced degree or other credentials on a business card or publication has a direct linkage to the childhood statement: "I know something you don't know." ("But just ask me and I'll bore you to tears with it.") Free and open traffic is the norm (at least in the free world) and there is something a bit sinister and suspicious about people or organizations who are secretive. Telling people to protect information just like any other asset doesn't work because they don't treat information like any other asset.

So human nature conspires against IP. So what? Not much, if the population of individuals with access to high-powered, widely connected, information- and process-rich systems remained at the levels of the early 80's. Not much if they could still have their human nature and access to that power controlled effectively by the technology and the administrative environment.

But those days have disappeared. Regardless of how much protective technology we can muster, the knee-jerk human reaction is to avoid or circumvent it because it constricts our freedom. Since people are a pivotal and primary component of distributed information systems, a successful IP program has to be designed around people, not around just the chips and fiber optics. *Distributed IP is psychology first, technology second.*

A Couple of Transitional Thoughts

Information protection is all about determining and verifying who is accessing an information resource, whether they are authorized to access it, and how they are accessing it. It's about controlling what they can and can't do with the resource and protecting its integrity and availability. The objective is to enable, strengthen and enhance, so all restrictions need to be balanced against the benefits to be attained. Blanket restriction of technologies and information without business justification is usually counter-productive and with certain exceptions, seldom lasts long. Therefore IP is becoming highly individual and situational. Different organizations will protect the same technologies differently. That, too, is a major change from the past.

In addition, IP is an ongoing process, not an event. It should anticipate, track and support business, human, environmental and technology changes. It should map to the overall strategies, architectures and implementations of the information systems—hierarchical, distributed or hybrid. The fondly remembered days of simply buying (and possibly even installing) a mainframe access control system and then forgetting about security never really existed—but even if they did, that image has absolutely no place in the distributed world.

Lastly, protection seeks to unify and envelop inside trusted domains. (Circle the wagons!) The more we decompose and distribute the information process, the more we also decompose and distribute protection. We make it more difficult to achieve consistent, coherent and comprehensive coverage. The more ad hoc our development, processing and transmission becomes, the more flexible and responsive the protective design and mechanisms have to be. The more the individual user dominates the information process, the more user-cognizant (even user-friendly) the protection process must become. The more complex, widespread and democratic the process, the greater the level and variety of potential threats.

It's a challenge. Portability, scalability, connectivity, interoperability and the freedom to choose among a wide range of vendors and offerings all conspire to make the protective process more complex. Let's move on to the next chapter and see what we have to work with to make effective IP possible.

Chapter 9

Information Protection—
Securing an Open System by Harry B. DeMaio

Press Inquiry to Willie Sutton, notorious bank robber:
"Why do you rob banks?"
Response: "Because that's where the money is."
"All technology should be presumed guilty until proven innocent."
　　　　　　　　　　　　　　　　　　　—David Brower

"If anything can go wrong, it will."
　　　　　　　　　　　　　　　　—Murphy's First Law

> In this chapter, we explore the major differences between protecting open systems and protecting the traditional hierarchical, single image, mainframe environments. We explain Information Protection (IP) architectures and consider some of the major architectural constructs that are important for effective protection. We note the heightened interdependence of IP architectures with other information processing architectures such as network, data, system and application. The architectural approach is highlighted because it is at the product-independent level that we can best enunciate our objectives and requirements. Of course, theory must ultimately adapt to realities and it is no easy task to match those requirements to existing or planned products such as OS/2, Novell Netware, Windows NT, the many flavors of UNIX and a universe of database and application packages. However, doing so is impossible without a clear set of architectural objectives to begin with.

> Finally we provide a list of functions no self respecting IP process should be without and finish with a collection of random thoughts on how to make an Open Systems IP program work.

Did Murphy, the great Law-Giver, really invent open systems? If you've been keeping current on the security incident reports in the popular press, especially about Internet, you might certainly think so. CERT, the Computer Emergency Response Team, a government-sponsored, national unit established to track, react and hopefully, even prevent break-ins and other attacks on public network systems, has reported thousands of known or deduced attempts.

That number should not be astonishing when you consider the vast size of the Internet. There are, after all, thousands of networks (*networks, not nodes!*) within the Internet. The accurate population, topology and dimensions of the Internet are not known, and they change so rapidly that measurement, if a trustworthy technique existed, would be onerous and expensive. Since there is really no one in charge of the Internet, much of the fundamental management information and characteristics that would be more readily available (perhaps) for a proprietary net are more difficult, if not impossible, to come by. There are also several thousand more networks operating on or through other semi-public nets. And, of course, many networks have multiple inter-network connections.

Some observers believe the security incident rate on Internet and on distributed systems generally may be vastly understated. Many incidents are not made public for (what else?) security reasons. The *undetected* volume is just that—undetected—but most experts believe it is substantially larger and considerably more widespread than the reported numbers.

One thing is more certain—the intent of those attempting the break-ins on public networks appears to be increasingly malicious. While the curious browser out for an electronic joy-ride or simply lost in the virtual maze will always be with us, an increasing number of attempted break-ins seem to be deliberately targeted and seriously purposeful. Why? Ask Willy Sutton. Because that's where the information is. Many organizations are beginning to put their applications and data that are mission critical, financially material, content sensitive and "attractive." Examples are numerous, including credit reports, telephone numbers, addresses, credit card numbers, telephone card numbers, and so on.

Of course, the Internet and Open Systems are neither synonymous nor coterminous. And there are plenty of well-controlled distributed networks on and off the Internet. Open systems need not be *wide* open systems. Unfortunately many begin life that way.

Hostile and Benign Environments— Prudence or Paranoia?

Evidence on the Eleven O'Clock News notwithstanding, most of us still have trouble dealing with the concept of hostility, especially hostility directed toward us. The difficulty in accepting its existence is exacerbated if most of our prior experience has been relatively benign. That statement has special application to most experienced information technology users. One of the bequests of mainframe-based legacy systems is a subconscious assumption that the system is inherently safe (or safe enough for our purposes). That assumption is made on the basis of a combination of physical, procedural and logical protection under the direction of a small population of trusted management and operations personnel. This assumption was never valid in the data center-based world. In open distributed environments, you make that assumption quite literally at your peril.

Physical, procedural and logical protective measures can no longer be taken for granted. The small population of data center managers and operating personnel has been expanded to include a much larger universe of known *and unknown* participants. Portability, dial-up, cellular and radio connections contribute to environmental unpredictability. Should open systems technology be presumed vulnerable until proven otherwise? In many of today's environments, the answer is Yes. But that need not lead to paralysis or rejection of the technology. Nor should it lead to a surrender of controls. It means that protection must be consciously and purposefully added to the environmental design. How? Let's drill a little deeper.

IP in Open Distributed Environments

In the last chapter, we discussed the fundamentals of Information Protection (IP). Now, let's examine what happens when IP and Open Distributed Systems meet. We'll follow up with brief functional descriptions and conclude with an examination of some of the IP tools and techniques that are available for distributed environments.

As we've noted, when you change the basic processing model from the traditional single image mainframe as profoundly as open systems does, there's every reason to assume that the IP model should also change. Unfortunately, that "no change" assumption is made over and over (often unconsciously) by major users. Eventually, they develop a frustrated realization that the largely transparent security mechanisms of the past are being replaced by a collection of functions and facilities that require planning, design, development and careful implementation. This required shift is not simply the result of technology changes. The fundamental process model describing how, where, and when systems are used and who has access to systems resources has changed in an open systems world.

Let's look at two major differences in Information Protection in an open systems threats and protection models.

Difference #1: Threats

In this new world, the threats (or at least the scenarios associated with threats) to system integrity, confidentiality and continuity change:

- *Consider the target.* While unauthorized attempts to gain access to information or process have been with us since the dawn of computing, until recently the mainframe as a physical and logical object of control could be easily defined. So the required defense perimeter was well understood and managed.

- *Compare a mainframe-terminal transaction* under the control of an application processor like CICS with that same transaction in a client/server implementation. Instead of two tightly connected endpoints operating in close affinity, we have transaction components interacting over a number of loosely connected nodes and paths. Each of these is probably aware of its neighbor processes but not necessarily aware of the entire process chain. However, since they all participate in some stage of the process they can all "contribute" to the aggregate vulnerability of the transaction. The number of points over which control must be extended in a consistent, orderly, comprehensive form increases sharply. That number will vary with the design of the physical and logical networks as well as with the application itself.

- *Certain classes of threat such as worms and viruses,* grabbing passwords on the paths using "sniffer" type devices, and spoofing (pretending to be a known, authenticated node path or process) are more likely in distributed environments. Worms and viruses are attacks which depend on the interconnection of systems to do their most severe damage (see Glossary). Don't forget that one form of interconnection still very prevalent is "sneakernet" (the manual transfer of data from one system to another). Diskettes are still one of the most dangerous sources of damage.

- *The sheer number of individuals and processes* involved magnifies the threat. Even if the ratio of incidents to users were to remain the same, a case that is by no means clear, the *absolute number* of incidents will increase along with the larger number of interconnected users and transactions. A decrease in both ratio and absolute numbers will come about only through carefully planned and applied protective measures.

- *Interconnectivity and interoperability,* by definition, extend the potential impact of any incident to a wider range of participants and participating processes. In these new environments, "no process is an island." An apparently simple problem can trigger a complex chain reaction with cascading results. This is true not only of technological but operating problems as well. Finding, defining and ultimately fixing the cause of a distributed system failure and all of its effects can be complex, frustrating and in some cases because of unpredictable results, dangerous. Inappropriate cures can sometimes turn out to be worse than the illness.

- *Magnitude of impact.* Because enterprises are putting greater and even full dependence on their distributed information systems, the business impact of an outage, compromise or integrity loss can often create a hard stop to the business process, instead of just a gradual decline.

- *Speed of propagation.* This is related to magnitude. In a complex, networked, interdependent environment, attacks, disruptions, or technical, administrative, operating or management errors can spread rapidly and replicate themselves in a variety of forms and results. Even after remedial action has been taken, residual faults can reappear and trigger rapid, repeat problems. While by no means the only example, many viruses often reappear in systems and networks after apparently having been eradicated.

- An obvious corollary is *reaction time.* How rapidly can the process recognize a compromise, outage or integrity fault and its dimensions? How swiftly and effectively can the process react and regain control? How quickly can normal or at least acceptable status be restored?

- *Reliance on single stream processes.* Distribution does not necessarily imply redundancy of process or alternate paths. In today's lean and mean environments, process redundancy, whether technology-based or otherwise, is often subjected to the strongest budget scrutiny and doesn't always win out. As a result, many complex network structures have significant (and subtle) single points of failure.

Difference #2: Information Protection Models

In an open systems environment, there is a wider diversity of IP models and mechanisms than in a mainframe environment.

The mainframe model provides a *unified security process*, incorporating authorization, identification, verification, logging, accounting and incident alarms in one tightly linked functional set contained in the operating system and access control software. In open distributed systems each of these functions is very likely to be decoupled and separated into free standing processing activities on different platforms and applications. Synchronized, seamless, end to end control with mutual recognition by all of the involved processes is not automatic. In fact, synchronized control with mutual recognition becomes a fundamental protection design criterion in hardware/software development and selection. It doesn't always happen, especially when several (dozen?) vendors may be involved.

There are three characteristics in any open IP design and delivery system that can make it highly situational: IP design is derivative, dependent and subordinate. (See Figure 9.1.)

WHY IS INFORMATION PROTECTION ARCHITECTURE SO VARIABLE IN OPEN SYSTEMS?

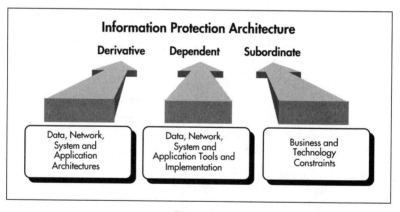

Figure 9.1

- *At the architectural level, IP design is derivative.* This means IP must follow the characteristics of the data, network, platform, application and presentation architecture. For example, whether it is possible to treat each node and path of the network as a trusted entity depends largely on the nature of the network's architecture.

- *At the implementation level, IP design is dependent.* Although there are an increasing number of specialized software packages that can (and usually should) be used to help achieve distributed security, there is still a great need to use and rely on the security, control, backup and recovery functions built into the various platforms, DBMS, network, application and presentation services that are planned or in use. Frequently, the IP specialist may be faced with trying to assemble an integrated protection environment out of existing functional parts. It may be do-able but it's seldom desirable.

  For example, to effectively classify and protect data, you should be able to build on a well designed and robust data architecture and DBMS providing unambiguous and consistent object identification, well protected relational functions and linkages and a comprehensive set of dictionary or repository processes. Similarly, for passing authorization, identification and verification between nodes across network paths, we have to assume that an effective system for handshaking and recognition exists at the protocol, session, and transaction level.

  The most effective way to deal with derivation and dependence is to include IP requirements in the early stages of overall architecture and design before firm commitments are made to specific platforms and implementations. This inclusion won't automatically cure protection mismatches but it will unearth the issues (and possible solutions) early enough to be given appropriate consideration and priority before developing, selecting and modifying platform, network, database, application and presentation products.

- *Finally, IP processes are subordinate to the needs of the business.* IP processes must operate within the overall constraints of the business and technology. With the possible exception of defense environments in which entire processes can be shut down in the presence of "contamination" or compromise, most organizations balance the level of protection against other considerations such as speed, capacity, ease-of-use, function, administrative overhead and, of course, cost. The number of viable IP options can turn out be very small indeed unless some early balancing of objectives and priorities takes place.

In considering these characteristics, we must stress one other fact. In the normal course of events, few business managers or technical designers and implementers will give protection a high priority unless explicitly directed to do so. Neglecting IP is not a management or process flaw as much as a fact of human and institutional nature. IP does not come naturally to most people or organizations. Free access and "getting on with it" does.

Architectural Considerations

Let's first examine some of the architecture and design elements that must be considered for protection in open distributed systems. We'll follow with a look at some of the required or more desirable IP design objectives. After that we'll discuss the nature and use of some available tools and mechanisms.

The IP Architecture Building Blocks

These are the conceptual building blocks which make up the basis of any IP architecture. They can be deployed in different configurations and modes. Many individual products can be used to implement them.

- **Trusted nodes and trusted paths**. In this instance, trust means that each successive network node need not re-verify the identification (and possibly, the authorization) of the process seeking service once the initiating node has done so. In a trusted network, any transaction sent from Point A to Point B can be assumed by Point B to be authentic. The reason for this assumption is that the initiating node (A), any intermediate nodes, and the path can be demonstrated to be reliable through analysis of their design and controls. Although common in the mainframe world, network trust is often impossible in Open Systems, especially with public networks like the Internet. In the absence of demonstrable trust, each node must act as a self-protective island, independently requiring verification and determining on its own the authorization of the incoming traffic or use the services of a known and trusted surrogate (see *Third Party Authentication*).

  Clearly, establishing "domains of trust" is advantageous because it cuts down on the security overhead and user irritation. Unfortunately, too many organizations operate in a trusted mode without sufficient evidence that the trust is warranted. However, even in some global and complex networks, it is possible to construct trusted links within an untrusted network.

- **Points of Identification**: These are the logical and physical locations where the user or process is identified, typically with a login ID. Most organizations assign a permanent ID to users or processes for use throughout the enterprise's own network. A different ID may be required for service on other networks. Just look at the number of alternative addresses printed on the business cards of public network users to get an idea of how individuals can collect IDs.

  There are three major dimensions to the Point of Identification:

  - The number of times the user must supply the ID
  - The number of times the ID is checked
  - The number of places the ID is checked

  An increasing number of security systems use scripts for supplying the user's ID (but hopefully not the password). These scripts reduce the number of times the user must be directly involved. However, each node in the process may check the ID as the transaction traverses its territory.

- **Points of Authentication or Verification**: As described above, the ID process is not enough. You must be able to verify that you or a process acting for you is truly the one identified. Reusable passwords (the kind we all key into the system) have been serving this purpose for years but with rapidly declining effectiveness. There are far too many password attacks and spoofing techniques (capturing and using a valid password to gain unauthorized privilege) in use today.

  The so-called "one time password" is a device that issues a unique password or other verifier that is good for only one specific session. Therefore, the danger of someone capturing a password and reusing it is vastly reduced, if not totally eliminated. In addition, password traffic should always travel in encrypted form and should therefore be useless to an interceptor. *No passwords "in the clear" (unencrypted) beyond the workstation (and even inside the workstation) should be a basic security design criterion.*

- **Points of Authorization**: Identification and authentication establish who you are. Authorization determines what privileges you will be granted by each of the processes and resources you approach. In a distributed environment authorization can be handled centrally or on a distributed basis (hybrid arrangements are also possible.) Updating privilege files and access control lists on each processing node (or intelligent switch) in a complex network can be a massive, error-prone job and may require almost constant maintenance.

If the enterprise can establish and maintain one authorization file from which all nodes in the system are fed, the process of privilege update is greatly enhanced and simplified. If an employee changes jobs and therefore privileges, that fact need only be reflected in one place. However, regardless of where it is maintained, that privilege information must still be available to all of the nodes from which you are likely to request service.

Today, many servers and subsystems and even some distributed applications require their own authorization files for access control. Several software products on the market manage multi-platform authorization by establishing interfaces with the various access control facilities in use throughout the net and providing them with update information automatically.

Question: As an alternate, can the "privilege information" travel with each user request for service as an extension of the trusted password or password equivalent? It could, if it can be protected and if it can be translated accurately by the target subsystem. But for repetitive usage, local privilege files at the node are usually more efficient than adding privilege information (and therefore overhead) to each service request. Most of today's systems do not transport authorization data with authentication data.

- **Points of Administration**: Where are the IP functions managed and how? In an open environment, this isn't a trivial question. It may well be that there is no single point from which all of the administrative function associated with protecting the network can be performed. A true client/server relationship of security administrative functions may have to be developed to map across the different processing domains being secured. Much depends on the nature and scope of the network operating system and applications in use. For example, each copy of Novell Netware 3.X sees the world as a single server and its attached workstations plus everything else, whereas Netware 4.x can adopt a more global view with detailed views of other servers and domains as well as its own. The administrative viewpoint of each version is significantly different. Points of administration for a particular function such as authorization or authentication may be different from the points at which the activity is actually performed. One server may be a physical location for several different logical points.

- **Modes of Accountability and Auditability**: These are the functions required to establish, manage and maintain an audit trail, establish transaction responsibility and enable transactions to be reproduced for purposes of examination and reconstruction. In today's open system product offerings, accountability and auditability features are the least understood, and least well designed or developed. Improperly designed audit and accounting functions can result in inadequate controls, intolerable overhead, or both.

IP Design Objectives

Now, that we have the architectural building blocks defined, what are some of the preferred design characteristics that we can expect to attain through effective design and implementation?

- **Economy of logon**: Sometimes loosely called "single sign-on," this process is directed toward reducing the number of times per session and per day the user needs to logon and present a password (or equivalent). Single sign-on is a design objective, not a system unto itself and can be achieved through the use of several of the techniques just described. True "single-sign-on" may not always be desirable. There may be processes and systems for which unique and individual ID and verification are necessary. Some of the same effects may be achieved by the use of one-time password devices.

  Do not confuse these two concepts. One-time passwords change the verification data each time a password is required. Without single sign-on, in the course of a day, you could use a one-time password device many times to re-verify your identity. Each time, the "password equivalent" submitted to the authentication mechanism will be different. On the other hand, single sign-on means you sign on only once per personal session regardless of the type of password mechanism you use.

  Single sign-on requires standardization and mutual recognition by processes. To achieve this standardization and mutual recognition, a layer of standardizing interface code applied at each node and perhaps for each application may be necessary.

- **Timely alarms and corrective actions**: Each node must be able to detect inappropriate action, identify the offending action for what it is, and, most importantly, transmit that information to the appropriate managing location and function for immediate response. If the warning never leaves the point of incident, it's like having working but disconnected fire alarms. They may make noise but they may not get the fire department's attention. Most of today's distributed systems are weak in this department. Today, most system-wide alarm and reporting systems are built, or at least rationalized by the using organization, supplementing existing vendor-supplied functionality.

- **Comprehensive, coherent, efficient, and consistent auditability and accounting**: As we indicated in the discussion on building blocks, it is more difficult to track, log, and, if necessary, reproduce multi-part client/server transactions, open connection transmissions or even remote procedure calls in an open systems environment than it is to perform the same functions in the single image model. Today, it is often necessary to use individual platform- or application-based logs and to reconstruct the transaction trail from the individual audit tools in each server or in each application. This process is usually very inefficient and ineffective.

- **Seamless IP administration from a single point**: This requirement is currently a much-to-be-desired dream. In its most basic form, it means all the protective functions work well together and can be managed as a single virtual entity from a single point. A number of standards activities are aimed at this objective. Obviously, IP administration closely aligns with and depends on network and process management. Here is a major example of a topic which should be incorporated into the architectural requirements and design specifications of any distributed system. But few, if any, of today's implementations can claim this characteristic, and have little protection as a result.

IP Tools and Mechanisms

If these are the architectural building blocks and desired objectives we seek to satisfy, what are the generic tools we have at our disposal to make it happen? Some of today's most effective tools include cryptography, third party authentication servers, and firewalls. While specific implementations may differ in detail from vendor to vendor, these tools are the subjects of functional and interface standardization at an industry level.

- **Cryptography** (synonyms: crypto, encryption). The principles, means and methods for rendering information unintelligible and for restoring encrypted information to intelligible form. Cryptanalysis is the converse process—breaking encrypted messages—usually without the owner's permission but not always. Lose or forget an encryption key and you'll see what I mean. Encryption is becoming an increasingly important IP tool, especially in distributed environments where conventional password-driven access control may not be effective or sufficiently strong.

Several Other Necessary Definitions

- **Encryption Algorithm**: A complex mathematical formula which combines the contents of a message with another unique string of data (Key) to create an encrypted message or decrypt previously encrypted data. Algorithms may be publicly known or proprietary.

- **Encryption Key**: A string of data which is mathematically combined by the algorithm with the message itself to encrypt or decrypt the message. Choice of key, key length and unpredictability of key contents are critical to the strength of the encryption process.

- **Key Management**: The administrative and technology-based techniques employed for creating, disseminating, controlling, maintaining and destroying encryption keys. This is one of the least understood but most critical aspects of encryption. Improper or inefficient key management can result in ineffective, dangerous and in many cases, overly expensive encryption processes. No encryption system should be adopted without a full understanding of the key management processes and costs.

A SHORT (AND RELATIVELY PAINLESS) TAXONOMY OF ENCRYPTION

Encryption can be examined in several different dimensions:

Purpose: Cryptography may be used for confidentiality, integrity and non-repudiation.

- Confidentiality is assured by making the information unintelligible to all but authorized individuals with the ability to decrypt the information.

- Integrity—This is a very important and often overlooked purpose of encryption. Most crypto mechanisms robust enough for serious commercial use are so designed that any change to the content of the encrypted message will make the entire message unintelligible, even to authorized individuals with the ability to decrypt. In a strict sense, crypto mechanisms do not preserve the message integrity as much as indicate whether integrity is still present. One technique described below can maintain the message in the clear but appends an encrypted "envelope" or "signature" which can be decrypted only if the message is unmodified. In this way, in the event of unauthorized modification, the message content is still identifiable even though it is known to be untrustworthy.

- Non-repudiation means that the message and its contents can be satisfactorily proven to have come from the indicated sender (and transmission point). This can be important in verifying major transactions.

Modes: As mentioned above, there are several basic modes of encrypting:

- Message or record encryption—the actual content is rendered unintelligible

- Digital envelope—the message is left in the clear but is used to develop a unique encrypted appendage which travels with the message and serves as an indicator of the integrity of the message. It is similar to the "hash total" used to ensure the integrity of a spreadsheet or other array of information

- Digital signature—similar to digital envelope but it includes in the encrypted appendage sufficient information to uniquely identify the sender or sending process. Additional data such as sequence numbers, time of day etc. can be added to the encrypted tag. A digital signature serves both integrity and non-repudiation. A digital signature can be added to an already encrypted message for further control and assurance.

Environment: Encryption is used to protect messages in transit (transmission) and data (including software) in storage. While the general techniques are the same for both, the length of time and the ways in which keys are kept and managed are very different. In the case of transmission, once the message arrives and is successfully decrypted, the encryption mechanism is disengaged and at least one level of key is discarded. In the case of storage, the mechanism and associated keys must be present and available for the life of the stored data. Let's look at transmission a little more closely.

Types of Transmission Encryption:

• End to end—The message originates in encrypted form and remains encrypted till it reaches its end point. Only the end users are involved in the process.

• Link—The message is encrypted, decrypted and re-encrypted at some or all of the intervening nodes in a network. This may be necessary for technological, contractual, legal or administrative reasons.

Crypto Techniques:

• Symmetric—The same algorithm and key (see below) are used for encryption and decryption. The Data Encryption Standard (DES) is a symmetric technique.

• Asymmetric—Two different keys are used for encryption and decryption. Public (or more accurately, shared) key algorithms are asymmetric. Asymmetric techniques are very useful for broadcasting or collecting information where the key to one side of the process is carefully restricted but the other side is more openly available to a larger population. A bank night depository is an appropriate analogy—the RSA public key method is the most popular asymmetric cryto technique.

• **Third Party Authentication Servers**: If no two points in an open distributed environment can clearly establish a restrictive domain of trust, you have several choices. Load each one up with the identifying characteristics of every other one and authenticate all traffic in detail. Administering and synchronizing such a process can be a nightmare (but it is being done in some environments). Choice two is to cross your fingers and hope everyone is honest. (Not a good idea!) Choice three is to establish a single authenticating authority that is trusted by all the other processes. Only this authority has to worry about the identification and verification and it in turn can send certificates of trust on behalf of all the processes seeking to interconnect. ("Any friend of Charlie's is a friend of mine.")

The third party process is complex. It employs encryption technology and some very detailed transaction processing. The authentication server itself must be carefully protected. Compromise or lose it and the jig is up. It can be a serious single point of failure unless it is made fault-tolerant. But it works in open environments where you cannot *directly* trust the path or the processes.

There are several different models for authentication servers. At the moment, the most popular is Kerberos (named after the 3-headed dog that guards the gates of Hell in Greek mythology). Developed and licensed by MIT, Kerberos mediates the authentication process. (See Figure 9.2.) After the user signs on at the workstation with a valid password or equivalent, Kerberos supplies the identified and verified user with an encrypted and trusted ticket, valid for the duration of the session, which can then be used to obtain specific application tickets and application session encryption keys, as needed. For the duration of the session, these electronic tickets or certificates can be presented by the client processes invoked by the user to the servers providing the required resources in lieu of direct re-verification by the user. In fact most, if not all, of this process is transparent to the user. The target application also verifies itself back to the client using the same technique. This too, is transparent to the end user sitting at the workstation. Recall the old image of the regal swan floating serenely on the surface while underwater there is a mad flurry of paddling going on. That's the third-party authentication process.

THIRD-PARTY AUTHENTICATION PROCESS—KERBEROS

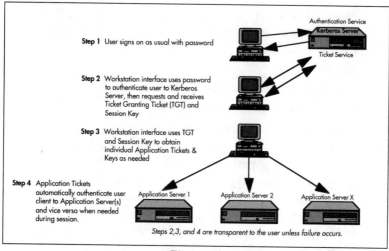

Figure 9.2

Kerberos is a major component of but not a complete single-sign-on system in itself (see *Economy of Log On*). Kerberos is also often mistakenly described as a complete access control system. It is not. The individual nodes still must determine whether access will be granted to the ticket holding process. Kerberos provides a trusted verification of the user's ID in untrusted environments. Since Kerberos can be rigorously demonstrated to be trustworthy itself, it is intended for use in open networks where establishing true domains of trust strictly on the basis of known nodes and users is not possible. Today, Kerberos runs only on a UNIX platform but can mediate authentication for other types of platforms It is not flawless and usually requires significant application interface modification. However, it is a very useful system that should be explored for all distributed environments.

There are several version of Kerberos in use. Version 5 is currently the functionally richest—but watch out, there are several implementations (flavors) in use. Another note: Kerberos isn't the only third-party authenticator in town. Other similar processes include the OSF/DCE Version 1.0 security mechanism (Figure 9.3), the European Computer Manufacturers Association's SESAME model, Digital Equipment's Authentication Service (DECdas) and IBM's NetSP.

OSF/DCE SECURITY

The Open Software Foundation's Distributed Computing Environment software offering contains a suite of related security features. Look for this "subsystem" as part of the DCE products.

It contains:

- Identification and Authentication through Kerberos Version 5
- Access Control List technology for authorization
- A registry data base structure for security information
- Secure Remote procedure calls with several authentication options and provisions for data integrity and confidentiality through encryption.

This package is about as close as you can come in today's open environment to a complete baseline security offering. Several vendors, such as IBM, Computer Associates and several of the UNIX suppliers have a somewhat broader architectural approach but all the slots aren't filled with products yet. OSF/DCE is very light in the audit and accountability departments and application interfaces still need to be developed by the user in many cases. It can be used to interface with mainframe processes.

Figure 9.3

- **Firewalls**: as the name suggests, firewalls are software or hardware/software combinations installed on a network server(s) to act as a controlled gateway between processes or network segments. The most common application of firewall technology is at the point of transition between private and public networks (such as The Internet). As usual, the term is used rather ambiguously by vendors to describe everything from enhanced access control software to elaborate, specially designed servers. They are an important addition to the protection toolkit but they are not all the same. Be careful.

Putting It All Together

So, at the end of the day what do we need to make it all happen? A set of effective tools and the will and discipline to use them. An effective family of protective mechanisms for mission critical, financially material and/or content sensitive applications in a distributed environment should include:

- An extensive suite of backup and recovery tools

- Non-reusable password technology

- File and transmission encryption, including digital envelope and signature

- Single sign-on mode of operation

- In untrustworthy open networks, a third-party authentication system

- Firewalls and gateways at points of contact with untrusted traffic

- Techniques for isolating compromised processes, processors and network components and unauthorized users and activities from the rest of the network

- Authorization management technology

- Anti-viral technology

- A full suite of audit, logging and journaling tools

- A consistent suite of network-wide alarm and incident reporting mechanisms

- Platform and server security test and measurement tools

- Application, system, data and network design tools that incorporate or support security and control functions

All of these functions are available as separate products and services or as embedded processes within application, network, platform, workstation, presentation and DBMS technologies. The trick is finding them and putting them together coherently to support your strategy and architecture. These technologies also require companion processes addressing ongoing training and awareness, incident reporting and handling and audit based on a consistent and comprehensive policy, standards and procedure structure.

Some Basic IP Design and Management Axioms for Distributed Systems

If this was 1894, the following statements might have been embroidered and displayed as needlework samplers. As we move toward 2001, they could appear on the electronic sampler—the screen saver.

- People are the most important component in any distributed IP process.

- There is a strong affinity between Quality and Protection. The more closely they cooperate, the more effective both programs will be.

- Most open distributed environments should be considered untrustworthy and potentially hostile until proven otherwise.

- Classify your data resources according to business impact and customize your protective strategy and architecture to meet those classifications.

- Seek and eliminate all *significant* single points of failure and use business as well as technological metrics to determine significance. This includes facilities, paths, nodes, switches, processes and...*people.*

- Develop comprehensive, specifically tailored Business Continuity Plans for each business process including but not restricted to the information technology—AND TEST THEM THOROUGHLY.

- Examine and test the backup and recovery functions of each platform and process including such items as file mirroring, RAID disk arrays, autosave techniques etc.

- Install, use and keep virus protection mechanisms up to date. Year-old virus detection will not recognize the latest flavors.

- Passwords should not appear in the clear beyond the workstation (and preferably not within the workstation, either).

- One-time password technology should be used whenever and wherever it is cost effective.

- To the extent possible, objects, rather than paths, should be the preferred focus of control.

- Make a serious survey of encryption technology and its application to your distributed environments. The odds are you'll need it if you really want to achieve high levels of integrity and confidentiality. Encryption technology can also contribute to continuity.

- Every IP model is as different as the using organization. Don't copy other protection schemes in detail. Learn from models and best practices but design your own IP strategy and architecture to fit your needs.

- Develop an explicit IP policy and supporting standards and procedures, publish them and develop awareness and measurement programs to support them.

- IP begins at the workstation. It doesn't end there.

- **Finally, and most important, distributed IP must be designed and implemented along with and as part of the overall development process—retrofit no longer works.**

Summary

Entire books have been written on this topic and there will be more to come. In these two short chapters, we have attempted to demonstrate how IP issues, processes and mechanisms are different in distributed environments than in a single-image mainframe environment. We have also pointed out the necessity to elevate IP to an equal level with the other design objectives of the system and network in order to protect information and manage continuity and integrity risks in an open environment. Inappropriate or improperly designed and implemented protection can be self defeating and even dangerous.

The real issue is in striking a balance between the cost of IP and potential losses. (See Figure 9.4.)

BALANCING IP COST AND RISK

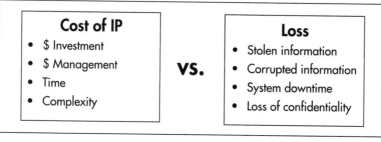

Figure 9.4

The open systems arena need not be wide open, and with proper design, IP can strengthen not inhibit the promises of the technology. That, after all, is why you're making the investment.

Chapter 10

Impact on Everyone—
No Function is an Island

*The shepherd drives the wolf from the sheep's throat for which the sheep
thanks the shepherd as his liberator, while the wolf denounces him for the
same act as the destroyer of liberty.*

—Abraham Lincoln

Nothing makes you more tolerant of a neighbor's noisy party than being there.

—Franklin P. Jones

In this section we discuss some of the changes in how information systems
are designed and built, open systems, and the impact of both on the end user
and the IS organization. Four major directions are converging in business
information systems: users are becoming more technology knowledgeable
and more involved, organizations are questioning the cost-benefit of technology, while at the same time, increasingly using technology to compete in the
marketplace. And, organizations are becoming more aware of the business
risk of computing systems as their enterprises become more dependent upon
them. As a result, users are becoming more involved in systems, the role of IS
is changing from one of systems manager and "owner" to infrastructure
provider and technology "consultant," and organizations are looking to open
systems to develop an integrated information infrastructure and leverage
down the unit costs of computing. All of this contributes to significant change
in the IS organization—in what it does, and how it does it. We take a look at
shifts in IS organizational responsibilities, spending, policies and procedures,
and organizational structure. Change, however, is not limited to the IS organization. It impacts everyone.

In today's computing business world, we are seeing the convergence of four major directions in business information systems:
shifting responsibility from IS to the users, focus on driving down
the unit cost of technology and technology services, realignment of
information and technology priorities within the business, and a
realization of the need to manage the business risk of reliance upon
technology. (See Figure 10.1.) These four courses are leading us to
a new view of the systems required to support the business and the
IS function needed to support the systems.

FOUR MAJOR DIRECTIONS IN
BUSINESS INFORMATION SYSTEMS

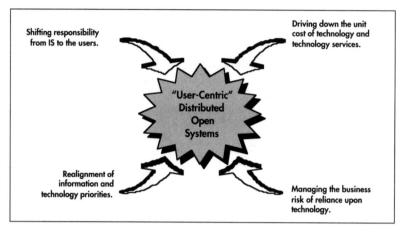

Shifting responsibility from IS to the users.

Driving down the unit cost of technology and technology services.

"User-Centric" Distributed Open Systems

Realignment of information and technology priorities.

Managing the business risk of reliance upon technology.

Figure 10.1

1. **Shifting responsibility from IS to the users**. The end user of systems is becoming much more knowledgeable and much more involved in systems. Technology vendors have been marketing directly to the end user, selling tools that capitalize on end user frustration with large IS backlogs and slow response to user requests. At the same time, IS has been working to get users to assume more of a role in systems development/selection and ultimately, more responsibility for the systems that are implemented. As a result, the end user is becoming more involved in systems design, technology selection, systems implementation, and in some cases, even assuming some development and support responsibilities.

2. **Driving down the unit cost of technology and technology services**. Organizations are questioning on the cost-benefit of technology. They are concerned about the cost of information technology and services. One problem is hidden costs. The Gartner Group estimates that 20-40% of decentralized business unit spending on information technology (IT) may be unrecognized because it is no longer being tracked and managed by the IS function. [Gartner Group, 1993]

    Another concern is the need to drive down the unit operating costs of information technology and services in order to deliver more systems functionality for the same total cost to the enterprise and to fund architectural updates. A large U.S. manufacturing firm is taking bold steps to reign in its IT costs. The company's goal is to fund the migration to new technology and new functionality by reducing the base unit cost of IT. Specific cost improvement targets were set for purchases, people, and data centers with an initial goal of reducing the overall cost of IT by 10%. IS management figures that the company needs to continue to remove 10-15% per year from the unit operating cost of IT to stay competitive and fund its infrastructure renewal initiatives.

3. **Realignment of information and technology priorities.** Paul Strassmann, author of the Business Value of Computers found in surveys of Fortune 500 companies that 52% of the organizations spent more money on IT than they made in profits. The CEOs of the companies rightly asked, "What did I get for the money?" In his surveys, Strassman found that the best companies didn't spend any more or less on IT than the worst companies—it was where they spent the money that counted. The best companies spent more of their information technology budget on mission critical operations systems than management systems. All other companies spent 60-80% of their information and technology on management information systems.[1] [Strassmann, 1990]

Time Warner and Nordstrom's are examples of companies placing emphasis on mission critical operations systems:

Time Magazine recently demonstrated some of the power of its technology in reporting personalized news. In the May 2, 1994 issue, the magazine debuted "individualized congressional reporting." Time printed personalized issues with a box in its Chronicles column containing the subscriber's name to catch the reader's eye and the voting records of their congressional representatives.

Nordstrom's, a Seattle-based department store chain, is an aggressive user of technology. The company announced plans to move into home shopping via interactive television. The company also announced a Visa credit card that will give customers discounts on purchases made at its stores.

---

[1]For the purposes of his expenditure comparisons, Strassman defined "operations" as those activities "essential for delivering products and services to today's customers." "Management" is defined as "everything not in operations."

Nordstrom's Visa card will be the retail answer to encouraging frequent shopper loyalty by giving escalating discounts as the shopper reaches successively higher annual accumulated purchase levels.

"Individualized reporting," "home shopping," and "frequent shopper rewards" all require sophisticated systems and intricate supplier relationships. These sophisticated systems are a "different breed" from accounting systems. They are highly interconnected and often involve exchanging information with suppliers and vendors from other organizations. These systems are also highly visible, change more frequently as the business environment changes, and require a much higher involvement and level of support from the users.

4. **Managing the business risk of reliance upon technology.** One other direction cannot be ignored. Organizations are becoming more aware of the business risk of computing systems. As their enterprises become more dependent upon systems and the technology market becomes more turbulent, they are seeking to manage that risk. On a system by system basis, risk is managed through redundancy, backup processes, and so on. On an overall technology direction basis, risk is managed by wrestling control over the technology direction of the organization away from the primary vendor and moving to more "open technology"—technology supported and perhaps provided by multiple vendors, minimizing dependence on any single vendor.

These directions are converging to change the role of IS in developing systems, in selecting and managing technology, and in managing the business risk of technology. Subsequently, the role of both users and the IS organization in developing and supporting systems capabilities is changing dramatically. Changes impact the policies and procedures for acquiring and building systems functionality. They also impact where IS budget dollars are going—and for what kind of technology. Ultimately, changes impact the purpose and structure of the IS organization itself. We will explore each of these areas. But first, let's take a closer look at the new breed of strategic, interconnected, cross-functional systems that are being designed and the expanded role of the user in creating them.

Changing the Focus to "User-Centric" Systems

In the start of this book, we discussed the new Era of Connectivity that has been spawned by the microprocessor. In this Era of Connectivity, our attention is shifting from accounting, management control, and operations support to decision support and sharing information across and among interconnected, dynamic work groups. (See Figure 10.2.)

THE ERA OF CONNECTIVITY

	Centralized Capabilities and Operations		Distributed Capabilities	
	1960's–70's	**1970's–80's**	**1980's–90's**	**1990's–?**
Systems Focus	Accounting and control	Operations support	Decision support	Workgroups, information sharing
Technology	Mainframe	Minicomputer/ Midframe	Desktop workstations/ Personal computers	Interconnected networks
Primary Users	Central, corporate	Departments and small businesses	End users	Dynamic workgroups, virtual collectives
Major Projects	Expansion and diversification of accounting functions	Decentralization of systems and new technology investments	New systems to support strategies for market leadership	Facilitate computing "collectives" or communities Support business partnerships
New System Capabilities	Data collection management reporting	Process support	Data access and analysis	Distributed access to common, shared, context-sensitive information
Alignment	Vertical—along management lines		Horizontal—along process lines	

Figure 10.2

At the same time, technology is becoming more powerful, more robust, and more "connectable," allowing IS to spend less time "making it work" and more time analyzing such questions as "what do we need?" and "what should we make it do?"[2]

As technology becomes more usable, our approach to designing systems is becoming much more "user-centric." Users are getting more involved in systems design and technology selection. And, we are beginning to design systems from the desktop back rather than from the mainframe out. (See Figure 10.3.) The "traditional" approach to designing systems is being turned on its ear.

---

[2]This is not to say that technology issues are becoming easier. Quite to the contrary, they are becoming more complex because of more powerful products, more options and greater choice, and the correspondingly greater number of decisions that must be made.

OUTSIDE IN VERSUS *INSIDE OUT* SYSTEMS DESIGN

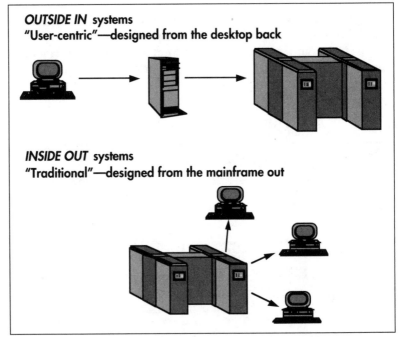

Figure 10.3

Outside in Systems Design

"User-centric" systems are designed from the *desktop back* or in other words, *from the outside in*. The design effort begins with describing how the user will interact with systems functionality. Although this may sound suspiciously similar to a more "traditional" *external systems design*, it actually differs significantly from the more traditional approach of producing (rather flat) views of screens and reports as a 'byproduct' of the functionality being designed. When designing systems from the outside in, analysts and designers begin with the "look and feel" of the systems. They describe a common *desktop* or set of functionality and navigation procedures *across* systems. Once the common desktop has been defined, it is used as the common user interface for all systems capabilities. Systems designers move backwards from the common desktop to describing systems functionality and data presentation in terms of the common desktop and user interface—relating systems functionality to what the user will be able to see and do.[3]

Inside out Systems Design

In contrast, *inside out* systems design really doesn't focus much attention on a common user interface and more specifically, common desktop capabilities across systems. Instead, the user interface is designed on a application-by-application basis as the systems functionality is designed and data defined. As such, systems are viewed from the inside out—"what will the system do?," "how will it do it?," and "what will the user see when it does whatever it is to do?"

The New "Superuser"—More Power, More Responsibility

An important benefit of user-centric, *outside in* designed systems is that the technology and functionality delivered to the desktop is much more powerful and usable by the end user. Users become "superusers," able to bypass IS for simple reports and ad hoc queries. Depending on the tools available at the desktop, the user may even be able to create more complex reports, queries, data, and logic routines, using the tools to do things that previously required a seasoned COBOL programmer. With a powerful desktop environment, users become more productive, more in control of their data and technology.

Along with more control comes more responsibility. As systems become more "user-centric," the user becomes more involved in systems design, technology selection, and sometimes, even in systems development, delivery, and support. The technology user has the opportunity to assume technology planning responsibilities, gaining more control over the technology direction and investment plan for the organization. The user becomes more responsible for the end product—both from a delivered functionality and total cost standpoint. And, as we pointed out in the preceding chapters, the user assumes an integral role in information protection strategies.

---

[3]This description of *outside in* systems design is not meant to imply a sequence of events, rather, a shift in emphasis. Actually, in order to do *outside in* systems design, an organization must have a strong technical architecture including a vision of the technology and standards that will be supported as well as a strong business systems architecture including data and process models. Otherwise, the *outside in* approach will collapse as new "unanticipated" functionality and technology is introduced to the environment. *"Outside in"* systems design might more appropriately be referred to as *"outside in—inside out," working both directions: from the desktop back and from the technical and business systems architecture out.*

Changing the Role of IS

As a result of the four major directions in business information systems and the increased role of users in systems design, delivery, and management, the role of IS is shifting from one of systems manager and "owner" to infrastructure provider and technology "consultant." Simultaneously, IS is assuming responsibility for the technology direction of the enterprise and for technology integration—a role previously fulfilled for organizations by the primary technology vendor. Let's take a look at some of the areas where IS is most impacted by the change in focus to operations-focused, "user-centric" systems.

Shift From Technology "Owner" to "Advisor"

As responsibility is transferred from IS to the user, the relationship between IS and the business changes dramatically. IS moves from "owning" and "managing" the technology to being advisors to the business on how the business can best use technology. While this role change is not caused by open systems, it is enabled by open systems. Open systems and the associated proliferation of desktop products and tools enables users to operate much more independently from IS than they were able to in the past. In the past, IS was needed to select, develop, and interpret technology to the business (it was mysterious stuff). Now, business users are able to select and use their own technology (within an overall connectivity and cost framework). This opens the door for IS to move into the role of *technology advisor* and *overall coordinator* of the investment in technology at an enterprise level—to select technology, integrate technology, facilitate resource sharing across business users, resolve technology issues, and plan and manage infrastructure investments.

The transition from IS as "technology owner" to "technology advisor" is a win-win situation for users and IS alike. Users are given more freedom and power on the desktop, more control over their computing resources, and better access to information. But, it cannot be stressed enough, along with greater freedom and control comes more responsibility. As more users step up to this responsibility and superusers are born through the use of open tools, IS becomes more productive and efficient as well. IS resources are freed to focus on technology integration, developing strategic applications, business process reengineering, customer service, and other services that add value to the organization.

Assuming Technology Leadership Within the Organization

In many industries, information networks and access to information are either the basis of heated competition or required for basic survival. Organizations in these industries know that they need to have more control over their own future and direction in technology. They are looking to IS to provide technology vision to the organization—to design and build information networks that create a competitive advantage or increase operational efficiency such as integrating business units to drive down costs. Open systems support the need of the enterprise to plan for the future direction and use of technology within the organization.

Open systems also support the need to manage the business risk of increased use of technology. Through the definition of standards and selection of standards-based technology (whether "open" or "proprietary/open"), the organization has greater freedom in setting an acceptable level of risk to the enterprise.

Expanding Technology Integration Responsibilities

In an open systems environment, the complexity of the technological environment increases with heterogeneous platforms and multivendor implementations. In this environment, the IS function assumes the role of technology integrator, a role formerly performed by the proprietary vendor. In this role, IS is responsible for establishing the technical foundation, communication and interoperation standards, to be supported by the organization. IS also assumes responsibility for selecting products that fit with the technical foundation, testing the products for interoperation within the technical foundation, and integrating those products into the environment. (See Figure 10.4.)

SHIFTS IN OPEN SYSTEMS TESTING RESPONSIBILITIES

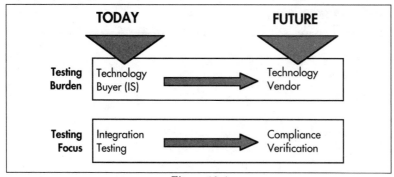

Figure 10.4

As technology vendors broaden their product and service offerings, IS is finding itself in the interesting position of being not only a customer of technology products, but also a competitor in the technology marketplace. Many technology vendors are now offering products and services previously created and performed by IS. The role of IS is shifting from one geared towards "creating" and "providing" technology and services to one recognizing where internal sourcing adds value and external sourcing is more economical.

IS/IT Budgets

Along with the shift in roles and responsibilities between IS and the end user, and between the primary technology vendor and IS, we are seeing corresponding shifts in IS spending. As organizations look to drive down the unit cost of information technology and services, they're looking to open systems to help, and spending an increasing percentage of their budget on open technology. A 1993 worldwide open systems market survey produced by X/Open foresees a dramatic shift in planned IT expenditures. (See Figure 10.5.)

PLANNED IT EXPENDITURES

	Current 1993	Planned 1996
Hardware-proprietary	28%	15%
Hardware-open	15%	20%
Hardware total	43%	35%
Software-proprietary	21%	16%
Software-open	11%	22%
Software total	32%	38%
Services	25%	27%
Total	100%	100%

Source: X/Open Market Research Report, 1993

Figure 10.5

The shift in IT spending from proprietary to open and from hardware to software and services is consistent with the major direction to provide more functionality, more information technology capabilities to the organization at a lower unit operating cost.

IS Policies and Specifics

The shift in the IS role from infrastructure "owner" to technology "advisor" brings with it required changes in many IS organizational policies and procedures. As we will see, in some cases, IS needs to establish a function and business processes to manage things that it previously didn't have the means to manage or the assigned responsibility to oversee—for example, defining and evolving the information and computing architectures and standards within the organization. In other cases, open systems and the converging directions to user-centric systems are causing IS to change existing operations.

Let's take a look at a few areas where either new policies and functions are needed, or significant changes to the "old way of doing things" are necessitated by open systems and the changing role of IS.

• **Definition and evolution of architectures and standards**

An open systems environment offers IS the opportunity to specify and manage the technology infrastructure at a standard interface level, rather than *only* at a specific vendor or product level. This offers IS the opportunity to guide the direction of the overall technology architecture while allowing end users the freedom to select individual vendor products that comply with selected standards. Of course, in today's technology world, there are some levels of the technology stack where "substitutable technologies" do not exist or, where decisions at one level force decisions at the higher level and specific technologies will need to be specified. For example, selection of a database platform may limit the selection of tools that can be used to access data.

Defining and evolving the computing architecture requires good design skills, solid knowledge of the state and direction of the technology marketplace, and business vision. It also requires participation on the part of the end user in defining an architecture that will be acceptable to the business. Many IS organizations are establishing an "architecture and standards" function to define and manage the evolution of the technical architecture. Many are also assigning responsibility for the information architecture (enterprise view of information) to this same function to facilitate the sharing of information and information resources.

- **Standards and technology monitoring, evaluation and selection**

    Understanding and "defining" the direction of the marketplace is an important process in the open systems world. With vendor alliances forming frequently around specific open standards, open proprietary standards, and technologies, the task is quite challenging. But, monitoring the direction of standards and technology is an important component in setting the overall technology direction for the organization.

- **Procurement policies**

    In an open world, the policies and procedures for procuring technology change. In order to manage the acquisition, integration, and support costs of systems, it is important to select technology that is consistent with the overall technology and business architecture. The most successful policies set standards and force the inevitable deviations from overall technology and business architectures to be justified on a product-by-product basis, based on business need.

    The 1993 worldwide X/Open market research report gave some insight into purchase policies around the world. (See Figure 10.6.) Europe and (quite surprisingly) Asia lead the world in purchase policies based on industry standards (Asia has lagged in acceptance of open systems in prior years). Companies from all parts of the world except Asia rely more heavily on selecting specific technologies than industry standards. Companies from all parts of the world rely more heavily on industry standards than international standards.

REGIONAL VIEW

Current Purchase Policies are based on...	Europe	North America	Industrialized Asia	Rest of World
Industry Standards	61%	33%	65%	46%
Specific Technologies	69%	77%	56%	65%
International Standards	56%	11%	40%	68%

(Respondents were allowed to check more than one answer.)

Source: X/Open Market Research Report, '93

Figure 10.6

One thing that stands out clearly in this chart is that North America lags the world in acceptance of industry and international standards—probably still viewing standards as overhead and limiting the (fierce) independence of technology vendors and programmers alike.

Overall, worldwide, organizations most often purchase specific technologies. (See Figure 10.7.) However, industry standards, in-house standards, and international standards are all used for more than 40% of technology purchases.

PURCHASE POLICIES—WORLD VIEW

Current Purchase Policies are based on...	Worldwide
Specific technologies	63%
Industry standards	50%
In house standards	46%
International standards	41%
Government requirements	33%
Specific vendors	11%

(Respondents were allowed to check more than one answer.)

Source: X/Open Market Research Report, '93

Figure 10.7

Whatever the rules, whatever the level, as the number of vendors and vendor products that can be considered for technology acquisition increase, it is more important than ever to define, manage, and maintain purchase policies.

- **Technology integration—testing and prototyping**

Technology integration is a major focus in an open system world. Industry and international interface standards can guide technology selection and development. "Branding" programs will help as both standards specifications and conformance test suites become more robust. But, today and in the near future, the burden of proof—integrating technology from multiple vendors—remains the responsibility of the implementing organization.

- **Internal standards adherence & verification**

Standards for common items, from end user "look and feel" to coding methods and techniques, are being defined and implemented in IS organizations as they embrace open systems. To achieve the benefits of standardization, IS departments also need to establish some sort of policy or means for *enforcing* the standards, restricting programmers and users alike from using "expanded functionality" and other non-standard, nifty enhancements vendors will and do provide to otherwise standard-compliant offerings. As organizations move towards interconnected, shared information systems and resources, isolated pockets of development and technology standards can no longer be tolerated. Without implemented and enforced development standards, the benefits of reduced training time, reusable modules of code, ease of integration, ease of portability, and so on, will all be a "pipedream."

- **Network design and management**

  In a distributed open computing environment, the role and importance of network design and management increase. The complexity of the network is significantly higher due to distributed functionality and heterogeneous equipment. Some of the areas that are more difficult to manage include: network capacity planning, asset management, day-to-day support, application distribution and version control, licensing, information protection and security.

- **Information protection and security**

  We dedicated a full two chapters to information protection and security in this book. But, it deserves to be mentioned again here. The topography and heterogeneous nature of a distributed open network information requires an increased emphasis on security and integrity. Attention needs to be elevated to logical security rather than relying on physical security with increased surveillance and integrity checking. Security and integrity concerns naturally rise in the open systems environment as access to data is broadened and the protective shroud of mystery surrounding proprietary systems is abandoned.

- **Vendor relationship management**

  Selecting vendors and managing vendor relationships is crucial to a successful IS strategy in an open computing environment. We have already discussed the use of role of vendor management in driving down procurement costs and developing a coherent, implementable technology architecture. Selecting vendors, establishing a good working relationship, sharing the architecture direction and understanding the technology directions of vendors, promoting standards, and negotiating contracts and performance agreements are all key elements to a successful vendor management program.

As the enterprise becomes more reliant upon technology, the success of the enterprise becomes more dependent upon how well its suppliers perform.

*   **Participation in standards organizations**

    Depending upon how "leading edge" the technology needs of the organization are, participating in standards organization efforts to define standardization requirements may be a new role for the IS function. At a minimum, the organization moving towards open systems will need to understand the state of standards and standardization efforts, select standards, and push for support of selected standards with primary technology suppliers.

The "Renaissance" IS Organization

We can't skip through this analysis of the impact on IS without commenting on changes to the structure of IS itself. As IS roles and responsibilities are questioned, realigned, and redefined, the next obvious question is, "how should the new organization be structured?" While each business situation and IS situation is unique, we can make a broad observation:

> *The renaissance IS organization needs to shift from a supply side model to a demand side model at a time when both the supply and demand sides of its business are changing.*

In economics, we learned about supply side systems. Supply side systems are internally focused, often almost completely ignoring the demand side. A supply side model focuses on the production factory—designing processes to make production as efficient as possible, and allocating scarce resources (people and equipment) to service the top few projects demanding attention until resources are expended. Remaining projects (regardless of priority or business need) remain unfulfilled.

A supply side model only works when you have a monopoly, or close to a monopoly on the goods and services provided by the supplying entity. Today, there isn't any portion of computing in which an entity can *maintain* a monopoly position. Alternative sources for products, and services, and even all aspects of the internal IS function itself are available to the organization and to end users. IS needs to pay attention to the open market axiom: the supply side can't add value—only demand adds value.

A "demand side" IS function focuses on value-added products and services. It pays more attention to its consumer (the organization and the end user), the products and services it will provide to the consumer, how it will produce those products and services, and the "market" in which it is competing (today's technology market—full of software products, packaged software, and services). A demand side IS function is focused on its relationship with the business and understands its strengths relative to the market. It makes decisions on a product and service level about whether that product or service is best done in-house—"in-sourced," or purchased from the marketplace—"outsourced." A demand side IS function assesses the full need of the organization then determines how best to fulfill the need, utilizing resources both internal and external to the organization.

As a matter of fact, we are seeing a realignment of IS organizational structures to reflect the shift in emphasis from supply side to demand side. A Gartner Group study of 140 IS managers reported 86% stated that their departments had been significantly reorganized in the past months. In most cases, the thrust of the reorganization was to move IT resources into the business units. [Gartner Group, 1993]

While the changing responsibilities and corresponding organizational structures of IS is a topic worthy of its own book, we can give a brief description of a new world, open systems supportive, "demand side" focused IS organization. (See Figure 10.8.)

EXAMPLE: DEMAND-FOCUSED IS STRUCTURE

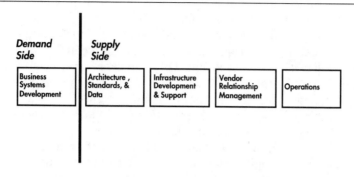

- The *business systems development* group is focused on fulfilling the needs of the business unit. Responsibilities may include designing, selecting, building, and integrating systems capabilities and the design, development, delivery, and support of the "user-centric" desktop front end to systems. The group would maintain business process models and may also support business process reengineering initiatives with business process design and support teams.

- The *architecture, standards, and data* group contains a relatively small number of high level designers and technologists focused on defining the technology infrastructure and the business information model (enterprise view of information) for the enterprise as a whole. The group would do basic research on technology and standards, staying abreast of technology developments. It would be responsible for defining the technology stack and planning the technology direction of the organization.

- The *infrastructure development and support* group contains highly skilled network and technology experts to select technology products and integration test, assemble/build, and implement the overall computing environment.

- The *vendor relationship* management function is a small number of people focused on developing and managing the relationship with vendors including qualifying vendors as suppliers, obtaining vendor information, and negotiating vendor contracts. This function is critical in driving down the purchase cost of technology and managing the overall quality of relationships with supplying vendors.

- The *operations* group is responsible for the execution and management of day-to-day computer operations.

Figure 10.8

We have discussed many of the responsibility shifts that may be experienced by IS in an open systems, demand side focused world. In this new world, IS will intensify its focus on its *own* business principles, business model, and processes. Functions that may not have existed in a proprietary world, such as technology management, will need to be established. Other functions, such as providing access to and protecting data will have new requirements and require new procedures. Vendor management will be a larger responsibility. And, IS departments will need to take a close look at their development methods and supporting tools.

The skills of the IS workforce will need to be enhanced to support new technologies, methods, design techniques, and development requirements. Standardized user interfaces and designs of application internals can cut training and development costs in the long run. But in the short run, the investment in learning, implementing and enforcing the standards is significant. Standardized technology platforms could allow outsiders to solve conventional problems while internal staff spends time with the unique and specialized needs of the business. However, programmers and management alike will find new skill requirements. Programmers may find that they need to be significantly broader in their technical expertise, or that they don't need their well-honed skills at coding basic applications and instead need more sophisticated technology integration and business skills. Managers may find themselves spending less time managing code development and more time planning the complete information environment. In both cases, decades of experience specifically applicable to managing and developing proprietary systems may become obsolete.

Organizational thinking is also at issue, particularly when migrating to an open distributed architecture. One writer, bemoaning slow progress towards implementation of open distributed computing theorizes:

> *"We seem doomed to manage the last generation of technology and unable to shift our views fast enough to form management cultures that can take advantage of the economics of distributed computing. We've become set in attitudes that hamper our ability to make proper investments. We sometimes spend more on managing a resources than the resource is worth...*
>
> *Many believe in the existence of two cultures: one centered on high-performance workbenches and object ori-*

ented tool kits and the other on mainframes and
COBOL. Some believe that these cultures of the 'future'
and the 'legacy' are irreconcilable." [Lorin, 1991]

Summary

The four major directions in systems design are converging,
demanding a renaissance in IS, attention to the demand side of IS,
and the development of a new breed of user-centric systems.

We can summarize the changes (albeit somewhat tritely) as
follows:

What's IN:	Usable, powerful, tool-based, "user-centric" functionality
What's OUT:	Inflexible, predefined, preformatted, rigid systems

What's IN:	User freedom and self-sufficiency
What's OUT:	Having to submit a request to IS for every new report or query

What's IN:	High user involvement in technology selection and management
What's OUT:	IS controlled technology

What's IN:	Lower technology acquisition costs
What's OUT:	Rising IS/IT budgets, hidden technology costs

What's IN:	Connective, distributed, open systems
What's OUT:	Isolated, proprietary systems

The change to the IS organization is significant. However, it is
not limited to IS. It impacts everyone. No function is an island.

Chapter 11

Case Studies—Added Dimensions

The method of enterprising is to plan with audacity and execute with vigor: to sketch out a map of possibilities, and then to treat them as probabilities

—Bovee

We are all in the gutter, but some of us are looking at stars
—Oscar Wilde

Most organizations are struggling to figure out what to do with respect to open systems architecture—how far and how fast to move. Case studies illustrate that each organization needs develop an individual approach to open systems—one that is appropriate for its situation—by evaluating the benefits, costs, and risks associated with migrating to an open systems environment against the required effort and the probability of successful implementation. And, each organization needs to understand the need to address the people issues of open systems—to challenge and change existing beliefs and practices, and to educate and train people in new ways of doing things.

When I was in Spaceland I heard that your sailors have very similar experiences while they traverse your seas and discern some distant island or coast lying on the horizon. The far-off land may have bays, forelands, angles in and out to any number and extent; yet at a distance you see none of these (unless indeed your sun shines bright upon them revealing the projections and retirements by means of light and shade), nothing but a gray unbroken line upon the water.

—Edwin Abbott, Flatland;
A Romance of Many Dimensions

In his book, *Flatland*, Abbott gives a wonderfully detailed and witty description of intelligent beings living in a two dimensional world from the viewpoint of a square in that world who has witnessed three dimensions (what he calls "Spaceland"). In his story, Abbott describes the community, social structure, and beliefs of two dimensional figures confined to a plane or other two dimensional space, with no awareness of anything outside that space and no means of moving from the surface on which they live. Abbott is both somewhat apologetic for the limitations of the awareness, vision, and thinking of the two dimensional beings and patiently understanding of the source of their beliefs. For example, he describes how two dimensional figures would observe the three dimensional phenomenon of a sphere:

> *They will only be conscious of the circle in which it cuts their plane. This circle, at first a point, will gradually increase in diameter, driving the inhabitants of Flatlands outwards from its circumference, and this will go on until half the sphere has passed through the plane, when the circle will gradually contract to a point and then vanish, leaving the Flatlanders in undisturbed possession of their country...Their experience will be that of a circular obstacle gradually expanding or growing and then contracting, and they will attribute to growth in time what the external observer in three dimensions assigns to motion in the third dimension.* [Abbott, 1992]

At the risk of digressing too far from the topic at hand, it is particularly interesting to explore Abbott's vision of Flatland knowing that during the present century, the works of Einstein, Lorentz, Larmor, Whitehead, and others have shown that at least four dimensions of space-time are necessary to account for the observed phenomena of nature. There are even some suggestions of the necessity of more than four. Abbott challenges the reader to extend the analogy of the sphere passing through Flatland to our three dimensional view of our own universe—Spaceland:

> *Assume the past and future of the universe to be all depicted in four-dimensional space and visible to any being who has consciousness of the fourth dimension. If there is motion of our three-dimensional space relative to the fourth dimension, all the changes we experience and assign to the flow of time will be due simply to this movement, the whole of the future as well as the past existing always existing in the fourth dimension.* [Abbott, 1992]

Imagine. Parallel space-time ribbons with the ability to traverse them at will![1] But now we surely digress.

The two-dimensional awareness of Flatlanders prohibits them from recognizing and understanding the impact of three dimensional space on their universe. For example, Flatlanders perceive light, but do not know its origin. In fact, it was in the old days that learned Flatlander men often investigated the question, "What is the origin of light?" with no other result than to crowd their lunatic asylums with the would-be solvers. Flatlanders simply could not comprehend the existence of light within their two-dimensional paradigm. Ultimately, they found open debate of such questions harmful to the peace and harmony of their two-dimensional existence. Flatlanders subsequently attempted to suppress such investigations by making them liable to a heavy tax, and then, finally, prohibiting them outright.

Flatlanders illustrate the straight jacket imposed on thinking by existing beliefs, existing paradigms. (Remember, *the fish does not know the water in which it swims.*)

There are some technologist and business minds that are perfectly content to design and select their information and technology within the limited dimensions of "proprietary-only" thought. That is one extreme viewpoint. Of course, at the other end of the spectrum there are also extremists that value regularity and order above all else, believing in uniformity and standardization of all things. However, in the middle (probably pushing a bit towards the standardization side) there are the business and technologist minds that seek to expand the dimensions of their information and technology architectures through the use of open systems concepts and standards. These minds are pragmatic leaders in the implementation of open systems, recognizing where "openness" provides value through regularity, consistency, flexibility, continuity, and competition, and where "proprietariness" adds value through uniqueness, and speed-of-availability.

This chapter tells the stories of several organizations that have committed their organizations to open technology. These organizations all set their course of action several years ago and are now well along the way. They speak of business, technology, and people challenges. They speak of the importance of defining the business needs and setting open systems goals to meet those needs. And, they

---

[1]This is not an easy concept for those of us whose consciousness is limited to three dimensions. Try as I might, the *Star Trek The Next Generation* episodes based on this theme always leave me with a headache.

speak of the importance of defining an approach to open systems that fits their particular organization. Most have sorted through technology and people issues to define their own path through open systems. They have also found that steering an organization towards open systems requires a level head, a steady hand and a strong belief in another dimension.

But, we'll let them tell their own stories.

Honeywell

Company Background

Honeywell is a global company that designs, develops, manufactures, markets, and maintains control systems for a variety of industries and markets. The Home and Building segment provides automation, energy management, environmental control, and security systems for buildings—as well as thermostats, gas valves, and other heating/cooling controls for industrial process and manufacturing automation. The Industrial business supplies automation and control products, systems and services—ranging from sensors to integrated control systems. The Space and Aviation Systems segment provides controls and guidance systems for commercial and military aircraft, space, and satellite applications.

Size: $6 billion revenue in 1993

51,000 employees in 95 countries on 6 continents
1,000 IS employees

Business Management Structure: Decentralized, but with growing recognition of the need for standards and for common processes in some areas. Honeywell is organized into three primary business units:

* Home and Building Control (HBC)

* Industrial Control (IC)

* Space and Aviation Control

There are further business breakdowns below this top level, especially in the Space and Aviation business. Each of the three business units is managed as a global business.

Information Systems (IS) Management Structure: Each major business unit has an IS function. Coordination is done through a corporate Central Information Systems organization. The IS function is headed by a Corporate Vice President.

Technology:

Mainframes
Bull DPS9000/GCOS	3
Unisys 2200/OS1100	2

Midrange
HP9000/UX	40+
(Bull) IBM/AIX	20+
DEC VAX/VMS	50+

PC
Apple	3,500+
IBM and compatibles	21,000+

Networks
WAN	TCP/IP on X.25
	Bull DSA on X.25
	Frame Relay
LAN	Novell Netware (standard)
	LANMAN (limited)

Factors in Choosing an Open Systems Strategy

Honeywell's systems mirrored the organization. They were developed within Honeywell's many business units and would not withstand the stress of changing the business practices. Many of the applications ran on outdated technology that the company was looking to replace. Honeywell decided that rather than replace outdated proprietary technology with new proprietary technology, it would rather move to open systems.

Key considerations behind Honeywell's move to open systems included:

- Provide common basis for migrating from fragmented, proprietary systems

- Allow flexibility to meet both local and global needs (scalability)

- Allow for time-phased implementation

- Take advantage of increasing availability of new application software on open systems

- Promote software portability and shareability
- Facilitate better integration with engineering and manufacturing computing applications (interoperability)

Approach to Open Systems Architecture

Honeywell was one of the earlier companies to make the decision to migrate to an open architecture. The management team interviewed a number of other companies to review their open systems strategies and, not finding much to learn from, in 1990 set about developing its own strategy.

Since then, Honeywell has created a set of corporate computing principles, defined a technical architecture, and published a set of technical standards. Business units are inventorying and assessing the technical and functional quality of their applications in meeting today's business needs. Common applications, to be used by most of the businesses worldwide, have been identified in a number of areas: human resources, finance, manufacturing, distribution, field support, and sales automation. A data architecture team has developed an enterprise-level data model and established a set of standard data elements which will be used across the common applications, and in most business unit specific applications. Maintenance of the architecture and standards is the responsibility of the Central IS organization.

Funding for the open systems migration is provided through savings and benefits gained from the new applications, and also through savings achieved in the traditional areas of IS. Honeywell IS consolidated its fifteen legacy data centers worldwide into three. Telecommunications were consolidated into a custom network agreement (Tariff 12) in the United States and efforts continue to find global or regional suppliers in other areas of the world. A vendor management program was started, aimed at creating worldwide agreements and achieving savings through discounts based on total company volume purchasing. And, Honeywell restructured IS work and reduced its head count.

When Honeywell embarked on its open systems strategy, management team members participated in several standards organizations and requirements groups including SOS (Standards and Open Systems Group.) The company has been a member of OSF for three years.

Experience With Open Architecture

Although Honeywell's commitment to an open environment remains strong, implementation has taken longer and been more difficult than planned. Open technologies and products, although successful in the test beds, are not always ready for implementation on a large scale. Changing the Honeywell culture has also been difficult. Building a consensus on common business processes and supporting information technology architectures has been challenging for a company accustomed to a very decentralized approach. And, consolidating the computing centers turned out to be a very emotional issue for the business units, with the business units feeling a loss of control.

The move to an open environment is complicated and long. Most of the applications supporting the company will have to be replaced as they are migrated because Honeywell does not want to see "the same junk on a different box." The enormous size, cost, and risk of the migration effort make it impossible to approach in anything other than an incremental manner. But, to undertake the effort in increments means to be under way for several years. Purchased package solutions take time to install and to interconnect. All-in-all, the package installations have gone well, and the distributed UNIX environment has been satisfactory.

Network management and systems management across the network are areas where Honeywell has had to devote a considerable amount of attention. Because of incomplete capabilities within all vendor products today, Honeywell has had to do its own integration. The company integrated products from multiple vendors to form its network and systems management infrastructure functionality.

Challenges

Honeywell sees the following challenges:

- An open architecture environment has significant complexity due to the number of components and the remaining incompatibilities between products.

- Industry standards are incomplete and developing at different rates. The original intent to migrate only to industry standards can't be implemented, and "stacks" of de facto standard products are being used "in lieu of" [de jure standard conforming] solutions.

- Integration of legacy and newer open systems is difficult during the transition period.

- Vendors are still trying to develop "lockins" around the standards. It is difficult to instill the discipline in the development environment required to stay away from "all those neat features."

- The skills of the IS staff need to be upgraded significantly to start using new technologies, techniques, methods, and tools.

- Vendor capabilities in assisting Honeywell in developing and implementing an open environment are limited.

Advice to Others

Honeywell has the following advice to companies moving to open systems:

- Base the plans for migration of applications on expected results for the business

  - Fund the migration through savings and other financial benefits

  - Time the migration to coincide with business process reengineering.

- Be prepared to face many interesting integration problems.

- Migrate your poorest applications first; don't risk failure on your most technically competent and/or functionally satisfactory systems. Save the best for last.

- Expect a long haul. The technology is not yet mature enough to be in a final state.

- However, after all of these warnings, don't be afraid to start either.

Honeywell contributors:

Bill Sanders, *Vice President of Information Systems*
John White, *Manager of Technology Supplier Relations*

Merck

Company Background

Merck is the world's largest pharmaceutical company. It describes itself as a company in transition in an industry that is in transition. The basic pharmaceutical business model begins with heavy research expenditures to identify, develop and test drug treatments—never knowing which investments will pay off. Those that do pay off are quite profitable, because the patent protection on the compound gives the company an effective monopoly on the treatment until the patent expires. Until recently, it was rare for two pharmaceutical companies to market patent protected products in the same therapeutic class. Because of this, the pharmaceutical industry had little price pressure and little competition within a therapeutic class. Pharmaceutical companies grew and prospered in this environment.

Today's environment is quite different. A phenomenon called *therapeutic substitution*, in which two or more companies market products in the same therapeutic class, has created head-to-head competition between patented products for the first time. Equally important, however, is that customers have banded together into buying groups large enough to extract price concessions from pharmaceutical manufacturers. As Merck faced these business issues, it changed into a company that placed much higher value on obtaining the proper information to make better management decisions. The company set off to re-engineer its business processes and retool its systems.

Merck is organized into several distinct divisions:

- Research and Development

- Manufacturing (Chemical and Pharmaceutical)

- Human Health Marketing

- Vaccine Marketing

- Agricultural and Veterinary Marketing

- Medco Containment Services

- Merck Medco Managed Care

- Corporate (Computer Resources, Legal, Public Affairs, Human Resources, Finance)

Size: $12 Billion in annual revenues for 1993
50,000 employees world wide
900 IS employees

Business Management Structure: Divisional operations reporting centrally.

Information Systems (IS) Management Structure: Centralized IS support, decentralized application development and support. IS has Systems & Programming (S&P) groups that perform systems development, package selection, and application support. Each S&P group is co-located with the Merck division it supports. IS also has a central services group that consists of systems and network operations, systems and network engineering, desktop support services, quality and security, architecture, re-engineering, and financial management.

Technology:

Mainframes/Supercomputer
IBM 3090	2
IBM ES9000	1
Cray	1

Midframes
VAX	100+
AS400	100+
Wang	80-
PC's (IBM compatible/Apple)	13,800+

Networks
Ethernet	4,500+ connections
Token Ring	4,500 connections
Clin Net AS400	60+ sites

Factors in Choosing an Open Systems Strategy

Merck chose to open its systems architecture for competitive reasons. In 1991, the company embarked on several substantial business process re-engineering efforts to streamline the organization and increase effectiveness. Merck wanted to create better lines of communications between interdependent business functions and organizations. The company understood that effective flow of information between the systems that support the business functions was a key to successful re-engineering of the business.

At the same time, Merck embarked on a program to strengthen and refresh its systems capabilities. The company hired a new CIO, established the IS architecture group, and began outlining its new systems vision.

Approach to Open Systems Architecture

Merck defines the new systems vision in four layers:

- Applications architecture

- Information architecture

- Technology Architecture

- IS Organization Architecture (how the IS group organizes itself to serve the corporation)

In refreshing the applications base, Merck IS adopted a "best of breed" strategy—selecting or building the best package to fit the needs of the various divisions. With a strategy of buying and integrating packages where possible rather than building from scratch, Merck could save 3-4 years on its timetable to new functionality. Merck also wanted to avoid compromising on functionality in the interest of integration. Users are very concerned about functionality and are actively involved in selecting the packages.

IS took on the challenge of integrating the best of breed packages. The packages needed to share data, so data synchronization between applications was an important goal. Even more important was the ability to convert data represented in the format of the source package into the format of the destination package. In particular, Merck wanted to avoid the burden of creating point-to-point interfaces between applications.

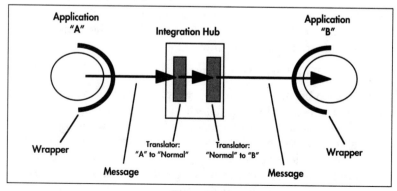

Figure 11.1

The architecture group developed a solution it called the Integration Hub. (See Figure 11.1.) The Integration Hub is a switch that routes messages from application to application. To use the Integration Hub, developers must write a "wrapper" for the application. This wrapper is the interface that the application exposes to the network, providing services that are available to other applications. The wrapper contains a list of permissible transactions or messages that the application is prepared to accept or transmit. These messages could contain updates to the data in the application or requests for information contained within the application.

The Integration Hub also contains translators that convert data to and from each application's native data representation into "Merck Normal Form"—the common Merck data representation. By making requests or updates through the Integration Hub, an application need not understand the data format of all the applications to which it interfaces. In only needs to know how to translate to and from the Merck Normal Form.

Succinctly, the Merck approach to open systems consists of business driven, best of breed applications that rely on an open architecture to interoperate in a heterogeneous environment.

Merck states that its primary goal is interoperability. The IS department is re-deploying its resources to support end-user needs by providing access to the information, and is building the integration hub to support its best of breed applications acquisition strategy. The IS department realized that because of the size and diversity of Merck operations, a heterogeneous computing environment was unavoidable and providing an integration layer was key to linking applications. The architecture group investigated available middleware technology and concluded that a single product did not exist that could be used to link a diverse set of packages—each with their own data, processes, and sometimes technology. In order to integrate best of breed packages, the first task had to be to design and build the integration hub (actually, to integrate the integration hub).

Experience With Open Architecture

The IS group has made a lot of progress towards its goals. The first group of best of breed applications for integration has been selected. And, development of the integration hub is under way—a prototype integration hub is operating in the lab and an integration techniques kit for software development has been distributed to the S&P units.

Longer term, Merck is looking toward newer technologies, such as CASE and object-orientation to leverage development efforts and solve some of the development cycle time and data organization and integration problems that exist today. In fact, Merck would not be surprised if the core of the integration hub eventually became a CORBA-style Object Request Broker (ORB).

In general, Merck IS is pleased with progress to-date and is moving forward.

With respect to involvement in standards organizations, key Merck IS personnel participated in the Standards for Open Systems group (SOS) when the group was actively developing its list of required standards. Merck IS used the opportunity to communicate Merck's needs and educate themselves. Now, Merck is more concerned with participating in standards organizations where products or standards do not seem to be converging on their own. For example, Merck is a member of the Shamrock Coalition and supports Shamrock's efforts to define document management standards.

Challenges

Some of the major challenges Merck IS is addressing include:

- Risk aversion— Although the IS group in general supports the direction and the integration hub approach, it is still necessary to convince individual projects to "plug" into the Integration Hub. To some, the integration hub approach is seen as more complex and risky than building bridges between packages on an interface by interface level. They need to be reassured that the Integration Hub will make integration jobs easier.

- Support from package vendors—Some package vendors do not provide an effective Application Programming Interface for getting data into and out of their packages. In addition, they are not always supportive of Merck's strategy of only using part of their overall offering (the "best of breed" part).

- Budgetary constraints—Merck IS is undertaking the challenge of refreshing the organization's application base, while Merck IS is also under pressure to reduce or contain costs.

- Training—Instilling IS personnel with the business and technical skills required to work within the new paradigm is an ongoing effort. Business function must win out over technical beauty—this is a particular challenge in an environment where technology is so seductive.

- Retooling—Getting the "word out in a gradual way." New techniques, methods, and tools are more effectively learned in an "apprenticeship" versus a classroom.

- Encouraging—Making the methodologies and procedures the "path of least resistance." Ultimately, new methods will be used only if they are perceived to be easier than other approaches. Tools must be found and created to support the methods and make them the easiest path.

Advice to Others

Merck has the following advice for others pursuing open systems strategies:

- Drive the open systems strategy from the business end. It is important to find a link to the business. The number of possible open systems strategies is infinite—it is a mistake to believe that an open systems strategy can be selected without driving the choice of strategy from the desired impact on the business. When business issues lead the analysis, it soon becomes clear which strategy is the best choice.

- Make sure when a strategy is chosen, that the requirements driving towards the strategy are clearly articulated. In Merck's case, the requirements were: "best of breed," "user-driven," "applications oriented," "architecture," working together in a "heterogeneous environment."

Merck contributors:

Charles Popper, *Vice President of Corporate Computer Resources*
Ian Miller, *Senior Director of Architecture and Emerging Technology*
Richard Bakunas, *Director of Infrastructure: Automation & Information Technology Department*

Home Depot

Company Background

Home Depot is a rapidly growing company with an impressive 35% annual growth rate over its short 15 year history. To date, Home Depot has done all its business within the U.S. although it just purchased a chain of stores in Canada and plans to expand its Canadian stores in the same format.

The home improvement industry is booming—it is currently estimated at $115 billion and according to the Home Improvement Research Institute in Lincolnshire, Illinois, the market will reach $142 billion in 1997. The "warehouse" home improvement store, emphasizing convenience and one-stop shopping, is now out-marketing, outpricing, and out-stocking local hardware stores and lumberyards. (Home Depot "megastores" carry up to 35,000 stocked items and 200,000 special order items.)

Home improvement has become a high-volume, low-margin business where controlling costs and providing customer service are the keys to success. Home Depot has aggressively leveraged a variety of information technologies to enable its stores to buy, supply, manage, and aggressively price its huge inventory of products. The company has become the category "killer" in the home improvement market.

Size: $9.2 Billion in 1993
45,000 employees

Stores: At end of 1994,
approximately 330 stores in the U.S.
approximately 13 stores in Canada

Business Management Structure: Decentralized. Stores operate as individual $35-50 million businesses. Store managers have profit and loss responsibility and accordingly, do their own replenishment orders, inventory management, and staffing. "Corporate" is a lean function providing support and consolidated reporting.

IT Management Structure: Centralized. Provides computing infrastructure, applications development, and support to the stores and corporate office.

Technology:

Store Configuration
HP9000/800 Series running HP-UX

HP terminals	16-32
Fujitsu/NCR registers	30-50
PCs (used primarily	3-6

for design applications such as
kitchen cabinets)

WAN

AT&T Interspan and SDN Services installed in 1994
(integrated voice and data using T1 access lines)
Hypercom IEN 3000/6000 series CPE
(router, FRAD, DSU/CSU, drop & insert mux, dial backup)
TCP/IP protocol over Frame Relay

Home Office

IBM ES9000	1

with MVS and DB2

Data General MV3500	6

(1 for each geographic division)

HP9000	15

with HP-UX and Informix

PCs with DOS/Windows	2,000

(Home Office and Divisional Offices)

LANs—Office Environments

Netware Servers	20+

running Novell
Ethernet segments bridged
Leased T1 lines to Division Offices

Distribution Centers

Terminals and printers—	2-3

linked to Divisional Data
General platforms over WAN

Factors in Choosing an Open Systems Strategy

Supporting sustained, explosive growth is a significant challenge to Home Depot's IT department. They cite four main reasons in their decision to pursue open systems:

- Flexibility—Home Depot planned to continue introducing technology in support of the decentralized store operations and needed to install store systems that could expand as new functionality was added. The scalability and flexibility of the midrange UNIX platform configurations has helped Home Depot expand store support as well as cope with rapid and sometimes unpredictable business growth.

- Cost—Midrange UNIX platforms were lower cost to purchase and install than expanding their mainframe configuration. Home Depot believes that they are paying a little more in infrastructure management to support the added complexity of a distributed network, but that open systems has represented a net gain to them in terms of cost.

- Interoperability—Home Depot has a set of legacy Divisional systems (on the Data General platforms) and Corporate systems (on the IBM mainframe) that they needed to connect with the stores' operational support systems. The ability of the various systems components to interoperate and evolve independently is critical.

- Data accessibility—Decentralized operations is the culture at Home Depot. Andy McKenna (President, Mid-West Division and former SVP of Information Services) says, "Our systems reflect our philosophy of having the store managers run the store." Making the information available to store managers to support their decisions is a high priority.

Approach to Open Systems Architecture

Home Depot decided to pursue an open systems direction late in 1991. They needed to make a decision on store systems because Data General MV 2500 and 3500 minicomputers in the stores were approaching capacity and limiting the company's ability to expand store functionality. Transaction volumes had been increasing steadily for the three years prior (transactions processed grew 80% annually for the period 1990-1992.) IT, after careful review of the alternatives, decided on a corporate-wide commitment to open systems:

- Stores would be ported to UNIX

- The corporate mainframe would be upgraded from a 3090 to an ES9000 and remain part of the long term architecture

- Divisional platforms would be next in line for replacement

Business management supported the new direction wholeheartedly. Home Depot IT was able to show that replacement of the store systems would be economical, providing about 10X the processing power at 1/2 the price of existing store systems. The initial step, bringing stores up on the new platform was a direct port of existing functionality, allowing quicker conversion of stores and creating a stable base for adding functionality in the future.

With business management support of the direction, IT designed and developed several architectural components to support rapid systems deployment. The architectural components are key to rapid systems development in that they allow development activities to focus on perfecting business logic and user interaction. Home Depot architectural components include:

* Application architecture—design of applications services based on creating common tools/routines to support a programmer's "workbench" and standardized screen presentation

* Data architecture—design of the data and repositories from an "enterprise" view

* Technology architecture—design of the network, platforms, and operating systems based on approved standards and creating an ubiquitous communications infrastructure

The IT function has a lot of autonomy in designing the technical infrastructure and selecting technology (as long as it works). Users participated in defining the technology architecture and participate in selecting technology and applications. Users are heavily involved in the definition and design of business logic. Home Depot has formalized the position of an "IT Liaison Director" to get user participation in IT from all aspects of the business: merchandising, stores and corporate.

Home Depot restricts its participation in industry standards committees. Instead, the company chooses to drive its standards requirements through its technology vendors and by actively speaking in favor of open systems standards at various conventions and conferences. It has developed a technology purchasing approach that focuses on end user functionality and fit with Home Depot's technical direction. But, that does not mean that standards are not important to the company. The question of fit with the Home Depot architecture is second only to satisfying end user needs. Architecture adherence has become a "cultural thing," mitigating the need to set up special review processes and procedures to check for compliance.

Experience With Open Architecture

Home Depot completed the migration of stores to the new platform in about ten months. In the following 1.5 years, IT has delivered significant new functionality to the stores. The company hired a substantial number of IT professionals to help with the effort, but it has been growing so rapidly, that it would have needed to add IT staff anyway. The company has also instituted on-going training programs to train legacy systems staff in the new architectures, technologies, and tools. The training programs have been very successful. The company has found legacy-skilled staff very willing and able to learn open systems and client/server concepts and technologies.

Challenges

Home Depot sees the following challenges:

*   Vendor adherence to open systems standards

*   Standards tracking—Who is really setting standards is confusing and interpreting standards that have been defined is difficult. Home Depot's strategy is to influence the standards process through its vendors

*   Network management in a distributed environment—particularly PCs

*   Application portability to ensure that hardware remains a "commodity"

Advice to Others

Home Depot has the following advice for others pursuing open systems strategies:

*   Don't believe vendor stories of open systems—prototype and investigate claims and plans.

*   Make it easier for IT staff to be compliant with the IT architecture than not. Home Depot has developed a lot of code as part of its "developers workbench" to support applications development.

*   It is not hard to train legacy systems people in new technologies and techniques when you give them the appropriate motivation and opportunities to learn.

- While it is true that open distributed systems are more expensive to manage, the extra management cost is minor compared to the benefits of flexibility, functionality and responsiveness to the business. Therefore, overall net cost is reduced.

Cost-wise, the company is pleased with its experience. And functionality-wise, Home Depot feels it is better positioned than if it had continued down the proprietary systems route. The experience is still relatively fresh. IT has been "heads-down" implementing the new direction for the last two years. Shortly, IT plans to re-address its plans—looking at distributed design issues and how to continue having a positive impact on the business. IT management states that the users give IT a great deal of freedom because of the perception that IT contributes to the competitiveness and profitability of the business.

Home Depot's commitment to open systems remains strong. IT representatives speak at industry conferences about their experiences (such as UniForum and NRF). According to Dave Ellis, Director of Network Services, Home Depot is a "vocal user of open systems."

Home Depot contributors:
    Dave Ellis, *Director of Network Services*
    Beach Clark Jr., *Senior Manager–Network Architecture*

Hyatt Hotels Corporation

Company Background

Hyatt Hotels Corporation was started in 1957. It is a wholly owned subsidiary of Hyatt Corporation that currently operates 87 hotels and 16 resorts in the U.S., Canada, and the Caribbean. Another subsidiary, Hyatt International Corporation, operates 48 hotels and 16 resorts in 31 countries.

In 1987, it was evident to Hyatt that the lodging industry was heading into a period of significant change and Hyatt set out to reinvent itself. The company's first step was to redo the technical underpinnings of the company in order to build an environment in which applications functionality could be developed and delivered rapidly. From 1987 to 1990, Hyatt concentrated on a building block approach to rebuilding its technical infrastructure as a basis for business innovation. In 1991, the lodging industry reported losses averaging $1,200 per room. It was clear that the real advantage (and perhaps even survival) would come to businesses that could respond quickly to market changes. Hyatt quickly embarked on a program to reduce costs, integrate operations, and focus on revenue producing sales activities. The company also moved boldly to offer new services and products in order to compete in a hotly contested market.

Some of Hyatt's major strategies include:

- Integrated sales and marketing teams that devise strategies and tactics to exploit Hyatt's strengths to the marketplace. The results are innovative packages such as "Business Plan" which provides travelers an office away from home while on the road.

- A national sales force that gives corporate customers a single contact to handle all of their bookings, regardless of the property location.

- Reminding all Hyatt employees of the service side of Hyatt's business with "Hyatt In Touch Day." Once a year, Hyatt turns its corporate headquarters management into the field in company-wide game of musical jobs that this year resulted in one executive vice president playing doorman at the Grand Hyatt in Washington, DC, and another playing waiter at the Hyatt Regency Irvine, in California.

- Using technology to support its focus on customer service. Hyatt has implemented a sophisticated voice messaging system designed to appeal to business travelers and a 1-800-CHECK-IN phone check-in service. The company is also testing automated check-in kiosks and is eyeing future applications of technology, such as concierge services.

Hyatt's IS department was faced with the challenge of rapidly developing systems and applications to integrate Hyatt's operations and support the new services and products.

Organization

Hyatt Corporation operates three main business units:

- Hyatt Hotels Corporation (U.S., Canada, Caribbean)
- Hyatt International Corporation
- Regency Systems Solutions and others

Size:
Hyatt Hotels Corporation
1993 sales in excess of $2 Billion
45,000 employees
150 IS employees

Business Management Structure: Centralized

IS Management Structure: Reflecting the structure of the organization as a whole, the IS function is centralized, with applications developed centrally and distributed electronically. The Hyatt Hotels IS organization, Regency Systems Solutions (RSS), supports the reservations function for the international division, as well as all functions for the domestic division.

Technology:

Centralized Systems
    Pyramid Servers running Unix   5
    HP9000/800 Series running HP-UX   3

Distributed Systems
    AT&T 3B2 running Unix   50
        (to be replaced by 1995)
    HP9000/800 running HP-UX   50

PC
    Intel-based PCs   2000+

Networks
    WAN   TCP/IP
    LAN   Ethernet, Novell

Note: Regency Systems Solutions regularly evaluates the Hyatt technology base as part of a 3-4 year refreshment cycle. The expectation is to completely replace 4-year-old equipment.

Factors in Choosing an Open Systems Strategy

Hyatt Corporation was going through significant business change. The company needed to be able to experiment with new service offerings and respond quickly to market opportunities and developments. RSS was facing several major development projects to support the company's efforts to integrate its operations. RSS also needed to be able to develop quick prototypes and modify applications as the company tested new service offerings. This all translated into the requirement that Regency Systems Solutions be able to develop applications quickly and cost-effectively. Open systems was an important component of the Hyatt strategy to develop a technical infrastructure supporting rapid development of applications. RSS was attracted to open systems because of the availability of high productivity software and the cost and flexibility of open systems products. RSS also saw the ability to select a platform from several competing hardware vendors as an important leverage point as it embarked on its strategy.

Approach to Open Systems Architecture

While Hyatt has been a pioneer in developing an enterprise-wide open systems architecture since the mid-to-late 1980s, the company's approach to open systems has been pragmatic—driven by the business need for significant new functionality. Hyatt wanted to build a consistent environment for rapid application development. With the number of programmers on its staff, the management felt that they needed to pick one environment and go with it. Reliability was also a factor. RSS wanted to build an environment that could not be crashed by programming errors. RSS decided to let the development tools and database environment drive the choice of open systems products. The choice was driven by how quickly the RSS staff could experiment, develop, and modify applications functionality.

Experience With Open Systems Architecture

The company's first experience with an open platform was a project to install a UNIX-based hotel management package. After initially considering continuing with proprietary hardware platforms, Hyatt chose to implement a UNIX-based package solution because of the cost advantages and hardware flexibility. During 1988, this solution was rolled out to 75 sites, implemented on a mixture of AT&T and HP platforms. By 1990, more than 95 hotels had systems installed.

The UNIX-based hotel package was the pivotal, initial move in the direction of non-proprietary platforms. But, far more significant was the project that followed shortly after: analysis of relational DBMS options for future development of all central and distributed applications. In reaching its decision, Hyatt was particularly motivated by the potential productivity gains from using the 4GL tools offered by open systems vendors. Hyatt selected Informix after evaluating four RDBMS vendors and kicked off the first project for its new development platform: building a replacement for the then 10-year old sales and marketing application. Again the flexibility advantages of the open platform were apparent, allowing Hyatt to change the underlying hardware platform as requirements changed. Ultimately the new sales and marketing application was implemented on a Pyramid platform.

By 1989, Hyatt's mainframe-based central reservation system was 7 years old and required replacement to respond to significant market and competitive changes. Lacking a packaged solution option, Hyatt elected to partner with AT&T and Informix to develop a system over a very aggressive 10-month development schedule. At the time, with Hyatt's three main competitors developing similar replacement systems on traditional mainframe platforms, this project represented a significant management commitment to the "high-risk" open systems architecture. In addition to developing the custom application, Hyatt replaced the existing trio of networks connecting its central and hotel systems with a single star-configuration network based on TCP/IP. The close partnership with Informix for software development, along with strict scope control, were critical to the success of this project.

Hyatt's most recent development project is the implementation of a client/server Sales Automation system using the Powerbuilder application development tool. This project has again demonstrated a benefit of the open architecture, allowing Hyatt to employ leading-edge development tools which deliver significant business benefits in terms of ease-of-use and reduced time-to-market with new products and services. This project also has built upon the creation of a wide area network infrastructure which facilitates data interchange among all Hyatt locations, allowing sales personnel in one location to review the availability of function rooms in all other Hyatt hotels.

RSS has been very effectively leveraging its building block foundation strategy. Since 1991, the year the new open technical foundation was largely in place, Hyatt IS has been able to *speed up its system delivery rate by a factor of four*. Hyatt IS productivity has been steadily increasing. RSS is now implementing 6-8 major releases per year.

Challenges

Hyatt points out that continuing challenges are different than initial challenges. RSS sees the following challenges as it continues to implement open systems:

- Maintaining the discipline to keep the architecture relatively narrow. With so many products to choose from, the temptation is to get sidetracked with each new set of capabilities that comes out. RSS advises that it is best to select a strategy and stick to it. It is better to select quickly and start getting 85% of the possible benefit than to delay implementation by studying technology products only to finally squeeze out a little more productivity but lose time in the process. Gordon Kerr, Senior Vice President of RSS smiles and explains, "There are two things that you should take time when selecting—spouses and consultants. The rest can be chosen with deliberate speed." Hyatt follows an approach of restricting the organization to only 1 or 2 products within a technology class.

- Continually refreshing the technology. Hyatt reevaluates its hardware strategy every 2-3 years and refreshes hardware every 3-4 years. Software is on a longer cycle to keep the complexity level down. RSS plans to refresh the database and development environment every 5-6 years.

- Keeping developers continually challenged is also difficult. Open systems and good project management are the keys to keeping developers challenged. RSS keeps projects short, 3-6 months, so that both the projects and the people stay focused on business benefits. The easy-to-learn 4GL environment and small project teams allow RSS to give exciting challenges to new people with some degree of more "seasoned" oversight. This helps Hyatt face the challenge of being a prime target for recruiters.

- Regency Systems Solutions is a separate Hyatt subsidiary, with a new goal of selling systems development services to other hotel companies. This new focus, while clearly an outgrowth of the organization's well-developed emphasis on business benefits, brings with it a new set of organization challenges.

Advice to Others

Hyatt has the following advice to others:

- Being the first to employ new technologies is okay, as long as the risk is matched to a significant potential business reward. Hyatt will embrace technology innovations only if it can clearly identify a significant business justification and it has ways to manage risk all the way through implementation.

- Close partnering with a vendor is an excellent strategy for managing the risk of a project, particularly if the project represents a potentially critical reference for the vendor. It is often easier to convince the vendor to change than to change vendors.

- In making the transition from a proprietary to an open architecture, start small but with an application that has a significant business impact.

- Embrace standards at a high level, but use them primarily as a proxy for assessing the integration capability of vendors' products. While Hyatt clearly recognizes the importance of standards, the IS organization lacks the resources to devote substantial time to influencing new standards' development.

- Along with the move away from a proprietary architecture has come significant IS employee turnover as skill requirements have changed. All of the mainframe operations staff and 80% of the mainframe development staff have left Hyatt for mainframes elsewhere. Responding to the challenge of meeting the need for open environment skills, Hyatt has developed a recruiting approach which emphasizes 25-50% hiring and developing new college graduates, rather than attempting to bring in experienced hires for all positions. The speed of learning 4GLs, Powerbuilder, and other high productivity development tools makes new hires productive in six months.

Hyatt contributor:
   Gordon Kerr, *Senior Vice President of Regency Systems Solutions*

Summary

Each organization attempting to implement open systems faces issues that are unique to that organization. The urgency of the move varies, dependent upon the state of existing systems and needs of the business. The business direction and information needs will also influence how an organization chooses to approach open systems. And, ultimately, the speed at which the organization can absorb the change meters its ability to implement open systems concepts.

Some determining criteria influencing an organization's approach to open systems, the urgency with which it pursues the goals, and success of its efforts are depicted in Figure 11.2 (in a multi-dimensional view, of course.)

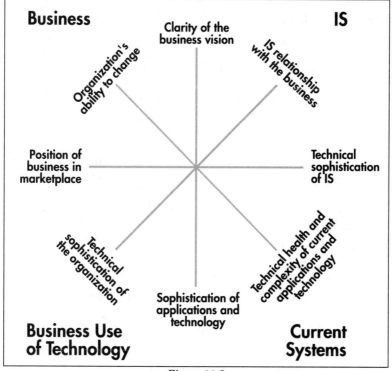

Figure 11.2

If we explore the radii a bit further, we may come up with the following characteristics that are of importance in developing an open systems direction:

Position of the Business in the Business Market

- The health and competitiveness of the business
- The importance of technology to the business at a strategic level
- The uniqueness of the business applications and technology needs
- The availability of software packages that support the business needs

Clarity of the Business Vision

- Degree of clarity of the business direction
- Degree of widespread understanding of the business direction

Sophistication of Applications and Technology

- The importance of technology to the business at an operational level
- The alignment of current systems functionality with the business direction (systems support of the business)

Technical Health and Complexity of Current Applications and Technology

- The technical health of systems functionality
- The complexity of systems functionality
- The level and condition of technology installed
- The degree of homogeneity or heterogeneity of the current technology set

Technical Sophistication of the Organization

- The technology awareness of business systems users
- The technology awareness of business leaders and management

Technical Sophistication of IS

- The level of technology awareness within the IS function
- The level of leadership and vision within IS

IS Relationship With the Business

- The nature of the relationship between the IS function and the business (e.g., the level of shared vision and goals, the degree of partnership, the degree of trust, etc.)

Organization's Ability to Change

- The degree of *leadership* versus management within the business
- The degree of common or dispersed leadership within the business
- Awareness of the business need to change
- Business tolerance of change
- The degree of centralization or decentralization of the IS function
- The level of investment in existing systems
- The ability to invest further in systems

Each organization needs to evaluate the benefits, costs, and risks associated with migrating to an open systems environment against the required effort and the probability of successful implementation in order to develop an approach that is appropriate for its situation. And, each organization needs to understand the need to address the people issues of open systems—to challenge and change existing beliefs and practices, and to educate and train people in new ways of doing things.

The narrator of Abbott's Flatland was a square—a figure rather high in the social pecking order of beings that valued regularity above all else. Yet, this visionary, enlightened square suffered years of imprisonment and the even heavier burden of general incredulity and mockery as a result of his awareness of another dimension and his attempts in turn to communicate his vision to other Flatlanders. The square languished in prison and became a martyr to the Truth, absolutely destitute of converts. He was never able to raise the awareness of his universe to match his own.

On the other hand, the stories of these organizations have a different theme: one of success in changing the way information and technology are designed, selected, and implemented. And one of success in changing how technologists and businesses work together to evolve the role and use of information and technology. The stories point to the need to pioneer—to challenge, define, and implement new architectures, new processes, new organizational units, and new technologies. But, they also speak loudly and clearly about the need to educate—to build awareness of another dimension that can be added to their use of information and technology.

These IS leaders asked business management and IS personnel alike: Do you have an open mind?

What's well begun is half done.

—Horace

Chapter 12

"Opening" Systems—
Opening the Business

Pooh looked at his two paws. He knew that one of them was the right, and he knew that when you had decided which one of them was the right, then the other one was the left, but he never could remember how to begin. "Well," he said slowly—

—A.A. Milne, *Winnie the Pooh*

> In this section, we combine material from earlier chapters with advice from our case studies to explore the issue of how to begin opening up a systems environment. The section begins with an overview of the major issues concerning IS executives today, then introduces a high level IS planning model, and points out a few key considerations in the Information & Technology (I&T) planning process. We continue with a vision of how open systems can help achieve IS goals and an overview of contrasting approaches to technology acquisition in the pursuit of open systems. We then get down to business and discuss some of the practices that have contributed to opening systems.

Business management guru, Peter Drucker, once said, "Long range planning doesn't deal with future decisions, but the future of present decisions." But, as Winnie the Pooh observed, the first decision is where to start the thought process. Let's begin by taking a look at the issues CIOs are most concerned with today.

In the 1994 edition of its annual survey of CIOs, Deloitte & Touche found:

- Business process reengineering remains a strong force for change—with the average number of initiatives per company at 3.2 per year, down slightly from 4.4 in 1992.

- Legacy systems are a growing problem. CIOs report that limitations of existing systems rank second only behind resistance to change as an obstacle to successful business process reengineering. Respondents also reported that 69% of their applications are running on old or outdated technical platforms. They expect to replace or radically improve more than 87% of these applications.

- Client/server is on the rise—Participants reported a five fold increase in the number of applications running on client server architecture—up from 5% in both 1991 and 1992 to 27% in 1993. Respondents estimate the percentage of applications running on client/server architecture to be 57%.

- Globalization will affect information systems on a wide scale. 82% of respondent companies with international operations expect a significant increase in information system integration, and the majority of these companies have very little integration today.

- Information service budgets are relatively flat—increases averaged only .4% in 1993, down from 3.0% in 1991 and 3.5% in 1992. Industry average IS budget increases ranged from 8.5% for Insurance to 4.2% for Banking and Financial Services, to 3.8% for Health Care, to 2% for Retail and Distribution, to -4.4% for Manufacturing, to -5% for Energy, Oil, and Gas.

- Open systems are on the rise. 71% of all respondent companies are now pursuing an open strategy, 90% expect to be pursuing open systems by 1995, and 39% expect to be "very open" by 1995. [Deloitte & Touche, 1994]

The CSC 1994 Survey of Top IS Management Issues ranked responses from North America and Europe as follows in Figure 12.1.

1994 Rank	Issues: North America	Issues: Europe
1	Reengineering business processes through IT	Reengineering business processes through IT
2	Aligning IS and corporate goals	Cutting IS costs
3	Organizing and utilizing data	Aligning IS and corporate goals
4	Instituting cross-functional information systems	Instituting cross-functional information systems
5	Creating an information architecture	Organizing and utilizing data
6	Improving the systems-development process	Improving the systems-development process
7	Updating obsolete systems	Creating an information architecture
8	Integrating systems	Improving the IS human resource
9	Improving the IS human resource (tie)	Managing dispersed systems (tie)
10	Changing technology platforms (tie)	Promoting the IS function (tie)
—		
15		Moving to open systems
17	Moving to open systems	

Source: CSC Survey 1994

Figure 12.1

The CSC survey findings also corroborated an anemic budget increase for IS in 1994, averaging 2.3%.

One doesn't need surveys to know that the major issue facing the IS organization is more work—caused by business change, business process redesign, quality initiatives, and an aging systems base—with roughly the same budget. Do more, with less! It is clear that IS cannot simply "speed up" what it is doing. It must do something different. (Out of the frying pan and into the fire!)

Changes in the business environment are forcing companies to re-invent themselves to survive. Changes in the business are forcing IS to re-invent itself to survive. In IS, as in business, innovation is the watchword. But again, which paw is the right one?

Michael Porter outlines four key ingredients related to the capacity to innovate:

- Having a core of sophisticated customers nearby

- Having a critical mass of key suppliers nearby

- Having some good competitors nearby (real innovation occurs where emotion, pride, and economics mix)

- Having very specialized pools of skills and an infrastructure that is highly tailored to the business—concentrated skills create an advantage [Insights, 1993]

In relating Porter's requirements for innovation to today's IS department, we can see that the core of sophisticated customers is not a problem. Today's end user is becoming more sophisticated every day. In some cases, end users are more up-to-date on new technologies than IS personnel. Finding competition, also, is not a problem. The IS function is beginning to experience competition from the marketplace. In the early 1990's, outsourcing data center operations has become a viable, and acceptable option to running internal centers. Software packages have multiplied and most growing industries now have a wealth of packaged software offerings. The market for systems integration services has grown so rapidly that most hardware vendors, software vendors, software service organizations, and consulting organizations all offer systems integration services. And, the increasingly sophisticated end user technology consumer is frequently becoming the direct marketing target for all kinds of technology products and services, often sidestepping the IS organization altogether.

But, we can also see a few missing ingredients in Porter's recipe for innovation. While the raw number of technology suppliers is high, the number of suppliers whose products could work with the plethora of products in our heterogeneous systems environments is much more limited. Here is one area where open systems play a big role in supporting the IS organization. Open systems standards and standards-based products grow the number of suppliers from which products can be selected and key supplier relationships forged—presenting more choices to the IS organization. Another missing innovation ingredient is that many IS organizations do not have a strong system for developing human skills—educating IS employees and developing workplace skills and knowledge on new technologies and new production processes. Also, many IS organizations do not have a strong infrastructure that allows them to assimilate and take advantage of technology innovations—without having to swap out major portions of the infrastructure. These IS organizations are not investing enough in building the infrastructure—information reservoirs, pathways, tools, and processes—to support innovation. In many ways, today's IS department is in a harvesting mode—focused on operations—rather than in investment mode—focused on development.

As important, or more important than efficiency is the ability to innovate. And innovation requires an investment in infrastructure.

As businesses seek innovation, they are becoming more dependent upon information. And, they are becoming more open—seeking to exchange information more freely both within the business and between the business and its suppliers and customers. Subsequently, Information and Technology (I&T) capabilities are becoming important to the competitiveness of the business—as a key requirement for information exchange. Information Systems are moving from being a support function and an enabler of business strategies to also being a driver of business strategies; Information and Technology planning is moving from being a secondary, trickle-down function, to being an integral part of business planning; and, open systems are becoming a more important part of I&T planning.

Before we discuss specific open systems strategies, let's briefly take a look at what's involved in Information and Technology planning.

An Overall I&T Planning Model

Key components of I&T planning include a statement of the business objectives and goals, related I&T objectives and goals, a view of the systems functionality and capabilities to support business goals, and a view of the IS organization and the services it will provide. (Figure 12.2.)

AN I&T PLANNING MODEL

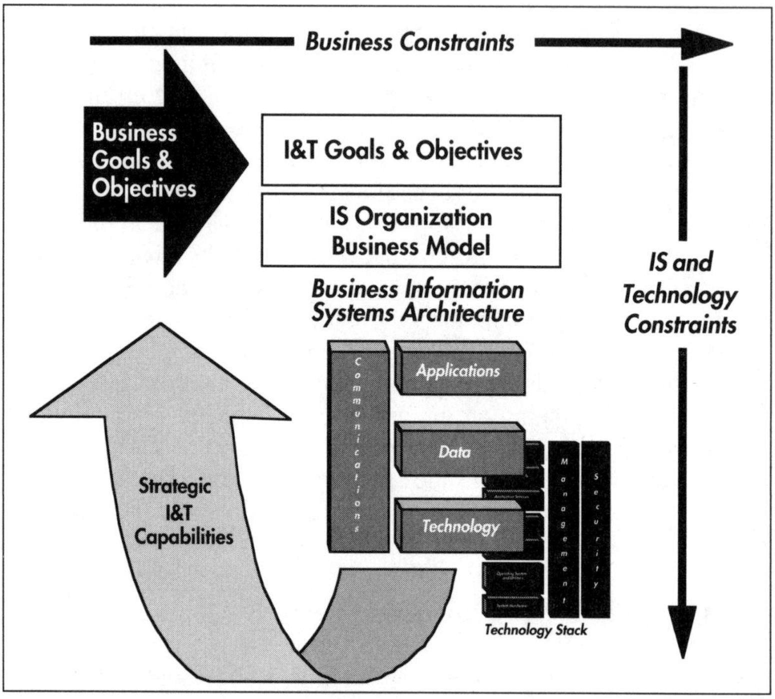

Figure 12.2

- **Business Objectives** drive the objectives of all functions within the business. While this may seem obvious, tremendous difficulties lie in both the definition communication and maintenance of business goals:

  - In definition—in explicitly outlining business goals in such a form that they are usable in guiding the goals of all the business functions.

  - In communication—in clearly communicating business goals to the business functions and employees in such a form that they are actionable and influence decisions and behavior.

  - In maintenance—in keeping the objectives of all the business functions in sync as changes occur in the business.

  IS executives responding to the CSC survey have rated "aligning IS and corporate goals" as one of their top four concerns for the full seven years CSC has produced the survey—clearly indicating "room for improvement" in this area.

- The **Business Information Systems Architecture** defines the business view of systems—the portfolio of applications, data, and platforms that define the current and future state of information systems in the organization. Behind the business information systems architecture is a technical view of the systems technology (technology stack) that builds up to and supports the business information systems architecture.

- The **IS Organization Business Model** defines the work processes, operations, structure, and skills of the IS organization to execute its strategies.

- **Constraints** come in many forms—but basically, they fall into two broad categories:

  - Business constraints—including such items as investment/capital availability, state of business operations, technological awareness, customers and competitors of the business and how the business needs to respond to their demands and directions.

  - IS constraints—including such items as budget and capital availability, current technology assortment, technology knowledge, relationship of IS with business, state of technology, etc.

- **Strategic I&T Capabilities** are the positive influence of IS strategies on business competitiveness. Depending on the industry and the business use of technology, information and technology can not only enable business strategies, but also drive and influence business competitive strengths and strategies.

Key Considerations

Several key areas influence the sense of urgency and degree of change to be addressed in I&T planning, as well as the degree of freedom IS has in making changes. Three of the most influential are:

- Business competitive issues
- Current technology support of the business
- Relationship of IS to business

Business Competitive Issues

We began this book with a description of how tumultuous the business environment is today (Introduction chapter). Indeed, a quick scan of some of the top selling business books in 1994 confirms the sense of change. (See Figure 12.3.)

SELECTED TOP SELLING BUSINESS BOOKS—1994

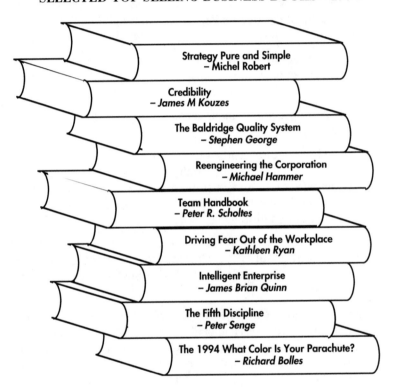

Strategy Pure and Simple
– Michel Robert

Credibility
– James M Kouzes

The Baldridge Quality System
– Stephen George

Reengineering the Corporation
– Michael Hammer

Team Handbook
– Peter R. Scholtes

Driving Fear Out of the Workplace
– Kathleen Ryan

Intelligent Enterprise
– James Brian Quinn

The Fifth Discipline
– Peter Senge

The 1994 What Color Is Your Parachute?
– Richard Bolles

Figure 12.3

Businesses are responding with a series of initiatives aimed at making themselves more competitive. Some popular programs include:

- *Business Process Reengineering* (BPR)—engineering radical change into a business process or business operations

- *Continual improvement programs*—programs focused on continuously improving processes and operations (less radical than BPR)

- *Total Quality Management* (TQM)—programs focused on the results of business processes and operations—and improving the processes and operations to improve the results

- *Organizational change programs*—programs to help businesses learn how to learn and change

Common targets of these business initiatives include cycle time, costs, business processes, and quality. (See Figure 12.4.)

COMMON BUSINESS GOALS

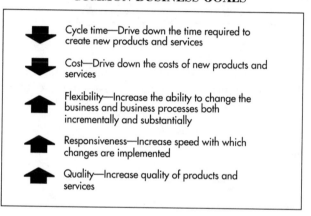

Figure 12.4

The bottom line in many industries with rampant change is an air of unpredictability. It is not clear what the next competitive threat will be or where it will come from. In today's market, the ability to change, quickly and continuously is a strategic capability. The ability to innovate is imperative. The ability to use and exchange information is a basic requirement. Information systems access and technical capabilities are critical to an organization's ability to compete in an unpredictable market.

Current Information & Technology Support of the Business

Along with the growing recognition of the importance of technology, there is also a growing awareness of the current state of I&T support of the business. Often there's a gap between what is and what the business wants. A portion of that gap can be attributed to the difference between what the business wants and what it can afford or what technology can do (we can all dream, can't we?) But often, admittedly, a portion of that gap stems from what the information and technology capabilities are and what they could be.

The state of current I&T support of business may be described on continuum from "in danger of imminent collapse" to "in sync and running smoothly." (See Figure 12.5.)

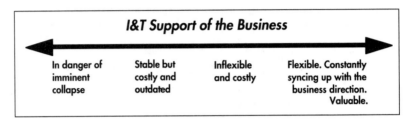

Figure 12.5

Crises may exist at any level of the business information systems architecture in terms of the current assortment of technology supporting capabilities at that level.

IS crises may include:

Short-term crises:

- Technology stability and/or vendor support of the products

- Support of business operations (design crisis)

- Cost

Short-term/long-term crises:

- Choice: vendor product options—availability of applicable, usable packages, tools, etc.

- Connectivity and interoperability—ability to interoperate with other applications, share data, connect with other platforms, and communicate with other platforms (heterogeneous environment)

Long-term crises:

- Scalability—ability to grow, shrink, spread as business changes

- Flexibility—ability to change as the business changes

- Stability—as a base upon which to build functionality and capabilities—technical viability

- Vendor viability

- Cost

Crises (and lack of crises) will cause IS organizations to have differing levels of urgency in considering the need to act and the speed with which action should be taken. The degree of openness of the current technology assortment limits or enhances the dimensions of the actions that can be taken.

Moving from the left side of the support continuum to the right side involves building the infrastructure capabilities to support on-going business change and assimilate technology advances. It is also requires building an organizational culture that supports change.

Relationship of IS to Business

The relationship between the IS function and the business affects the degree of freedom the IS function has in taking action and effecting change. While there is no question that users need to drive definition of business information needs and participate heavily in designing, testing, and implementing systems functionality, there are questions about how involved the user community should be in selecting individual technology products and standards. When technology product decisions are left to the IS function, the technology assortment of an organization is generally more standardized and easier to support. When users drive technology product decisions, the technology assortment of an organization is generally more diverse, less integrated, and more difficult to support.

When the IS function is in a "high trust" position, it has more freedom in setting the technology direction of the organization and assembling and integrating the technology assortment. It is more likely that a coherent technology strategy can be articulated and achieved. When the IS function is in a "low trust" position, users naturally become more involved in IS operations, technology selection, and development activities (if they care about technology support) and the more diverse the technology assortment generally becomes. In a "low trust" position, it is less likely that a coherent technology direction can be articulated and followed.

Planning Basics

So, back to the question at hand (or at paw?): "Where do we begin our efforts to open up systems?"

First, we need to outline what we want to achieve. Then we can look at where and how open systems can contribute to our efforts and discuss alternative approaches.

Business is issuing a series of challenges to the IS function. We might generalize those challenges into the following six points. (See Figure 12.6.)

Business Challenges to IS

- Identify and deliver technology that sharpens business competitiveness
- Deliver significant new functionality—quickly
- Continuously change systems functionality to support business
- Integrate business units and work teams
- Drive down unit costs
- Manage business risk

Figure 12.6

What We are Trying to Achieve: IS Goals

In responding to the business challenges and aligning with the strategic business goals, the IS function might lay out a set of goals that strategically align with the goals of the business. (See Figure 12.7.)

IS Goals

Cycle time—Drive down the time required to create new applications functionality and systems capabilities

Cost—Drive down the unit costs of systems capabilities, functionality, and services

Functionality—Provide more functionality to support business operations and decision support

Flexibility—Increase the ability to change systems capabilities, both incrementally and radically, not just once but over time

Responsiveness—Increase speed with which new functionality and changes are implemented

Quality—Increase quality of products and services

Stability—Increase the stability of the base infrastructure and technology

Ability to rejuvenate—Increase ability to incorporate new technology and new design approaches into technology base and systems capabilities

---

Figure 12.7

To react to rapid market and business changes, IS departments are striving to drive down their own cycle time—the time it takes to deliver new systems functionality. In response to the "do more with less!" imperative, IS functions are looking to cut the unit cost of systems capabilities and deliver more functionality within roughly the same budget. "Quality," one of today's watchwords in business, is every bit as important as a goal in the IS function. Newspapers and magazines are full of stories about the very real costs of quality breaches in technology products and services.

The last four goals deal with building an infrastructure that supports innovation. IS organizations are looking to improve the flexibility of systems and the ability of the IS organization to quickly respond to business needs. They are also looking to improve the stability of the technology base and the ability to assimilate new technology developments as they become attractive.

In focusing on the information and technology infrastructure, IS is recognizing the need to move from individual heroics to more structured approach to dealing with connectivity and integration. In other words, changing from developing connectivity between applications and products on an interface by interface basis to developing a framework for connectivity.

Open Systems Axioms

Open systems contribute to the proposed IS goals in many ways. Let's briefly revisit the axioms of open systems we introduced in previous chapters in the context of their contribution to IS goals and challenges:

> **Axiom #1: Standardization at any layer in the technology stack makes the layer directly below exchangeable.**

Standardization at any layer in the technology stack creates the ability to substitute technology at the layer directly below. And, the ability to substitute technology creates competition, which in turn drives down prices. Technology acquisition costs can be driven down at the layers in the technology stack where several competitive alternatives are available. The existence of competitive alternatives also reduces the risk of reliance on the technology direction or economic viability of an individual vendor.

> **Axiom #2: Products are valuable at a point in time, but architectures are valuable over time.**

Understanding the technical architecture of a product and industry/market support for the technical architecture (i.e., proprietary, ported proprietary, proprietary/open, or open), leads to a better view of the future of that product. In assessing technology products, remember: you are not only buying a product, you are also (and often more importantly) buying an architecture. Market support for that architecture will enhance or complicate connectivity, interoperability, and the ability to integrate collections of products from multiple vendors.

This statement also holds true for the architecture of business information systems. IS organizations are also learning, as technology vendors are, that architectures are valuable in planning for and servicing business computing needs over time. The fit of that architecture into your technology architecture will either enhance or complicate your information integration and distribution efforts. And, specifying the technology architecture (the technology stack) helps weather short technology product lifecycles.

Axiom #3: Technology leads, standards follow.

This axiom points to the design choices in the technology stack.

To optimize technology costs and technology stability, select innovation where innovation gives an advantage (where innovation is worth the proprietary premium). Use open and proprietary open standards wherever possible to take advantage of lower cost and longer technology planning horizons.

Axiom #4 (new): Componentization and logical independence reduce complexity.

At the root of open systems is the concept of dealing with the complexities of the computing environment by defining and organizing component functionality and technologies, then defining "standard" functionality supported by the components and "standard interfaces" between the components. This concept of logical independence provides the opportunity to add, refine, and evolve components independently of the others.

The concepts of componentization and logical independence can be extended to data and application architectures.

The concepts of componentization and logical independence are not limited to technology products. They can also be applied to the organization of the functional components of data and applications. If standard interfaces (functions and access methods) are defined, each layer of the business information systems architecture can be evolved independently. Applications can be changed to support changing business processes without redefining the data that is used by the applications. Data structures can be modeled after the business and take advantage of the increased stability of an organization's data relationships over the stability of the processes using the data. Standard industry data and process models may be used to support non-unique or routine functions, further limiting the time an organization's IS department needs to spend defining and maintaining data structures and applications. Technology platforms can be changed as processing and data access volumes and performance requirements dictate without extensive effort to redefine and migrate data and applications.

Where and How Open Systems Contribute

Open systems can contribute directly to the goals of IS. (See Figure 12.8.) Open systems can be used to drive down technology costs, and reduce the risk of reliance on a single vendor. Because of industry definition/support of standard architectural frameworks, open systems enhance the connectivity and integration of technology products, help stabilize technology platforms (or at least, contribute to the understanding of where stability may or may not exist), lengthen planning horizons, and reduce the overall complexity of the computing environment.

HOW OPEN SYSTEMS CONTRIBUTE TO IS GOALS

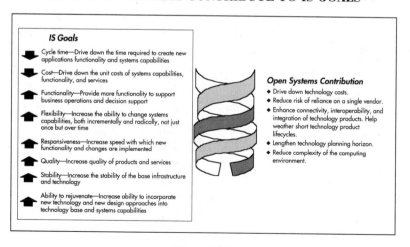

Figure 12.8

Some Big Decisions

Several big decisions affect the definition of an open systems strategy. These decisions form the basis for a statement of I&T policies or principles that guide the process of defining the business information systems and technology architectures, setting an open systems direction, and selecting component technology.

Largely "Make" or Largely "Buy"?

This question involves developing an understanding of whether IS should focus on building applications functionality or purchasing and integrating packages. Some factors in making this decision include:

- How industry-standard are the business practices of the organization (versus "signature" business processes that differentiate the organization from its competition)?

- How strong is the market for package applications supporting industry standard business practices?

- How urgent is the business need for new information systems capabilities?

The real impact of this decision is one of emphasis on the IT infrastructure and strategy for integration (Figure 12.9): whether to focus on developing a tools workbench for creating functionality or on middleware for linking applications.

CRITERIA INFLUENCING MAKE OR BUY DECISIONS

Criteria Influencing Make or Buy Decisions

	Largely "Make"	Largely "Buy"
Business Processes	Business processes and practices are unique, or "signature"— they differentiate the business from its competition.	Business processes and practices are generally consistent with industry versions.
Packaged Applications Availability	Market for packaged applications is small with few competitors or perhaps poor/ unstable industry economics.	Market for applications is strong with many choices for major systems.
Business Need for New Functionality	Less Urgent. Basic needs are satisfied by existing systems.	Extremely urgent.

IS Emphasis on Infrastructure and Integration

I&T Infrastructure	Emphasis on building support for systems ment including logical data and process model repositories, design and programming tools, development workbenches, etc.	Emphasis on building an integration develop- infrastructure—providing support for building applications interoperability, data sharing, and other interfaces.
Integration Focus	Interfaces between applications built within the framework are standardized through the framework. Interfaces with "outside" packages are built bit by bit—on an individual interface level.	Interfaces between packaged applications are accomplished through the development of a standardized approach to interfaces and integration.

Figure 12.9

In reality, most IS functions need to plan for and design an I&T infrastructure that supports both custom development and packages. Most organizations cannot afford to exclude packages from their technology assortment, and cannot rely exclusively on outside vendors to service their every computing need.

Degree of Data Sharing?

What is the degree of current and desired information integration across business functions and what is the approach for data sharing? This issue is not so much a decision as it is an understanding of the issues and statement of the design objectives around the approach for distributing and integrating data while preserving data integrity in the process.

Degree of Data Accessibility?

This big decision is related to defining the data-sharing philosophy. It involves outlining the type of data accessibility an organization wants to support and how it will support it. Factors influencing the decision include:

*   Percentage of "knowledge workers" requiring decision support type capabilities versus operations workers requiring more structured support of business operations

*   Level of user technology sophistication

*   Degree of information openness and access the business wants to provide

Innovation Versus Standardization?

From a technology point of view, where do you need innovation and uniqueness in technology? Or, to restate the issue: where do you want the cost benefits and stability of standardized technology (tempered of course, by the availability of suitable technology products), and where do you need the more rapid innovation and uniqueness of proprietary technology, and can you afford it? Answers to these questions may differ at each layer of the technology stack, and indeed for specific components within the layers.

Few or Many Vendors?

Do you want the benefits of being able to select technology from the broader array of offerings from many vendors or the reduced technology integration and management headaches of limiting products to those of few vendors? This decision is generally a highly charged one—particularly in organizations where the IS function is in a "low trust" situation. Generally, technology integration is more manageable (and indeed, more possible) as the number of vendors is limited. Another benefit is that by limiting vendors and vendor products, you can generally get better performance out of both the products and the vendors themselves. But, it is advisable at a minimum to keep the threat of substitution real to optimize technology costs and vendor performance. In a homogeneous computing environment, the cream won't rise to the top! (Even just the threat of heterogeneity may cause you to be able to identify cream.)

Standardize on Products or Standards?

This big decision is related to the decision on vendors. It is also generally highly sensitive and political, particularly in organizations with users that are very technologically knowledgeable. Standardizing on products minimizes the technology integration burden and lowers technology acquisition costs while standardizing on standards maximizes the technology selection. The technology environment becomes more complex as more products are added— not just in terms of technical integration and interoperability issues, but also regarding associated asset management, licensing, versioning, and vendor management issues. On the other hand, in environments where the IS organization is in a "low trust" position and where users lead technology selection, product features are more important to them than the integration and management issues. Often IS organizations have no choice but to rely on standards for integration.

Exploring these big decisions helps an IS function develop a clearer vision of the technology needs of an organization and prepares it for developing an open systems direction.

Getting Down to Business

The bottom line of all this discussion on business needs, IS goals, big decisions, and so on is this:

> *In pursuit of opening systems, planning is more important than ever.*

Implementing and managing technology in an organization has never been easy—and the wild, escalating pace of technology development along with the advent of distributed computing and open systems has made the job more difficult than ever.

Let's summarize the advice from our case study organizations and our planning discussion into a few brief, but key initiatives.

> *Everything has been thought of before, but the problem is to think of it again.*
> —Johann W. Von Goethe

■ **Clearly define business competitive issues and goals**

Understand the business competitive issues, goals, and major initiatives. This step is key in understanding where technology contributes to business competitiveness, as well as in identifying and complying with constraints imposed by the business and the business market.

■   **Understand the role of technology in the organization**

Technology may be a support mechanism for business operations, an enabler of business operations and strategies, or a driver of business competitiveness. It is important to understand the implications of I&T on business operations and the competitiveness of the business, today and in the future.

■   **Be candid about the current state of I&T business support**

Confront basic questions such as:

•   What is the current state of technology within the organization?

•   What is the current state of I&T support of the business?

•   Where is the I&T competence? What competence exists inside and outside of the IS organization? Is the technology competence inside or outside the business?

Be candid about any crises that may exist (or alternatively, ecstatic about a lack of crises).

■   **Understand the state and direction of the relationship of the IS function with business**

The state of the IS relationship directly impacts the degree of freedom the IS function has in setting and following a technology strategy. Overall, the IS function can play many roles in technology acquisition, development and integration, support, and management. Open systems most directly impact the potential roles of the IS function in technology acquisition. (See Figure 12.10.)

■   **Define I&T goals in terms of business objectives**

State I&T goals in such a way that they directly relate and support the business objectives. Make sure that any I&T strategy chosen is driven from the desired impact on the business.

POTENTIAL IS ROLES IN TECHNOLOGY ACQUISITION

Technology Provider	IS selects and provides all technology including applications.
Infrastructure Provider "Select Core Technology Products"	IS selects and provides core technology—users select applications within the core technology framework—e.g., users can choose technology from a list of technologies supported by IS.
Infrastructure Integrator "Select Core Technology Standards"	IS provides standards and an information infrastructure—users participate heavily or drive selection of applications and core technology—e.g., users may drive selection of technology from the top of the technology stack down to the operating system layer (or further) as long as that technology is consistent with standards in the infrastructure framework defined by IS.

Figure 12.10

■ **Clearly outline I&T initiatives**

Translate the I&T goals into very specific IS initiatives. Initiatives should be stated in such a way that it is possible to answer the following questions:

• To IS management: How does the I&T initiative contribute to one or more objectives of the business?

• To an IS employee: Will the outcome of this work contribute to one of the I&T initiatives? (If not, drop that project and pick up something that will.)

The important thing is to stay in sync and focused on the goals of the business. Because of the complexity and rapid change of technology, it is easy to begin following technology for technology's sake, rather than for the sake of business. Remember the advice of Winnie the Pooh (speaking to Piglet of Owl),

> *...you can't help respecting anybody who can spell TUESDAY, even if he doesn't spell it quite right; but spelling isn't everything. There are days when spelling Tuesday simply doesn't count.*

> —A.A. Milne, *Winnie the Pooh*

■ Define the business open systems "participation" strategy

Depending on business competitive issues, the role of technology in the organization, and the state of technology standards, an organization has some options in the degree of "participation" in open systems. (See Figure 12.11.) If the technology needs of the organization are pushing the edges of the technology industry, the organization has no choice but to be more aggressive in the standards process and more generous in its contributions to industry efforts in pioneering the open systems vision. If the technology needs are less cutting edge, the organization can follow open systems pioneers and benefit from the perspiration of others.

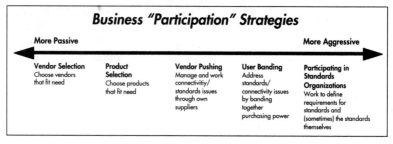

Figure 12.11

■ Define business information and technology architecture

As we have mentioned several times, there is a pretty big war going on about *how* to implement open systems. The two major camps are:

Purist—
Philosophy: Open systems are based on industry standards. One needs to select industry standards and select only products that adhere to those standards.

Pragmatist—
Philosophy: The goals of open systems and alignment of IS objectives with business objectives can be best achieved by picking and choosing through standards and products.

It should be noted that a pessimist camp still exists, although the numbers are dwindling:

Pessimist—
Philosophy: Open systems are not achievable, and even if they were, they would not be desirable—they would be too far behind the market in technology innovation.

Definition of the business information and technology architectures is where beliefs become actions.

■ **Define information protection approach**

Develop an approach or architecture for information protection that meets the needs of the business. Integrate the IP approach and architecture with I&T goals and architectures.

The largely transparent security mechanisms of the past are being replaced by a collection of functions and facilities that require planning, design, development, and careful implementation. In an open distributed environment, information protection must be integral to the overall architecture of systems, it cannot be effective as an after-the-fact add-on.

■ **Define the technology acquisition strategy**

Develop an approach to technology acquisition that balances the needs of the organization for technology innovation with the needs for connectivity, interoperability, and integration with the constraints of technology, the technology budget, and the state of existing technology.

Technology selection is becoming much more complex. It is complicated by the increased complexity of distributed computing, information sharing, and richer end user computing functionality. Selection is complicated by the broader range of offerings from a multitude of vendors. And, it is both helped and complicated by the increased activism of the end user.

The real challenge is to define technology evaluation and selection procedures that strike a balance between the benefits of using leading edge, innovative products and the benefits of using industry standard technology. Key considerations: control technology proliferation and preserve technical architecture without stifling innovation.

■ **Define the impact on the IS organization**

The pursuit of open systems necessitates changes in the IS organization: in planning, in defining the technology direction and architecture, in technology acquisition procedures, in technology testing and integration, in vendor management, and (potentially) in participating in setting the industry technology direction through standards bodies, to mention just a few.

■ **Define metrics & evaluation criteria for the IS organization and initiatives**

Define the mechanisms for managing the new IS organization. This involves establishing the metrics for the new organizational units, the IS initiatives, and the ever present question: "how should I&T-based benefits be evaluated?" The latter is a particularly sticky issue. However, if the evaluation of I&T-based benefits isn't reassessed as the IS direction is set, technology acquisition and development practices may actually be rewarded for being in conflict, rather than in sync, with business and I&T goals.

■ **Define key vendors and manage vendor relationships**

Define the vendor strategy (few or many vendors) and identify key vendor relationships:

> *Reality:* There is no way to completely insulate an organization from all vendors through the use of standards. At each and every point where proprietary technology is used, the vendor of that technology becomes important to the business.

> *Truth:* You really wouldn't want to totally insulate the business from key vendors, even if you could. At every point where you have a key supplier relationship, you gain leverage with that supplier, be that leverage through volume purchases with that vendor, or through the threat of substitution.

It is important to identify those vendors that are particularly important to your organization—for whatever reason, and carefully manage the relationship with those vendors.

For example, in today's technology market, database products are mostly in the ported proprietary category of our Openometer. This means that while you can achieve many of the open systems goals using a multi-platform database, such as Oracle, you are storing your information in a proprietary product. In addition, if you use the programming tools from Oracle, you are building your applications in a proprietary product. Not that this is bad. Quite to the contrary, Oracle offers a very functional, popular set of development tools. But, selecting to build applications in Oracle Tools means linking your applications and data to the technology direction, cost/performance curve, and economic viability of Oracle. Suddenly, Oracle Corporation becomes very important to your organization.

■   **Plan ahead and practice ahead**

There is a long lead time from square one to understanding the direction of the technology industry and being ready to assume a leadership role in introducing technology into the organization and managing its technology direction. Many successful IS organizations have established technology monitoring functions that monitor industry developments and testbeds or integration labs to test new products.

Choosing an Open Systems Strategy

Ultimately, in pursuing the goal of opening systems, an organization can follow one of three alternative paths towards open systems. (See Figure 12.12.)

APPROACHES TO OPEN SYSTEMS

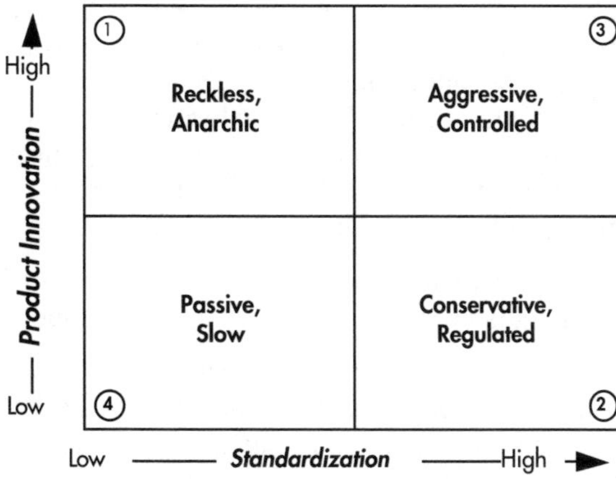

Figure 12.12

1.   Acquire technology products based on product features, without paying much attention to the standards and alternative platforms the technology runs/runs on.

We label this strategy *liberal, risky* because while it can help solve some short-term technology capability issues—it can be used to deliver a set of functionality or capabilities quickly—this strategy typically creates a long-term technology support and integration nightmare. Technology acquisition costs will be higher with this strategy both in the short- and long-term. Innovative, proprietary technology will command a premium in the market and connectivity/integration, support, and management costs will be high over the long-term.

Despite negative long-term consequences, this strategy can be very effective in overcoming inertia or solving an immediate crisis. *Heed the warnings, though!* The benefits of this strategy are short-lived and the organization that places itself in this box should plan a way out of it.

2. A second strategy is to describe a technical architecture based wholly on standards, shunning innovative technologies that lead the market in feature and function in favor of technologies that comply with industry standards.

    We label this strategy *conservative, regulated* because, although it preserves the technical coherence of the collection of technology products in the computing environment, it will continually employ technology that is behind the market in terms of features and capabilities. Technology acquisition costs will be lower under this strategy, but innovation will also be lower. This strategy may be a long-term position for organizations whose information technology needs generally lag industry state-of-the-art or organizations needing long technology planning cycles and stable costs.

3. A third strategy is to describe a technical architecture that consists of both industry standards and innovative technologies.

    We label this strategy *aggressive, controlled* because it attempts to strike a balance between innovation and standardization. This approach standardizes on products where standards don't exist, are not complete enough, are not stable enough, or don't suit the needs of the organization. This strategy may be a long-term position for organizations whose technology needs are more leading edge.

4. Remaining *passive, slow* is the "do nothing" approach and does not get an organization any closer to open systems.

    However, this strategy may be perfectly appropriate and the best choice for organizations whose current systems meet their business needs. Organizations without any immediate business need to change systems and technology will have no need to pursue open systems. The Open Systems strategy should be driven by the business direction and need.

The real challenge is to strike a balance between the benefits of using leading edge, innovative products and the benefits of using industry standard technology. Key considerations: control technology proliferation and preserve technical architecture without stifling innovation.

Summary

The choice of an open systems path should be based on an understanding of the business direction, business needs, technology needs, and the level of risk the business is willing to assume. In setting an open systems strategy, it is important to:

- Identify where open technology provides the greatest value to business

- Determine where proprietary technology is needed and appropriate

- Develop an objective and credible comparison of technology alternatives

- Develop a do-able, manageable implementation plan

- Identify and work within constraints of the business, the IS function, and the technology market as a whole

Opening systems is not easy. There is no one answer to how to proceed. Open systems are not the path of least resistance. And, it should be emphasized that "opening the business" is a decision that should come ahead of opening systems. You will not be committed to or successful in open systems unless you are also committed and successful in opening the business.

> *There is a man who has a business that manufactures concrete saws. He is the only manufacturer of a certain type of concrete saw in the country. He has no competition to speak of. He makes his saws out of steel and iron for weight and longevity. He could use cheaper materials, such as aluminum, but the saw wouldn't work right. It wouldn't be heavy enough to break through concrete*

and it wouldn't last as long. The man has no need to change his product or his business. He knows his customer, he knows the market, and he knows his business. The information systems supporting his business are over twenty years old. But, they service the business just fine.

If this man were to go through the analysis we just described, he would choose to stay right where he is.

Depending on where your business is, where your business is going, and the needs of the business, you may choose any of the three paths, or, to stay put. The key is, once you commit to how open your business will be, the open systems strategy falls right out. And, if the open systems strategy you choose places you in a box that is not a comfortable position, you need to set a strategy to move out of the box into one that suits your business needs better over the longer run.

Chapter 13

Closing

The Walrus and the Carpenter were walking close at hand;
They wept like anything to see such quantities of sand:
'If this were only cleared away,' they said, 'it would be grand!'

'If seven maids with seven mops swept it for half a year,
Do you suppose,' the Walrus said, 'that they could get it clear?'
'I doubt it,' said the Carpenter, and shed a bitter tear.

—Lewis Carroll

'Is there any other point to which you would wish to draw my attention?'
'To the curious incident of the dog in the night-time.'
'The dog did nothing in the night-time.'
'That was the curious incident,' remarked Sherlock Holmes.

—Sir Arthur Conan Doyle

A friend of mine once told me a story from his childhood. During the summer, he and his best friend used to fish every afternoon. While fishing they would throw rocks into the lake. They claimed that without the interruption of rocks, fish would have no concept of the world outside their familiar environment of water, seaweed, sand, plants, and other fish. So, by throwing rocks into the lake, they were teaching the fish about God.

Open systems concepts are a bit like rocks thrown into the technology industry. Through market demands for interconnectivity, interoperability, portability, and the like, technology vendors are learning about the world outside their particular products, clients, symbiotic partnerships, and competitors. Likewise, open systems concepts are waking up IS departments around the world to a broader view of systems and technology and the role of technology in the organization.

At the same time, an "open" system, like beauty, like art, like religion, is in the mind of the beholder. There is a perception angle to open systems. That is one reason why the concepts are so difficult to define—and to grasp. In order to create open systems, you need to envision where they benefit your organization, establish parameters for the choices ahead—then create your own definition of open systems, and decide how you will implement them. *Open systems are as much about how you choose to address your business priorities and subsequently how you assemble and build systems as they are about the technology you acquire.*

Open systems have come a long way since the concepts were introduced some 15 years ago.

Open systems are a reality. Real technology, real products exist. Standards organizations, technology vendors and technology users are sorting out their roles. Corporations, both large and small are implementing open systems and benefiting from their efforts.

Open systems still have a long way to go. The road is rocky. Implementing open systems is not easy. Maintaining the dual focus of implementing the new while maintaining the legacy environment may be an overwhelming task. The trick is to create a process where past investments in systems are protected, yet where new investments contribute to the desired future rather than perpetuating the past.

The scope of the change imposed on IS by open systems concepts will be beyond many technologists. Many CIO's estimate that the percentage of their staff that will not make it through the transition to open systems and the new IS mission ranges from 20-50%. These are difficult realities—requiring thoughtful strategies to guide the people and the organization through the transition.

Organizations that have taken the plunge and are implementing open systems caution followers to be clear in your intentions, plan for uncertainty, and tolerate failures.

Until open systems concepts and supporting technologies are more mature—easier to select, assemble, interconnect, manage, and support—every project undertaken in an "open" manner will have an R&D component. Every project will need to devote attention to making sure that the hardware, software, and communications facilities are all working together.

Until an open computing environment is turnkey—completely defined, workable, performance proven, and accepted and supported by a preponderance of technology users and technology vendors—both technology vendors and technology users will balk at the prospect. Within the implementing organization, both technologists and end users will also balk at the unknown and uncertain aspects of open systems as well as the fundamental changes both enabled and forced by open systems. Implementing an open computing environment requires significantly changing what IS does and how it does it.

The real question is how long will (or should) reluctance to change be tolerated?

It is not surprising that we are having difficulty standardizing computing communications and interfaces—facsimile machines provide an interesting object lesson on the pains and timeframe of standardization:

> Buyers today can go to an electronics store, pick up a fax machine based on feature and price, and be relatively worry-free about whether it will be able to communicate with other faxes. However, it took a while to get fax machines to this state.

> The first facsimile machine was designed in 1843, by Scottish physicist, Alexander Bain. For the first 100 years, there was virtually no market for the machines. Beginning in 1941, fax machines began to sell to press associations and the government. (They were particularly useful for sending news photos during the war.) The first U.S. "standard" on office fax was published in 1966 by the Electronics Industry Association.

> The following is quoted from the standard document.

> *Each manufacturer has designed his facsimile equipment used for message communications to fit the requirements of his customers and the natural characteristics of the types of mechanisms employed when operating on a private line basis. The same equipment was initially used when operation of facsimile equipment on a regular telephone call basis became available. Operation between some of these equipments was not possible due to differences in the facsimile equipments. This Standard specifies machine characteristics which will ensure interoperation.—EIA* standard RD-328 [McConnell, 1989]

> Even with this standard, the received copy might be stretched from the original size or could have parts near the edge of the page missing, but, for the first

time, diverse fax units were able to communicate. Each manufacturer stayed within the wide tolerances required to get the standard, but did not convert to the "recommended for eventual standard" items. Clearly, there was an acute need for a facsimile standard to one set of performance specifications instead of interoperability.

Subsequent facsimile standards were developed in:

1968—CCITT Group 1 Fax Recommendation

1976—CCITT Group 2 Recommendation

1980—CCITT Group 3 Recommendation

1984—CCITT Group 4 Recommendation

Once facsimile manufacturers got their act together and expanded from the proprietary fax mindset, the marketplace exploded.

Estimates of the number of fax machines in the U.S. at various points in time include:

1941—A small number of fax units were made for news photo use

1965—Xerox placed an order with Magnavox for 25,000 units

1975—100,000 units in the U.S.

1987—7 Million Group 3 faxes in the U.S. [McConnell, 1989]

Faxes were created to exchange information and it took us over a hundred years to start using them, *then almost another fifty to move from proprietary communications to standardized communications.* With computers, the original focus was on computing—operations contained within the machine. As the business environment is challenging organizations to integrate, both internally and externally, organizations are learning that there is real power in information exchange.

If our experience with faxes can be used as an indicator, it will take a while yet to sort through the computer standards and the processes for defining and evolving them. But it will happen.

The head of the Architecture Group in a large IS organization recently described the technology direction of his organization and how they were introducing "architecture," standards, client/server, UNIX, TCP/IP, Oracle, Windows, and so on into a former exclusively mainframe organization. He said "We're not talking about 'Open Systems' here—the concept is too esoteric. We are implementing practical technologies that conform to industry accepted standards in order to enhance the accessibility of our information and to build applications that are usable and will support our business as it goes through the changes it is facing." He was right. They are implementing practical technologies that conform to industry accepted standards to enhance the accessibility of their information.

They are also implementing open systems.

The move to open systems is inevitable. The futures of business and technology are beginning to converge. Open systems are an enabler for dramatically increasing the usability and flexibility of systems as well as driving down the unit operating costs of IS.

We are coming to the realization that open systems simply "must be"—they are underpinnings of the future where business and technology (finally!) meet.

Two closing thoughts:

He who can take advice is sometimes superior to him who can give it.

—Karl von Knebel

On the other hand, if you can tell the difference between good advice and bad advice, you don't need advice.

—Dr. Laurence J. Peter

APPENDIX

Standards Groups

This appendix contains a listing of formal organizations, associations and government entities, as well as informal groups and alliances that claim to, or are reported to participate in standards creation, adoption, or influencing. This list is inherently incomplete and inaccurate. We have assembled contact addresses and telephone numbers wherever possible to help you find more current information than can be provided here.

ABI—Application Binary Interface Consortium

Description

The ABI Consortium, founded in July 1990, was established to promote Mips Technologies Inc.'s RISC architecture as a development environment. The consortium published the Mips ABI, which describes the Mips-specific extensions to UNIX System V Release 4 operating system. [abstracted from Garry, March 15, 1993.] The consortium maintains a reference platform for testing applications that implement the extensions. If a program successfully runs on the reference platform, it is guaranteed to work on all other machines that implement the ABI. [UNIX Review. June 1993]

Membership

Silicon Graphics, AT&T/NCR, NEC, Pyramid, Control Data Systems, Tandem, Sony, Siemens Nixdorf, and Olivetti.

Contact

Silicon Graphics
2011 N. Shoreline Blvd.
Mountain View, CA 94039
(415) 390-3033; Fax: (415) 969-6327

ACE—Advanced Computing Environment Consortium

Description

ACE was founded in 1991 with the aim of producing inexpensive yet powerful RISC-based workstations that will support thousands of commercial and technical applications [Eibisch and Jubley, 1991]. While ACE largely collapsed with the withdrawal of Santa Cruz Operation (SCO) and Compaq, it may now have the support of Sony, Toshiba, and NEC. However, ACE currently appears to be defunct. [Lavin, 1993]

Mission

The initiative was designed to broaden the use of advanced microprocessor-based systems while protecting customers' investment in today's computing environments [88Open Consortium, 1991]. ACE had hoped to port both MS Windows NT and SCO UNIX to the MIPS processor to begin the new generation with an alternative to Intel. [Lavin, 1993]

Membership

ACE was founded by 21 vendors led by Santa Cruz Operation (SCO), Compaq, Microsoft, MIPS Computer Systems, and Digital Equipment Corp. By the end of 1991, ACE had over 200 members including hardware and software vendors, third-party hardware and chip vendors, and system integrators. [Eibisch, 1991]

Conformance Testing

No information indicates that ACE does conformance testing.

Miscellaneous

Key elements of the ACE initiative include a unified UNIX operating system environment (ACE UNIX), Windows NT, full support for x86-based, industry-standard PCs and PC systems, and a standard specification for MIPS reduced instruction set computing (RISC) microprocessor-based computers. [88Open Consortium, 1991]

ACM—Association for Computing Machinery

Description

ACM is an international society made up of developers and users of information technology. They recently inaugurated a magazine entitled StandardView, whose sole topic is standards. ACM has a Technical Standards Committee with the purpose of empowering members—as individual technical experts—so that they may actively participate in the standards-making process. [Rada, 1993]

Contact

Ms. Lillian Israel
Director of Marketing and
Membership Services
ACM
1515 Broadway
New York, NY 10036
(212) 626-0530; Fax: (212) 944-1318

ACM European Service Center
Avenue Marcel Thiry #204
1200 Brussels, Belgium
32-2-77-49602; Fax: 32-2-77-49690

ANSI—American National Standards Institute

Description

A nonprofit, privately-funded membership organization founded in 1918, ANSI coordinates the development of U.S. voluntary national standards in the private sector. ANSI is the U.S. member body to ISO and IEC. Standards are not developed by ANSI but by technical and professional societies, trade associations, and other groups which have been accredited by ANSI and submit their standards to ANSI for approval. [ANSI, November 1993]

Mission

The objectives of ANSI are threefold: to coordinate the development of U.S. voluntary national standards and perform as the U.S. member body to the nontreaty international standards bodies, to serve both the private and public sectors' needs for voluntary standardization, and to provide voluntary standards system and conformity assessment activities that will contribute to the health of the economy and the competitiveness of the U.S. industry in today's changing global marketplace. [ANSI, November 1993]

Membership

The membership of ANSI includes approximately 1,300 companies, 30 government agencies, and over 250 technical, trade, labor and consumer organizations. [ANSI, November 1993]

Direction

Some of the key functions of ANSI are:

- Coordinate the self-regulating, due process, consensus-based U.S. voluntary standards systems

- Administer the development of standards and approve them as ANSI standards

- Provide the means for the U.S. to influence development of international and regional standards

- Disseminate timely and important information on national, international and regional standards activities to U.S. industry

The benefits derived from such functions are:

- Provides national and international recognition of standards for credibility and force in domestic commerce and world trade

- Assists companies in reducing operating and purchasing costs and ensures product quality and safety

- Provides national and international standards information essential for marketing worldwide

- Promotes a self-regulated and strong privately administered voluntary national and international standards system. [ANSI, November 1993]

Conformance Testing

ANSI accredits certification programs of competent U.S. organizations, but does not certify products and services. [ANSI, November 1993]

Address

ANSI (U.S)   ANSI (Europe)
11 West 42ND Street   Brussels
New York, NY 10036   Avenue des Arts 50
(212) 642-4900   1040 Brussels, Belgium
                                 011 322 513 6892

Miscellaneous

ANSI designates standards as American National Standards when it finds that principles of openness and due process have been followed in the approval procedure and when it finds that a consensus of those directly and materially affected has been achieved. [ANSI, November 1993]

AOW—Asia-Oceania Workshop

Description

AOW was created in 1988 to assist in the development of internationally harmonized specifications for OSI and to ensure acceptable interoperability based on OSI. The workshop serves as a forum for OSI and Open System Environment (OSE) experts in the region. [AOW, November 1993]

Membership

Organizations that wish to promote interoperability of information processing in the Asia/Oceania region. [AOW, November 1993]

Conformance Testing

AOW does not do conformance testing, but harmonization of Profile Testing Specifications is done through the activities of the PTS-SIG. [AOW, November 1993]

Address

Interoperability Technology Association
for Information Processing (INTAP)
Asia-Oceania Workshop
(c/o) Interoperability Technology Association
for Information Processing (INTAP)
Sumitomo Gaien Building 3F
24, Daikyo-cho
Shinjuku-ku, Tokyo 160
Japan
81 3 3358 2721; Fax: 81-3-3358-4753

Miscellaneous

AOW is organized with a Council, Plenary Meetings, a Technical Liaison Group (TLG), several Special Interest Groups (SIGs), several Special Groups (SGs), and several Project Teams (PTs).

SIG activities include Document Filing and Retrieval, Directory, File Transfer Access and Management, Local Area Network, Message Handling Systems, Manufacturing Message Specifications, Network Management, Open Document Architecture, Profile Test Specifications, OSI Transaction Processing, Virtual Terminal, and Wide Area Network.

There is only one Special Group now—OSE-SG (Open Systems Environment). There are no Project Teams so far. [AOW, November 1993]

APS—Asynchronous Protocol Specification Alliance

Description

An industry consortium [with the intent] to establish an Application layer standard for the transmission of multimedia X.400 data over existing voice telephone lines. The group will attempt to focus efforts to address the demand for X.400 communications, including Electronic Data Interchange, electronic mail, voice, images, and fax and binary files, via phone lines. [Digital News & Review, 1992]

Membership

Isocor (OSI messaging software vendor) and Maxware (division of Norwegian Telecom).

Address

Isocor
12011 San Vicente Blvd.; Suite 500
Los Angeles, CA 90049
(310) 476-2671

ASR—Automatic Speech Recognition Workgroup

Description

This technical workgroup is the first Signal Computing System Architecture (SCSA) workgroup to be formed. Their charter includes defining an open API to meet the needs of developers seeking to incorporate speech recognition into call-processing applications. They will define the Device API for automatic speech recognition software and hardware. [EDGE On & About AT&T, 1993]

Mission

The goal of the group is to define an ideal, non vendor-specific standard that will allow users to easily incorporate speech recognition into their systems, regardless of the underlying technology. [EDGE, 1993]

Membership

ASR is composed of representatives from leading speech recognition technology companies including Voice Processing Corp., Voice Control Systems, and Dialogic. [EDGE, 1993]

CBEMA—Computer and Business Equipment Manufacturers Association

Description

CBEMA develops and advocates public policies beneficial to the information technology industry in the U.S., participates in all pertinent standards programs worldwide, sponsors ongoing industry councils to improve the business operations of members, and provides a forum for executives to work issues across national borders. [CBEMA, November 1993]

Mission

CBEMA's mission is to ensure that public and standardization policies reflect CBEMA's member company interests and promote information technology. Progress is measured by:

* Policies that support companies freely competing to provide information technology in the U.S.

- Policies and actions enhancing the global competitiveness of U.S.—owned companies in the industry

- Policies and actions enhancing the strength of the information technology industry in the U.S.

- Policy makers considering CBEMA views essential

- The development and use of voluntary standards to support information technology products and services. [CBEMA, November 1993]

Membership

CBEMA membership consists of 26 companies active in standardization activities. [CBEMA, November 1993]

Conformance Testing

No information indicates that CBEMA does conformance testing.

Address

CBEMA
1250 I Street NW; Suite 200
Washington, DC 20005
(202) 737-8888

Miscellaneous

CBEMA does not publish standards in its own name, but participates actively with national standards bodies. CBEMA is also a member of ANSI, serving on ANSI's Executive Standards Council. Member companies of CBEMA participate in JTC1 and other IEC committees.

CBEMA promotes standards through: publicity in association communication and the technical and trade press, reference to and incorporation of standards in member company and internal technical publications, and implementation of standards in member company products. [CBEMA, November 1993]

CEN—European Committee for Standardization

Description

CEN (European Committee for Standardization), CENELEC (European Committee for Electrotechnical Standardization), and ETSI (European Telecommunications Standards Institute) are responsible for standardization activity in Europe. These three groups formed the Information Technology Steering Committee (ITSTC) to coordinate and monitor the preparation of European information technology standards, including telecommunications standards. [CEN, November 1993]

Mission

To prepare European Standards in non-electrical fields. [Breitenburg, 1990] and to promote the Open Systems Interconnection Basic Reference Model (ISO 7498, 1984) in Europe, a standard which permits the interconnection of both similar and disparate computer systems. [CEN, November 1993]

Membership

Membership consists of 19 national standards organizations of countries belonging to the EC and the European Free Trade Association. [CEN, November 1993]

AENOR; AFNOR; BSI; DIN; DS; ELOT; IBN; SIS; STRI; IPQ; ITM; NNI; NSAI; NSF; ON; SFS; SNV; UNI

Conformance Testing

CEN members have designed a framework for certification of IT hardware and software (ECITC). CEN also has a framework for European certifications known as CENCER. CENCER may issue a European mark of conformity to standards, or the mutual recognition of test results and inspections. [CEN, November 1993]

Address

CEN
Rue de Stassart, 36
B-1050 Bruxelles
Belgium
+32 2 5196811

CENELEC—Comité European de Normalisation Electrotechnique

Description

The European committee for standardizing open electrotechnical systems. CENELEC is the regional equivalent of the International Electrotechnical Commission. [Seybold, October 1992]

CCITT—International Telegraph and Telephone Consultative Committee

As of March 1, 1993, CCITT no longer exists; it has been converted into the new "Telecommunication Standardization Sector" (abbreviated "ITU-T"). [ITU, September 1993]

CEPT—Conférence Européenne des Administrations des Postes et des Télecommunications

Description

The conference on administering European postal and telecommunications standards. CEPT issued the Net2 standard. [Unisys, 1989]

Component Integration Laboratories

Description

Seven software publishers have formed a consortium [...] to produce a standard that will rival Microsoft Corp's Object Linking and Embedding (OLE). [Vizard, September 1993]

Membership

The consortium members are Xerox Corp, IBM, Novell Inc, WordPerfect Corp, Oracle Corp, Apple and Taligent. [Vizard, September 1993]

Direction

The consortium is expected to simplify matters for management information systems personnel because only two operating systems standards will dominate: OLE and Component Integration Laboratories' standard. Also, the existence of two standards may motivate the companies involved to keep their systems open. The consortium expects to create a developer's kit that will combine Apple's Bento object storage format, IBM's System Object Model and the OpenDOC program architecture.

COS—Corporation for Open Systems International

Description

Formed in 1986, COS is the only international not-for-profit consortium dedicated to the successful introduction of interoperable open systems networking products and services for the computer communications and telecommunications industries. COS has initiatives for many interrelated technologies including ISDN, TCP/IP, Open Systems transition and deployment strategies, electronic messaging, multi-protocol routers, and video teleconferencing. [COS, 1994]

Mission

Accelerate the implementation, deployment, and usage of standards-based, interoperable, open systems networking products and services. [COS, 1994]

Membership

Currently 70+ organizations participating (computer and telecommunications equipment vendors, service providers, systems integrators, and government and commercial users of information technology). [COS, 1994]

Members include:

Ameritech Services; AT&T Company; Bell Atlantic Corporation; Bell Communications Research, Inc.; Booz-Allen & Hamilton; Central & Southwest Services, Inc.; Computer Sciences Corporation; Defense Information Systems Agency; Digital Equipment Corporation; DSET; EPRI; Hewlett-Packard Company; HP/Idacom Electronics Ltd.; Life Cycle Technology Corporation; Motorola, Inc.; National Communications System; NIST; Northern Telecom Inc.; NYNEX Corporation; Pacific Gas & Electric Company; Southern Company Services, Inc.; Southwestern Bell Telephone Company; 3Com Corporation; Unisys Corporation; U.S. General Services Administration.

Conformance Testing

COS is involved in the setting of conformance testing standards, and has a product certification program of its own called COS MARK. COS MARK promotes high quality conformance and interoperability testing for OSI/ISDN products and services, and acts as an indicator of product interoperability to prospective product purchasers.

COS selects and implements test suite specifications profiles that are based on OSI/network/ISDN related standards. COS also works with open systems users to promote necessary requirements for enterprise, multivendor interoperability.

Address

Corporation for Open Systems International
8260 Willow Oaks Corporate Drive, Suite 700
Fairfax, VA 22031
(703) 205-2765; Fax: (703) 846-8590

COSE—Common Open Software Environment

Description

COSE is a catalyst to make current processes work faster. It is not a standards organization, or an organization of any kind. Instead, it is a process. COSE accelerates standardization through existing open system processes in such initiatives as OSF, POSIX, UNIX International, and X/Open. [Datapro, October 1993]

Some consider COSE to largely be a response from UNIX vendors to the competitive threat from Microsoft NT, which can run on numerous hardware platforms and may soon be able to run on RISC based machines.

The COSE catalyst is introduced in two phases of open systems processes. First, before formal specification submissions to industry bodies, COSE working groups are assembled to develop a recommendation for a specification. Second, after the specification is formalized, in some cases, cooperative product development is done to accelerate an initial product implementation. [Datapro, October 1993]

The reorganized OSF (Spring, 1994) will become the focal point for the year-old COSE initiative—finally giving COSE a home.

Contact

UniForum
2901 Tasman Drive, Suite 205
Santa Clara, CA 950544-1100
(408) 986-8840

Open Software Foundation
11 Cambridge Center
Cambridge, MA 02142
(617) 621-8700

Miscellaneous

COSE will accelerate standards in many technology areas. Initially, COSE vendors will concentrate on the following technologies:

- Common Desktop Environment (CDE). The CDE is being submitted to X/Open for incorporation into the X/Open Portability Guide. Commercial implementations are planned for 1994.

- Networking. COSE has identified three leading heterogeneous distributed computing technologies that offer services and tools that support the creation, use, and maintenance of distributed applications: OSF DCE, SunSoft ONC+, and Novell NetWare.

- Graphics. COSE supporters plan to provide a consistent graphics application environment across platforms through common APIs and interoperability protocols.

- Multimedia. COSE supports an infrastructure called Distributed Media Services (DMS) for distributed multimedia.

- Object Technology. COSE primarily supports the Object Management Group (OMG) efforts.

- Systems Management. A COSE working group is concentrating on defining a systems management framework and associated tools for systems management. [Datapro, October 1993]

DMTF—Desktop Management Task Force

Description

The DMTF is an open industry group established in 1992 to create a standard for desktop management. [EDGE: Work-Group Computing Report, July 1993]

Mission

To establish an industry standard for desktop management. [DMTF, 1993]

Membership

Includes eight charter members—DEC, HP, IBM Corp., Intel Corp., Microsoft Corp., Novell Inc., SunConnect, and SynOptics Communications Inc.—and more than 300 participating members. [DMTF, 1993]

Contact

(503) 221-2945

Miscellaneous

The DMTF has shipped version 1.0 of its Desktop Management Interface (DMI).

The DMI facilitates the management of desktop computers—either as standalone systems or linked into local networks. It will benefit vendors of hardware and software products by providing a uniform interface through which all consoles or applications can manage any DMI-compliant product. This uniform interface will simplify component and application management and make it easier for vendors to develop interoperable products. [EDGE: Work-Group Computing Report, July 1993]

These products span five major groups: PC platforms, such as desktop systems and network servers; hardware and software components, such as operating systems, spreadsheets, databases, word processors, video cards, fax modems, and network adapters; management applications—networked and local; networked and standalone peripherals, such as printers, scanners, pointing devices, mass storage devices and CD ROM players; and management consoles based on industry standards. [DMTF, 1993]

To date, the DMTF's effort has focused on management of IBM compatible PCs. However, the architecture incorporated in the DMI is intentionally open for porting to other environments. [DMTF, 1993]

A developers' version of the DMI—for DOS, Windows, Windows/NT, and OS/2—was delivered at the DMTF Developers' Conference October 18, 1993. [DMTF, 1993]

DSIS—Distributed Support Information Standards Group

Description

The Distributed Support Information Standards (DSIS) Group is composed of leading computer industry companies who are jointly promoting the development of international standards for service and support information. [DSIS, 1994]

The standards being promoted by the DSIS Group will address the concerns of organizations responsible for service, support, and management of networked systems. [DSIS, 1994]

Membership

The current members include Bell Atlantic Business Systems Services, Inc., Hewlett-Packard Co., ICL PLC, Microsoft Corp., and Sun Microsystems Computer Corporation. Several other companies are contributing to the group's activities. [DSIS, 1994]

Contact

Raymond Edgerton; Chairman, DSIS Group
Bell Atlantic Business Systems, Inc.
50 E. Swedesford Rd.; PO Box 3004
Frazer, PA 19355-0704
(610) 296-6159; Fax: (610) 640-9277

Miscellaneous

The DSIS Group is working with other standards organizations, including the Internet Engineering Task Force and the Open Software Foundation. The requirements identified by the DSIS Group will be provided as input to these Organizations to avoid redundant or conflicting work. [Levine, August 1993]

ECMA—European Computer Manufacturers Association

Motto: Standardizing Information and Communication Systems. [ECMA, July 1994]

Description

ECMA, founded in 1961, is a non-commercial, non-profit organization headquartered in Geneva, Switzerland. It is organized around technical committees, which cover particular areas of work and maintain liaisons with other active institutes around the world. Endorsed ECMA standards are submitted to these institutes for publication as International and/or European IT standards. ECMA is exclusively dedicated to the cooperative development of standards applicable to information and communication systems. [ECMA, July 1994]

Mission

"To develop, in cooperation with the appropriate national, European, and international organizations as a scientific endeavor and in the general interest standards and technical reports in order to facilitate and standardize the use of information processing and telecommunication systems.

To encourage the correct use of standards by influencing the environment in which they are applied.

To promulgate various standards applicable in the functional design and use of information processing and telecommunication systems." [ECMA, July 1994]

Membership

Two classes of membership exist within ECMA: Ordinary Members are companies that develop, manufacture, and market data processing equipment, and Associate Members are companies that have an interest in specific subjects dealt with by one or more ECMA technical committees. Presently there are approximately 25 Ordinary Members and 15 Associate Members. [ECMA, July 1994]

Conformance Testing

ECMA does no conformance testing.

Address

ECMA
114 rue du Rhône
CH-1204 Geneva
Switzerland
41 22 735 36 34; Fax: 41 22 786 52 31
E-Mail: Helpdesk@ECMA.CH

Miscellaneous

ECMA functions much like a smaller version of ISO/IEC JTC 1. It is made up of approximately 12 technical committees and 8 task groups. Eighty standards produced by ECMA have been endorsed by ISO/IEC and thirty by ETSI. The ECMA Portable Common Tools Environment (PCTE) Standards have been accepted as ISO/IEC standards. [ECMA, July 1994]

EWOS—European Workshop for Open Systems

Description

EWOS is an informal association of seven organizations that was created in 1987 for the purpose of drawing up documents to be incorporated in the standardizing process at international or European levels. EWOS has "associated standards body" (ASB) status. [Breitenburg, 1990]

Mission

EWOS's objectives are to serve as a truly open European forum for the development of OSI profiles and definition of the corresponding conformance testing specifications. [Macpherson, 1990]

Membership

Members include representative European federations of technology suppliers and user organizations: Cooperation for Open Systems Interconnection Networking in Europe (COSINE), European Computer Manufacturers Association (ECMA), European MAP Users Group (EMUG), Open Systems Interconnection Technical and Office Protocols (OSITOP), Reseaux Associes pour la Recherche Europeene (RARE), and the Standards Promotion and Application Group (SPAG), in conjunction with the European standards institutions, CEN and CENELEC. [Breitenburg, 1990; Macpherson, 1990]

Direction

Proposed mandates include: study of a general framework for the elaboration of IT functional standards; X/Open portability guide; use of OSI in the library community; application of OSI-based solutions in the medical field; and remote access to databases. [Macpherson, 1990]

Conformance Testing

EWOS has adopted a General Policy for work on conformance testing specification standards. An expert group on conformance testing has been created to formulate proposals regarding the execution of the mandate and further work on the subject. [Macpherson, 1990]

Address

EWOS
Mr. Jacques Rega, Director
Second Floor; 13, rue Brederode
B-1000 Brussels
Belgium
32 2 511 7455; Fax: 32-2-511-8723

Miscellaneous

EWOS development results are put into formal proposals called EWOS Documents (EDs) which serve as direct proposals to the standards bodies for adoption as European Prestandards (ENVs) or Standards (ENs). Other useful information which is not intended for standardization is put into EWOS Technical Guides (ETGs). ETGs aim at facilitating the correct selection, use, implementation, and coherent further development of additional standards or pre-standards.

Technical activities are managed by the Technical Assembly whose members include approximately 120 experts from 79 European and U.S. companies. These members are users, suppliers, standard institutes, government agencies and academics. [Macpherson, 1990]

EWOS has established the Open System Environment Implementors Workshop (OIW) as the open forum for systems vendors and integrators to discuss various paths to interoperability. [Heffernan, 1992]

Fibre Channel Association

Description

The Fibre Channel Association is a group of Fibre Channel service providers, equipment vendors, research and engineering organizations that support the foregoing, users, and other interested parties promoting the acceptance and implementation of Fibre Channel technology and applications, based on national and international standards. The intent of this Association is to support the rapid advancement of an efficient and compatible technology base that promotes a competitive Fibre Channel marketplace. [Fibre Channel Association, 1993]

Mission

The worldwide promotion of Fibre Channel as the technology of choice for a simple migration to and deployment of the "Gigabit Highway." [Fibre Channel Association, 1993]

Membership

Principle members include: AMCC, AT&T, Cypress Semiconductor, Emulex Corp., ESL Inc., Fujikura Technology America, Corp., Hewlett Packard, IBM, Interphase, Corp., Methode Electronics, Siemens Gibre Optic Components, StorageTek, Sum Microsystems, Tandem Computers, TriQuint Semiconductor, and Unisys. [Fibre Channel Association, 1993]

Address

Fibre Channel Association
12407 MoPac Expressway
North 100-357; PO Box 9700
Austin, Texas 78766-9700; (800) 272-4618

IDAPI—Independent Database Application Programming Interface Group

Description

This group is attempting to establish IDAPI as a data access standard in competition with Microsoft Corp. sponsored Open Database Connectivity (ODBC) standard. IDAPI resides between an application and its data to provide access to both SQL and non-relational navigational databases. [Moser, 1993]

Membership

Original members: Borland International Inc., IBM, Novell Inc., and WordPerfect Corp. Other members include: Cincom Systems Inc., Fulcrum Technologies, Ingres Corp., Informix Corp., Sybase Inc., and Unix System Laboratories Inc. [Moser, 1993]

IEC—International Electrotechnical Commission

Description

IEC was set up to facilitate the coordination and unification of national electrotechnical standards. Founded in 1904, the IEC also publishes international standards. [IEC, November 1993]

Mission

"The object of the Commission is to promote international cooperation on all questions of standardization and related matters, such as the verification of conformity to standards in the fields of electricity, electronics, and related technologies, and thus to promote international understanding. This object is achieved by issuing publications, including international standards." [IEC, November 1993]

Membership

IEC members are national committees from approximately 48 participating countries (only one committee is allowed per country). National committees are expected to be as representative as possible of all electrical interests in their representative countries: manufacturers, users, governmental authorities, and teaching and professional bodies. [IEC, November 1993]

Conformance Testing

- IECEE: IEC System for Conformity Testing to Standards for Safety of Electrical Equipment

- IECQ: IEC Quality Assessment System for Electronic Components [IEC, November 1993]

Address

ANSI, U.S. National Committee of the IEC
11 West 42nd Street
New York, NY 10036
(212) 642-4936; Fax: (212) 398-0023

International Electrotechnical Commission

3, rue de Varembe
P.O. Box 131
CH-1211 Geneve 20
Switzerland
41 22 734 01 50; Fax: 41 22 733 38 43

Miscellaneous

IEC organization includes a Council, Committee of Action, Technical Committees, Central Office and Advisory Committees. The Council, on which all national committees are represented, administers the operations of the IEC. The Committee of Action performs tasks delegated by the Council, and takes all necessary action to ensure operation of IEC technical work. The Technical Committees are set up and approved by the Council on the recommendation of the Committee of Action. [IEC, November 1993]

IEEE—Institute of Electrical and Electronic Engineers

Description

Founded in 1963, it has over 320,000 members and is the world's largest technical professional organization with members in 150 countries. The institute is a leading authority in areas ranging from computers, aerospace and telecommunications to electric power, consumer electronics and biomedical technology. [IEEE, December 1993]

Mission

To enhance the quality of life for all people through the constructive application of the theory and practice of electrical engineering and computer science. [IEEE, December 1993]

Membership

IEEE membership includes engineers, scientists and students in electronics and allied fields. The Computer Society of the IEEE has over 90,000 members. [IEEE, December 1993]

Conformance Testing

No information indicates that IEEE does conformance testing.

Address

IEEE
445 Hoes Lane, PO Box 1331
Piscataway, NJ 08855-1331 USA
(908) 562-3800

Miscellaneous

IEEE is responsible for publishing over 20 percent of the world's available literature on electrotechnology and is recognized as a world leader in the development and dissemination of industry standards. IEEE's product line consists of more than 600 active standards with approximately 80 new standards published annually. [IEEE, December 1993] IEEE processes for developing standards include:

* All standards activities fall under the direction of the Standards Board. All standards are developed by various technical committees of IEEE societies

* The IEEE Standards Manual and IEEE Standards Style Manual list procedures for new standards projects and submittal of completed standards for approval

* Standards Coordinating Committees (SCCs) have been established by the Standards Board

* Before long-term work on a standard begins, New Standard Project Authorization Requests must be submitted to the Standards Board for approval

* All standards completed by a committee must be submitted to the Standards Board with the results of a vote by all committee members and a summary of the makeup of the committee. The latter is done to ensure that the work was done by a balanced representation of the industry involved

* Published standards are submitted to ANSI for consideration as national standards

- The IEEE Communications Society (COMSOC) has a Standards Liaison and Coordinating Committee, which brings together all COMSOC standards activities to ensure compliance with the IEEE Standards Manual. The committee also checks to avoid duplication of effort by various COMSOC technical committees [IEEE, December 1993]

ISO—International Organization for Standardization

Description

A worldwide federation of national standards bodies, founded in 1947, with a Central Secretariat in Geneva. A non-governmental organization, it develops international standards for voluntary implementation, covering virtually all technical fields except electrical and electrotechnical standardization, which is dealt with by the IEC (International Electrotechnical Commission). With regard to information processing standards, ISO and IEC in 1987 set up JTC 1, Joint Technical Committee, Information Technology. [ISO, November 1993]

Mission

Promotes standardization and related activities throughout the world to facilitate the international exchange of goods and services, and to develop cooperation in the spheres of intellectual, scientific, technological, and economic activity. [ISO, November 1993]

Membership

ISO is made up of 96 national standards bodies, one from each country. These standards bodies are the most representative of standardization in their respective countries. More than 70% are governmental institutions or organizations incorporated by public law. The remainder have close links with the public administration in their own countries. The membership total includes 20 correspondent members, which is normally an organization from a developing country which does not yet have its own national standards body, and one subscriber member which is an organization from a small country with very limited financial resources. [ISO, November 1993]

Conformance Testing

ISO itself does not carry out any testing, inspection, auditing, assessment, certification, or registration of materials, products, systems, or services. However, ISO/CASCO (ISO Council Committee on conformity assessment) develops guides on various aspects of conformity assessment and related activities. [ISO, November 1993]

ISO/CASCO's terms of reference are to:

- Study means of assessing the conformity of products, processes, services, and quality systems to appropriate standards or other technical specifications

- Prepare international guides relating to the testing, inspection, and certification of products, processes, and services, and to the assessment of quality systems, testing laboratories, inspection bodies, certification bodies, and their operation and acceptance

- Promote mutual recognition and acceptance of national and regional conformity assessment systems, and the appropriate use of international standards for testing, inspection, certification, assessment, and related purposes. [ISO, November 1993]

Address

American National Standards Institute
11 West 42nd Street
New York, NY 10036
(212) 642-4900

ISO
1 rue de Varembo
Case Postale 56
CH-1211 Geneva 20
Switzerland
41 22 734 1240

Miscellaneous

ISO's technical work is carried out by 2,678 technical bodies comprising 182 technical committees, 633 subcommittees, 1,838 working groups, and 25 ad hoc study groups. The Organization had published approximately 9,000 international standards by the end of 1993. [ISO, November 1993]

The development of international standards begins in the technical committees, where working drafts are refined into committee drafts. These are then circulated for study within the technical committee concerned. When an agreement based on consensus is reached, the text is registered by the Central Secretariat as a draft international standard (DIS) and circulated to all ISO member bodies for voting. When a DIS is approved by 75% of all members voting, it is accepted and published by ISO as an international standard. ISO standards are reviewed at intervals of not more than five years.

In addition to international standards, ISO publishes technical reports, handbooks, guides, study documents, and reports on progress of its work within the technical committees, as well as various publications such as ISO Bulletin, on the work of ISO and its members, and ISO 9000 News, on the ISO 9000 quality management and quality assurance standards.

ISO collaborates very closely with its partner, IEO (International Electrotechnical Commission), particularly in the field of information technology, through joint groups such as JTC 1 (see entry) and ABTT (Advisory Board on Technological Trends). [ISO, November 1993]

IAB—Internet Activities Board

Description

IAB is an informal group which focuses on producing standard specifications revolving around the Internet protocol suite, the SNMP, the structure of management information (SMI), and the management information base (MIB) used in managing Internets based on transmission control protocol internet protocol (TCP/IP). [Hickerson, 1992]

IAB oversees the Internet Society, who has primary responsibility for the development and review of potential Internet Standards. [The OSINetter Newsletter, 1993]

Membership

The IAB is composed of senior researchers who, for the most part, are the designers and original implementors of the Internet suite.

Direction

IAB is currently working on standardizing tasks related to print, software, user, and user group management. [Hickerson, 1992]

IAB recently proposed a change to the Internet protocol which involved switching over to Connectionless Network Protocol (CLNP) from the seven-layer OSI standard. Due to heated reactions against this proposal, the IAB decided to back off on the CLNP approach. However, Internet has been growing rapidly and some changes will be necessary. Any change made to the Internet will affect TCP/IP basic protocols. [Baker, 1992]

The Internet Society (ISOC) has transferred the authority to approve final standards to the Internet Engineering Steering Group (IESG) from the IAB. [Gerishanker, 1992]

Miscellaneous

The Internet suite of protocols was sponsored by the U.S. DoD and grew out of early research into survivable multimedia packet-networking sponsored by the Defense Advanced Research Projects Agency (DARPA). At the time, there was only one network, called the ARPANET, which connected a few dozen computer systems around the country. With the advent of different networking technologies, such as Ethernet (trademark of Xerox Corp.), Packet Radio, and Satellite, a method was needed for reliable transmission of information over media that do not guarantee reliable, error free delivery of information. Thus, the Internet suite of protocols was born. [Rose, 1990]

IAB has become part of the Internet Society (ISOC), where the IAB Board of Trustees has agreed to work toward establishing a cooperative relationship with the International Telecommunications Union (ITU). It is hoped by the ISOC that the de facto Internet standards may gain formal acceptance in the international community. [Press, 1992]

ITU—International Telecommunication Union

Description

The ITU became a specialized agency of the United Nations in 1947, and is headquartered in Geneva. Its responsibilities include the regulation and planning of worldwide telecommunication, the establishment of operating standards for equipment and systems, the coordination and dissemination of information required for the planning and operation of telecommunication services, and the promotion of and contribution to the development of telecommunication and related services. [ITU, September 1993]

Mission

The three main functions carried out globally by ITU:

- standardization of telecommunications

- regulation of telecommunications (mainly for radio communications)

- development of telecommunications [ITU, September 1993]

Membership

ITU membership is composed of national governments represented by their post and telecommunication administrators. [ITU, September 1993]

Certification Testing

No information indicates that ITU does conformance testing.

Address

Place des Nations
CH-1211 Geneve 20
Switzerland
41 22 730 5111

Miscellaneous

ITU meets at a Plenipotentiary Conference at intervals of not less than five years. The conference constitutes the supreme authority of the ITU and lays down general policy. ITU members also hold World Administrative Conferences to consider specific telecommunication matters, and Regional Administrative Conferences to reach agreement on regional issues.

The world is divided into three ITU regions to best meet the requirements of different countries. The regions are: Europe and Africa, the Americas, and Asia and Oceania.

ITU has undergone some major changes as summarized:

- As of 1 March 1993, CCITT does not exist anymore; it has been converted into the new "Telecommunication Standardization Sector" (abbreviated "ITU-T"). The former Plan Committees have been abolished, the GAs activities have been transferred to the Development Sector, and the Telecommunication Standardization Sector how deals exclusively with the standardization of telecommunications. [ITU]

- Likewise has the former "CCITT Secretariat" been converted into the "Telecommunication Standardization Bureau" (TSB). [ITU]

- Standardization of radio communications (carried out in the former CCIR, now the "Radio communication Sector"), is being transferred progressively to the Telecommunication Standardization Sector. [ITU, September 1993]

JSA—Japanese Standards Association

Description

The Japanese Standards Association (JSA) is a private nonprofit organization that plays a leading role in the promotion of industrial standardization and quality management. Established in 1945, JSA has published over 400 specifications relating to standardization, quality management, quality engineering and technology. [88Open Consortium, 1991]

Mission

JSA's objective is to generate industrial standardization and quality control for all industry. JSA pursues six activities:

- Publication/distribution of the (JIS), the English edition of JIS, monthly magazines, related books, standards materials, and other publications.

- Generation of standardization and quality control.

- Education and consultation on standardization and quality control.

- Study and research of standardization and various engineering techniques.

- Cooperation in international standardization activities. [Macpherson, 1990]

Membership

JSA has more than 10,000 corporate members. [88Open Consortium, 1991]

Conformance Testing

No information indicates that JSA does conformance testing.

Address

Japanese Standards Association
1-24, Akasaka 4-chome
Minato-ku, Tokyo 107
Japan
+03-3583-8001

Miscellaneous

Japanese Industrial Standards are national voluntary standards for industrial and mineral products. Compliant products can be marked JIS certified. [88Open Consortium, 1991]

JSA set up three computer technology standardization committees in July, 1993. They are the "Object-Oriented Standardization Survey/Research Committee," the "Software Development Support Tool Survey/Research Committee," and the "Security Technology Standardization Review Committee."

JTC 1—Joint Technical Committee—Information Technology

Description

JTC 1 was formed as a joint ISO-IEC committee which integrated existing ISO and IEC subcommittees dealing with generic information technology work. [Macpherson, 1990]

Mission

Standardization in the field of information technology. [Macpherson, 1990]

Membership

Members are national bodies, or countries eligible for membership through their existing membership as member bodies of ISO or national committees of IEC. [Macpherson, 1990]

Direction

JTC1 manages the development of generic information technology standards, coordinates ISO and IEC technical committees dealing with other aspects of information technology, maintains appropriate liaisons with other internal standards bodies and user groups, and undertakes long-term planning. JCT 1 also develops common ISO-IEC procedures for standardization of information technology based on proposals of the ISO-IEC harmonic working group. [Macpherson, 1990]

Conformance Testing

No information indicates that JTC 1 does conformance testing.

Address

Secretariat ISO/IEC JTC 1
American National Standards Institute
1430 Broadway
New York, New York 10018
(212) 642-4900

Miscellaneous

JTC 1 publishes international standards under ISO and IEC logos. JTC 1 establishes subcommittees which study assigned parts of the work program. The subcommittees are structured into four technical groups:

• Application Elements

• Equipment and Media

• Systems support

• Systems

Working Groups (WGs) are established if there are one or more approved projects for a JCT 1 subcommittee, or to undertake specific tasks.

The Information Technology Task Force (ITTF) provides support for JTC 1 activities, however, it is not a part of JCT 1 structure. ITTF responsibilities include:

- The day-to-day planning and coordination of JTC 1's technical work relative to IEC and ISO.

- The supervision of ISO and IEC constitutions and rules of procedure. [Macpherson, 1990]

Kaleida Alliance

Description

The Kaleida Alliance is an on-going, open organization for manufacturers who agree to support, promote and license ScriptX. In the long run, all OEM licensees of ScriptX will participate in the alliance. [EDGE: Work-Group Computing Report, May 1993]

Membership

Charter members are Apple Computer Inc., IBM, Hitachi Ltd., Toshiba Corp., Mitsubishi Electric Corp., and Creative Technology Ltd. [EDGE, May 1993]

Message Handling Service (MHS) Alliance

Description

The goal of the MHS Alliance is to assure interoperability of products intending to use Novell's Message Handling Service.

Membership

Novell and 19 other vendors including Da Vinci Systems Corp., Futurus Corp., Reach Software Corp., and Powercore Inc. [Brandel, 1993]

MOSES—Massive Open System Environment Standard

Description

[...] MOSES organization is trying to address the paucity of system management tools for open operating environments. [Desmond, 1993]

Membership

Millipore Corp, Northern Telecom, Sequent Computer, Oracle Corp, Burlington Coat Factory, and US West's NewVector Group. [Desmond, 1993]

Address

Mike Prince; MIS Director
Burlington Coat Factory
Lebanon, NH
(603) 643-2800

Miscellaneous

Among the five major issues that MOSES hopes to resolve are data backup and recovery, task scheduling, change management and alarming. The tasks are divided amongst group members and an Unix Data Center Special Interest Group has been organized for member communication and to enable other interested parties to join the discussion. [Desmond, 1993]

Multiuser DOS Federation (MDOS)

Description

Formed by a consortium of hardware and software vendors to help users easily integrate a variety of multiuser DOS products. [Sherer, 1992]

MDOS released a white paper that outlines a standard to help developers write software that works with multi-user DOS environments and hardware from diverse vendors. One section of the white paper covers the new Serial Card/Software Environment Interface Specifications. This describes three potential standards: how multiuser I/O boards interface with multiuser operating systems, how device drivers obtain services from the multi-user environment and the way the multiuser environment obtains services from the add-on I/O boards. [Sherer, 1992]

NIST—National Institute of Standards and Technology

Description

The National Institute of Standards and Technology was established by the United States Congress and is a principal agency of the Commerce Department's Technology Administration. NIST's main goals include: aiding U.S. industry through research and services contributing to the public health and safety, and supporting the U.S. scientific and engineering research communities. [NIST, November 1993]

Mission

To assist industry in the development of technology needed to improve product quality, to modernize manufacturing processes, to ensure product reliability and to facilitate rapid commercialization of products based on new scientific discoveries. [NIST, November 1993]

Conformance Testing

NIST coordinates the development of technical and data standards and conformance tests for the Continuous Acquisition and Life-Cycle Support (CALS) standardization effort. Originally started in the Department of Defense (DoD), CALS is a government and Industry strategy to transition from paper-intensive, non-integrated weapon design, manufacturing and support processes to a highly automated and integrated mode of operation. [88Open Consortium, 1991] Most recently, NIST established an Enterprise Integration Office to facilitate promoting CALS solutions to the commercial sector. [NIST, November 1993]

Address

NIST
Gaithersburg, MD 20899

Miscellaneous

The Computer Systems Laboratory (CSL) is one of NIST's major science and research components. CSL's programs seek to overcome barriers to the efficient use of computer systems, to the cost-effective exchange of information and to the protection of valuable information resources in computer systems. Its technical work is carried out in five divisions: Information Systems Engineering Division, Systems and Software Technology Division, Computer Security Division, Systems and Network Architecture Division, and Advanced Systems Division. [NIST, November 1993]

Network Printing Alliance

Description

The alliance was formed to promote a new spec for communications between LAN-based distributed printers and PCs. Called the Network Printing Alliance Protocol, the spec establishes a format for printers to send messages to the host PC or print server that controls network printing. NPAP also provides a base set of printer-to-host specification commands to exchange status, control and configuration information, regardless of the page description language, printer technology and communications interface. [LAN Computing, 1993]

Membership

More than 50 member companies. [LAN Computing, 1993]

NMF—Network Management Forum

Description

NMF was formed in the late 1980s with the goal of promoting movement in a common direction toward interoperability standards for network management. [NMF, November 1993]

Mission

MF's scope is to promote worldwide acceptance and implementation of a common approach to the management of networks and systems from the perspective of the services they deliver by devising specifications and working with other industry forums. [NMF, November 1993]

Membership

There are four classes of membership: Board, Associate, Corporate, and Affiliate. Affiliate members include users, universities, and nonprofit organizations. Membership consists of almost 120 worldwide telecommunications and computer suppliers and service providers. [NMF, November 1993]

Direction

NMF's scope has expanded to encompass all of the issues in providing the marketplace with service management solutions for multivendor, multidomain, multitechnology, multiapplication network and systems. [NMF, November 1993]

Conformance Testing

NMF works with other organizations as part of the OmniPoint partnership to define conformance and testing requirements. [NMF, November 1993]

Address

Network Management Forum
1201 MiKemble Avenue
Morristown, NJ 07960
(201) 425-1900

Miscellaneous

NMF developed a program called OMNIPoint (Open Management Interoperability Point) in conjunction with 15 other consortia and groups from around the world. OMNIPoint is a comprehensive framework for managing networks and systems from the perspective of the services they deliver to end customers. It is a combination of existing and emerging management standards and technology designed to improve the processes for managing telecommunications and information systems.

By providing a strategy, technical specifications and procurement and development guidance, OMNIPoint makes it possible for managers to improve service quality, reduce costs, and fulfill service-level agreements with their end customers. The goal of OMNIPoint is to make advanced, integrated, and automated management happen across the industry, as fast as possible, at the least cost, and at the least risk. OMNIPoint 1 was released in August of 1992. Additional specifications are due out in early 1994. [NMF, November 1993]

OIW—Open Systems Environment Implementers Workshop

Description

A workshop sponsored by NIST.

Mission

OIW recently expanded its charter to address all issues related to Open Systems instead of just Open Systems Interconnect Networking (OSI). [UI, 1992] The scope of OIW meetings will now address operating systems, databases, graphics, user interfaces, data interchange and software. [Houser, 1991]

Conformance Testing

No information indicates that OIW does conformance testing.

Miscellaneous

The proposal to expand the OIW charter was the idea of the Senior Executives for Open Systems, a group of information technology executives from a number of leading American companies. Their motivation was to speed the development of products based on vendor-neutral standards. [Houser, 1991]

OIW has adopted the common programming interface for communications (CPI-C) technology as its recommended application programming interface (API) for transaction processing. The vote to adopt the technology, developed by IBM and embraced by the X/Open consortium, marks the first time the OIW has agreed to support a specification not based on an international standard or standards development project. [Heffernan, December 1992]

OMG—Object Management Group

Description

An international organization with members representing vendors, software developers, systems integrators and end users. OMG was founded in 1989 and has become the industry focal point for standardization of distributed systems.

OMG is a nonprofit corporation dedicated to maximizing the portability, reusability and interoperability of computer software. The members are committed to creating a framework and supporting specifications for commercially available object-oriented environments. The group has adopted the Object Request Broker (ORB), a standard for sending messages across client/server networks for application integration and development. [OMG, November 1993]

Mission

OMG was founded with the specific aim of specifying a framework for software applications based on object-oriented methods that would cater to the interoperability of application over mixed networks of computer hardware and operating software. [OMG, November 1993]

Membership

Membership includes companies, universities, and groups that number over 439+. Some notable members are: [OMG, August 1994]

AT&T, Eastman Kodak, GE Advanced Concepts Center, MIT, Microsoft, Sun, IBM, HP, Digital, and Lotus.

Conformance Testing

Performs conformance testing with X/Open. [OMG, November 1993]

Address

OMG Inc.
Framingham Corporate Center
492 Old Connecticut Path
Framingham, Ma 01701
(508) 820-4300; Fax: (508) 820-4303
E-mail: OMG @ 0MG-ORG

Miscellaneous

OMG's Object Request Broker (ORB) provides the mechanism by which groups of objects may communicate with each other and be accessible throughout a network; it is the transport mechanism throughout a network. It receives requests from objects, directs them to the target objects whose services were requested, and passes responses to the objects that issued the requests. [OMG, November 1993]

OSF—Open Software Foundation

Description

The Open Software Foundation (OSF™) is an open systems technology delivery organization with the objective of enabling users of information technology to exploit that technology to fundamentally improve the way they do business. OSF supplies software to make information technology easier to learn and easier to use, while enabling various vendors equipment to work together, sharing applications and information across distributed, open computing environments. OSF has created a coalition of vendors and users working together to provide the best available open system technologies.

The Open Software Foundation (OSF™) is a not-for-profit R&D organization. OSF was founded in 1988 by major computer vendors to help accelerate the adoption of open systems. Today OSF is an international coalition of 400 organizations—vendors and users—who work together to identify, acquire, enhance, and implement open systems technologies. Headquartered in Cambridge, MA, OSF has more than 200 employees worldwide. [OSF, August 1994]

OSF's hardware-independent software offerings are the OSF/Motif® graphical user interface and the OSF/1® operating system, the OSF Distributed Computing Environment (DCE), and the OSF Distributed Management Environment. [OSF, December 1993]

Mission

OSF's mission is to be the leading supplier of a complete, innovative, and equitable open systems environment to the worldwide computer industry.

OSF adheres to seven guiding principles:

- Offerings based on relevant industry standards

- Open process to actively solicit input and technology

- Timely, vendor-neutral decision process

- Early and equal access to specifications and software

- Hardware-independent implementations

- Reasonable, stable licensing terms

- Technical innovation through universities and research [OSF, December 1993]

Membership

OSF has over 400 members, with membership open to any organization. Members include systems manufacturers, hardware system vendors, independent software vendors, semiconductor manufacturers, service companies, industry consortia, educational institutions, public and quasi-public entities, and consulting and research firms. Some noted members include:

Barclay's Bank, PLC; Cray Research; Daimler-Benz, AG; Data General Corporation; Digital Equipment Corporation; EDS; Groupe Bull; Hewlett-Packard; Hitachi, Ltd.; IBM; Intel; Motorola; NASA; Nippon Telegraph and Telephone; Sony Corporation; Stanford University; Sun Microsystems; TransArc; World Bank; Xerox Corporation. [OSF, August 1994]

Conformance Testing

Through the OSF Certification and Trademarking Program, licensees of OSF technologies may obtain the right to use the "OSF Certified" seal and the OSF technology trademark to promote products that conform to OSF specifications. [OSF, August 1994]

Address

Open Software Foundation
11 Cambridge Center
Cambridge, MA 02142
(617) 621-8700

Miscellaneous

OSF provides an open forum in which people in the computer industry—consumers as well as providers—meet to discuss and debate open systems issues. Through member meetings and special-interest groups, members identify technical and business issues for OSF to consider. For example, members help shape the evolution of OSF technologies and relate their experiences with those offerings in an effort to promote the acceptance of open systems in various industries.

On March 23, 1994, OSF announced a progressive new business and operating model which includes new technology processes and provides increased opportunities for both end user and vendor participation. Major system vendors have joined together in endorsing the new organizational structure and business model as the focal point for promoting and accelerating the delivery of open systems enabling technologies.

In the newly-defined organization, emphasis shifts to a more project-oriented operating model. Technology projects will be separately funded and individually managed multi-company development initiatives. This will enable more customer-specific technology issues and requirements on a much more timely basis.

The new model's development process introduces the Pre-Structured Technology, or PST, process. The PST process is the successor to what has been widely known as the "cose" process, taking the best elements of that process and formalizing them within the OSF infrastructure. Moving the "cose" process into an organizational framework is a crucial step forward in uniting the industry around a focal point for open systems.

In addition to a source code implementation, each technology project will produce a specification which will be made freely and publicly available. The specification, along with test suites, will be submitted to X/Open, and other relevant industry standards bodies, as appropriate. [OSF, August 1994]

OSINET

Description

OSINET was established in 1984 to foster development, promotion, and deployment of OSI through activities related to interoperability testing. [Macpherson, 1990] In 1991, OSINET became a corporation and its day-to-day operations are handled by the Corporation for Open Systems under a management services contract. [OSINET, November 1993]

Mission

Its mission is to foster the development and use of OSI products through promotion of OSI as a means of interconnecting various computer systems, by providing interoperability tests for OSI protocols, by establishing a network for R&D purposes, and by maintaining an on-line register of the interoperability test results. [OSINET, November 1993]

Membership

Membership base consists of approximately 25 organizations—OSI product suppliers, users and government agencies.

Senior members include: Apple, AT&T, Bull, Control Data Systems, DEC, Hewlett-Packard, IBM, Northern Telecom, and Unisys.

Regular members include: Allied-Signal, Amdahl, Cray Research, MITRE, NCS, NIST, Proginet, Retrix, Soft-Switch, Tandem, Wang, and Wollongong. [OSINET, November 1993]

Direction

The OSIone Test and Registration (T&R) Service is the most densely populated OSI register today. With the additional test suite development in 1993 for Virtual Terminal, Directory Services and Network Management, and the use of the T&R Service in other regions, OSINET expects the Service to grow accordingly. Broader customer usage should stimulate more entries, and the Service should grow rapidly. [OSINET, November 1993]

Conformance Testing

OSINET is engaged in three different areas of activity:

- Research and development of test suits and the conduct of OSI interoperability testing

- Demonstration and promotion of the OSI technology

- Testing and registration of announced OSI products [OSINET, November 1993]

Address

OSINET
8260 Willow Oaks Corporate Drive, Suite 700
Fairfax, VA 22031
(703) 205-2797; Fax: (703) 846-8590

Miscellaneous

OSINET has three main organizational components:

- OSINET network: comprised of subnetworks, intermediate systems and end systems

- OSINET Steering Committee: establishes and manages OSINET, and determines and approves all projects

- OSINET Technical Committee: carries out all technical program work [OSINET, November 1993]

OURS—Open User Recommended Systems

Description

OURS formed in September 1991, is an end-user oriented group formed to do task-force investigations into interoperability, specifically in the areas of software licensing, security, multivendor education, and information exchange. [McMullen, 1993]

Mission

Promote interoperability of vendor products so that they may be easily integrated, managed, and maintained. [LaCroix, 1992]

Direction

OURS has formed several task forces to study crucial issues in today's information systems (IS) departments.

- Software licensing: IS managers are now realizing that inconsistent licensing arrangements are expensive and create confusion. OURS is lobbying to clarify pricing policies with software vendors

- Multivendor education and training: OURS is developing training guidelines and listing the types of training and certification available in LAN computing

- Information security: OURS is discussing standards that will allow security measures to reside across multiple systems

- Inter-vendor product specifications: OURS notes that vendors need to provide better information about how and which products work with each other

Membership

Included in the 17 charter members who represent over 150,000 users on enterprise-wide works are: [LaCroix, 1992; Ambrosio, 1991]

Avon Products, Inc.; Pacific Gas & Electric Co.; Shell International Petroleum; Sara Lee Corp.; The American Stock Exchange; The Center for Disease Control; Lufthansa German Airlines.

Conformance Testing

No information indicates that OURS does conformance testing.

Personal Computer Memory Cards Interface Association (PCMCIA)

Description

PCMCIA is trying to establish a standard for the small, dense memory cards needed for notebook computers and other small computers. The PCMCIA is an association of 250 vendors aimed at promoting the interchange of tightly packed integrated circuit cards in systems. The first standard was PC Card, which sets a standard for compressing expansion memory into an object slightly larger than a credit card. [Devoney, December 1992]

Point-to-Point Protocol Consortium

Description

PPPC promotes cooperation among networking product vendors and provides testing of interoperability under PPP.

- Providing implementation information so PPP can reach full standard status

- Contribute to the specification and implementations of open networking protocols

- Improve responsiveness to customer needs by having vendors cooperate to resolve inter-vendor problems [LAN Computing, 1992]

Membership

Comprised of both hardware and software vendors. [LAN Computing, 1992]

Portable Computing & Communication Association (PCCA)

Description

The PCCA is a non-profit organization formed to provide a forum for all companies and individuals interested in mobile computing and communications. [PCCA, 1994]

Mission

The purpose of the PCCA is to enable, develop, and promote the adoption of software and hardware standards for interoperable mobile computing and communications. [PCCA, 1994]

Membership

Advanced Micro Devices; Andrew Seybold's Outlook; AP Research; ARDIS; B&K Precision; Beaver Computer Corporation; Bell South Mobile Data; Burr, Egan, Deleage & Company; Compaq Computer; DCA; Dell Computer Corporation; EON; Fourth Wave Technologies; Ericsson GE; Geotek Communications; Hewlett-Packard Company; IBM PC Company; Intel Corporation; ITT World Directories/ITT Publitec; Lap & Palmtop Expositions; Lotus Development Corporation; McCaw Cellular Communications; Megahertz Corporation; Melard Technologies, Inc.; Metricom, Inc.; Microsoft Corporation; Motorola UDS; Mte 1/NWN; NEC Technologies, Inc.; Nokia Corporation; Personal Resources Corporation; Philips Semiconductor; Photonics Corporation; Pinpoint Communications, Inc.; RAM Mobile Data; Regis McKenna, Inc.; Research In Motion; Rockwell International; RSA Data Security; Traveling Software; TV Answer, Inc.; U.S. Army, Communications—Electronics Command; Walker Richer & Quinn, Inc.; Wildsoft, Inc.

Address

The PCCA
PO Box 924
Brookdale, CA 95007-0924
(408) 338-0924; Fax: (408) 338-7806

POSC—Petrotechnical Open Software Corporation

Description and Mission

POSC, a not-for-profit, membership corporation, is dedicated to facilitating integrated computing technology for the exploration and production (E&P) segment of the international petroleum industry. [POSC, 1994]

Membership

Founding Sponsors:

BP Exploration Inc.; Chevron Corporation; Elf Aquitaine; Mobile Oil Corporation; Texaco Inc.

Member Companies

ADB/Intellitic; Agip (ENI Spa); Applied Terravision Systems Inc.; ARCO; Australian Geological Survey Organization; BRGM; British Department of Trade and Industry; British Geological Survey; Bureau of Land Management (U.S.); Cambridge Arctic Shelf Program (Cambridge Univ.); Central Geophysical Expedition (Russia); Department of Energy (U.S.); Digital Equipment Corporation; DRD Corporation; Dwight's Energydata, Inc.; Edinburgh Petroleum Services Ltd.; Everest Technologies, Inc.; Gas Research Institute; The Geologic Service of the Netherlands (R.G.D.); Geomath International; Geomatic a.s.; Geoscene—Oilfield Systems Ltd.; Halliburton; Hewlett Packard Company; IBM Corporation; Inforama SA (France); Ingenierie et Informatique Interactive Graphique (31 G); INGEOMINAS; Institut Francais du Petrole; Intera Information Technologies; Kappa Engineering SA; Kestrel Data Management, Inc.; Kvatro-Notis AS; Landmark Graphics Corporation; Lighthouse Point Software, Inc.; Merak Projects Ltd.; Minerals Management Service (U.S.); Nancy School of Geology; Norsk Hydro a.s.; Norwegian Petroleum Directorate; Odin Reservoir Software & Services AS; Oilware, Inc.;Open Software Foundation; Oracle Corporation; Oryx Energy Company; Petroleos de Venezuela S.A. (PDVSA); Petroleum Exploration Computer Consultants Ltd.; Petroleum Information (PI); The Petroleum Science and Technology Institute; Petrosys Pty. Ltd.; Petrosystems; Petrotechnical Data Systems BV; Phillips Petroleum

Company; Platte River Associates Inc.; Pohlman and Associates, Inc.; PPDM; Prism Technologies Limited; Repsol Exploracion, S.A.; Rockall Data Services; Saga Petroleum a.s.; Sattlegger GmbH; Saudi Arabian Oil Company; Schlumberger Well Services Company; Shell Oil Company; Simon Petroleum Technology—Tigress; SINTEF; Statoil; Sybase Inc.; Sysdrill Limited; Terrasciences, Inc.; Texas A&M University (Petr. Eng. Dept.); The Information Store Inc.; TNO Institute of Applied Geoscience; Total Exploration Production; UK Atomic Energy Authority; UniSQL, Inc.; Univ. of Houston (Inst. for Improved Oil Recv.); Western Atlas International, Inc.; X/Open Company Limited; ZEH Graphic Systems; Z&S Consultants Limited. [PCCA, 1994]

Address:

Bill Bartz, President and CEO
POSC
10777 Westheimer, Suite 275
Houston, TX 77042
(713) 784-1880; Fax: (713) 784-9219

Compliance

A snapshot of the Conformance Statement Template is currently under member review as a first step toward certification of vendors' applications.[PCCA, 1994]

PowerOpen Association

Description and Mission

The PowerOpen™ Association is an international corporation whose mission is to deploy a binary compatible application base for PowerOpen compliant platforms. [PowerOpen Association, 1994]

Membership

Apple, Bull, IBM, Motorola, and Thomson-CSF incorporated the PowerOpen Association in February, 1993, with a shared vision that the PowerOpen Environment would become a widely accepted, RISC based, open systems environment. Harris Computer Systems and Tadpole Technology joined as founding principal members taking an active role in the Association's ongoing activity and launch. PowerOpen is open to all and is continuing to actively recruit additional members. [PowerOpen Association, 1994]

Address

Pat Riemitis
PowerOpen Association, Inc.
10050 North Wolfe Road, SW2-255
Cupertino, CA 95014
(408) 366-0460; Fax: (408) 366-0463

Miscellaneous

The consortium will create Application Binary Interface (ABI)-compliant platforms for the chip. PowerOpen plans to recruit independent software vendors, market the chip and license test suites for ABI software. ABI will be based on a new version of the AIX operating system. [Gillen, 1993]

SGML—Standard Generalized Markup Language Open

Description

SGML Open is a non-profit, international consortium of providers of products and services, dedicated to accelerating the further adoption, application, and implementation of the Standard Generalized Markup Language, the international standard for open interchange of documents and structured information objects. [SGML, 1994]

Membership

SGML Open

Sponsor Members:

(As of June 10, 1994)

AIS/Berger Levrault; Active Systems, Inc.; Arbor Text, Inc.; ATLIS Consulting Group; Auto-Graphics, Inc.; Avalanche Development Company; Data Conversion Laboratory; Database Publishing Systems Ltd.; Datalogics; Electronic Book Technologies, Inc.; Exoterica Corporation; Frame Technology Corporation; Fukrum Technologies Inc.; Graphic Communications Association; Grif SA; Hal Software Systems; InContect Corporation; InfoAccess Incorporation; InfoDesign Corporation; Information Dimensions, Inc.; InterCAP Graphics Systems; Intergraph Corporation; Interleaf Inc. (a subsidiary of Interleaf Inc.); Logical Design Solutions, Inc.; OMI Logistics; Open Text Corporation; Oracle Corporation (a division of Frame Technology Corporation); Passage Systems Inc.; Recording for the Blind; SoftQuad Inc.; STEP (Sturtz Electronic Publishing Gmbh); Texcel; US Lynx; Westinghouse Electric Corporation; WordPerfect Corporation; XSoft.

Address

Mary Laplante
Executive Director
SGML Open
910 Beaver Grade Road #3008
Coraopolis, PA 15108
(412) 264-4258; Fax: (412) 264-6598
E-Mail: laplante @ sgmlopen.com

SPAG—Standards Promotion and Application Group

Description

A Brussels-based group of computer vendors interested in promoting OSI. The group responds to customer objectives, establishes OSI conformance test facilities, develops profiles beyond specifications of the European Economic Community (CEN/CENELEC/CEPT), and seeks to reduce vendor costs while providing customers with better products and services. [Unisys, 1989]

SPAG is a firm supporter of current GOSIP-type initiatives by public procurement bodies throughout the world—in particular, the concerted effort made in Europe to progress the translation of procurer requirements for open systems, based on real business scenarios, into clear, unambiguous, user-friendly guidelines. [OSINetter Newsletter, July 1993]

Membership

Among SPAG's members are such US companies as IBM Corp., DEC, and Hewlett-Packard Co. [Masud, May 1993]

SQL Access Group

Description

The SQL Access Group was set up in 1989 to develop an architecture for communication between dissimilar relational databases, with the aim of creating complete multivendor database interoperability. [Computergram, 1992]

Membership

Membership includes Digital Equipment Corp., Informix Software Inc., Oracle Corp., Microsoft Corp., Lotus computing Corp., and X/Open Co. Ltd. [Computergram, 1992]

Conformance Testing

No information indicates that SQL Access Group does conformance testing.

SQL Access Group
P.O. Box 5559
Manchester, NH 03108

Miscellaneous

In May, 1993 the SQL Access Group published three specifications that have been approved by ANSI and ISO. The specifications are directed at:

- Standard SQL

- Call Level Interface (CLI) for C and COBOL

- Remote Database Access definition for communications between client and remote database servers. [Software Magazine, May 1993]

Standards and Open Systems (SOS) Group (a.k.a., Group of 10, Group of 20)

Description

SOS is an open systems user group that was formed in 1991. The aim of SOS is to force systems and software vendors to create products that allow interoperability between legacy and open systems. The SOS group has called on the major system vendors to work with the Open System Environment Implementors Workshop (OIW) to develop profiles based on available standards and publicly available specifications. [Heffernan, December 1992]

Membership

Du Pont Co.; American Airlines; General Motors Corp.; Eastman Kodak Co.; McDonnell Douglas Corp.; Motorola Inc.; 3M Co.; Northrop Corp.; Unilever United States, Inc. [Computergram, September 1991]

TIS—Tools Interface Standards Committee

Description

A consortium established by systems and applications software developers to set standard interfaces for 32-bit operating systems such as Microsoft Windows, OS/2, and UNIX. The committee hopes to improve portability of software tools of TIS compliant vendors. The committee will first focus on interfaces for debuggers, linkers, and loaders. [Garry, March 1993]

Membership

IBM; Intel Corp.; Borland International Inc.; Microsoft Corp., Lotus Development Corp.; MetaWare Inc.; Watcom; Santa Cruz Operation.

TPC—Transaction Processing Performance Council

Description

The TPC was founded in August 1988 by eight leading software and hardware companies. Prior to TPC's founding there were no commonly agreed upon benchmarks measuring database performance. [TPC, 1994]

Mission

The TPC is a non-profit corporation founded to define transaction processing and database benchmarks and to disseminate objective, verifiable TPC performance data to the industry. [TPC, 1994]

Membership

The TPC is open to any organization or company, including vendors and end users. [TPC, 1994]

Amdahl Corp.; AST Research; AT&T; Australian Government; Borland; Bull; Compaq; Convex; Cray Research; Data General; Digital Equipment Corp.; Electronic Data Systems; Encore Computers; Fujitsu/ICL; Hewlett Packard; Hitachi (SW); IBM Corporation; IDEAS Intl. Informix Software; Ingres Corporation; Intel Corporation; ITOM International; Microsoft Corp.; Mitsubishi Electric Corp.; NEC Corp.; Novel; Oki Electric Industry Co. Ltd.; Olivetti S.P.A.; Oracle Corp.; Pyramid Technology; Samsung; SCO; Sequent Computer; Siemens Nixdorf—Information Systems; Silicon Graphics; Software AG; Solbourne; Sony Corporation; Stratus; Sun Microsystems; Sybase; Tandem Computers; Toshiba Corp.; Tricord Systems; Unisys Corp.

Address

Kim Shanley, Administrator
TPC
777 North First Street, Suite 600
San Jose, CA 95112-6311
(408) 295-8894; Fax: (408) 295-9768

UniForum—The International Association of Open Systems Professionals

Description

Formally called \usr\group, UniForum is a nonprofit, vendor-independent association of UNIX and open systems professionals dedicated to the standardization, education and implementation of open systems. The association serves as a forum to exchange information about open systems, the UNIX operating system, software, and applications. [UniForum, November 1993]

Membership

Membership includes software developers, systems analysts, engineers, MIS directors, technical executives, VARS, end users, systems integrators, and software vendors. There are over 80 corporate sponsors and over 30 affiliate members from around the world Overall, UniForum has more than 6,500 members worldwide. Some notable corporate sponsors include.

Amdahl Corp.; Compaq Computer Corp.; Digital Equipment Corp.; Hewlett-Packard Co.; IBM Corp.; NCR Corp.; Open Software Foundation, Inc.; Sun Microsystems; Novell; Santa Cruz Operation; Oracle. [UniForum, November 1993]

Conformance Testing

No information indicates that UniForum does conformance testing.

Address

UniForum
2901 Tasman Dr., #205
Santa Clara, CA 95054-1100
(408)986-8840; (800)255-5620

Miscellaneous

Other UniForum activities include:

• Conducts research studies on the open systems market

• Provides technical services and publications, including a monthly magazine and the annual "Open Systems Products Directory," the only single source reference book for the industry

• Hosts an international trade show and conference dedicated to UNIX system products and services

• Co-hosts an annual executive symposium aimed at educating MIS executives on the importance of UNIX and open systems in the commercial computing environment [UniForum, November 1993]

UI—UNIX International

Note: UNIX International shut its doors in December, 1993, officially ending a five-year feud with OSF. The Parsippany, N.J. based consortium closed ostensibly because it had fulfilled its mission to standardize on Unix System V Release IV. [Unix World's Open Computing, 1994]

Description

Founded in 1988, UI was a nonprofit organization responsible for directing the evolution of the open systems environment based on UNIX System V, the industry-standard open operating system. [UI, 1991]

UI's primary focus was to generate product requirements. It generated and submitted product requirements to UNIX System Laboratories. In addition, UI released product requirements and specifications widely to the industry to allow for broad implementation. [Datapro, August 1993]

Membership

Membership grew to more than 300 companies worldwide, including system manufacturers and vendors, independent software vendors, system integrators, government organizations, end users, and universities. [Datapro, August 1993]

Some notable members included: [UI, 1991]

Amdahl Corp.; AT&T; Control Data Corp.; Fuji Xerox Co, Ltd.; Motorola Computer Corp.; NCR Corp.; Olivetti; Sun Microsystems; Toshiba Corp.; Unisys Corp.

Address

UNIX International
20 Waterview Blvd.
Parsippany, NJ 07054
(201) 263-8400

Miscellaneous

UI ensured that future enhancements and releases of System V contain features demanded by a changing marketplace and conform to specifications formed by industry standards organizations. UNIX System V code was produced and licensed by UNIX Systems Laboratories, now owned by Novell.

UI also developed the UI-ATLAS framework. The framework is a complete open computing environment that enables the development of distributed applications today and a clear migration path to object-oriented applications of the future. UI-ATLAS allows systems vendors and software developers to create competing, yet compatible products because it uses standardized Application Programming Interfaces (APIs) and reference technologies that specify how products are incorporated into the system. [UI, 1991]

UI released a document in early 1993 entitled "Roadmap for UNIX Systems and Related Technologies," that maps out the future of UNIX System 5. They planned to incorporate new technologies into the operating system, such as multimedia. UI planned to add a broad range of interoperability capabilities that focused on Novell Inc.'s NetWare, Apple's AppleTalk, and IBM's LU 6.2. Also planned was a federated naming system, a complete object management environment and improved Microsoft Windows graphical user interface emulation. [Fredric, February 1993]

UNIX Systems Group

Description

UNIX Systems Group is the result of the union between USL and Univel. Their immediate goal is to create a high-volume UnixWare desktop business. Novell is seeking to quickly challenge IBM's OS/2 and Microsoft Corp.'s Windows NT for leadership in the market for advanced 32-bit operating systems. [Software Magazine, September 1993]

USL—UNIX Systems Laboratories

Description

USL receives requirements and technical specifications for new versions of UNIX System V formulated by members of UI. USL then produces and licenses the operating system code [UI]. In early 1993, USL was acquired by Novell and became a wholly owned Novell subsidiary. Later in 1993, USL was united with Univel by Novell to form a new unit called UNIX Systems Group. [Software Magazine, September 1993]

USENIX Association

Description

The USENIX Association is the original non-profit membership organization of individuals and institutions with an interest in UNIX and other advanced computing systems. USENIX extends its support to the broad computing environment and to professional subspecialties such as software development and system administration. [USENIX, 1994]

Mission

USENIX and its members are dedicated to: problem-solving with a practical bias; research that works; and rapid communication of the results of both research and innovation. [USENIX, 1994]

Address

Toni Veglia
USENIX Association
2560 Ninth Street, Suite 215
Berkeley, CA 94710
(510) 528-8649; Fax: (510) 548-5738
E-mail: office @ usenix.org

Miscellaneous

USENIX sponsors conferences and symposia geared toward the more technical UNIX developer, system administrator, and user. The annual Winter Technical Conference features a refereed technical track, invited presentations, and a full tutorial program. Symposia devoted to various special-interest topics are held throughout the year. [USENIX, 1994]

User Alliance For Open Systems

Description

The User Alliance for Open Systems is a requirements interest group under COS that worked to identify and solve OSI's most significant problems within the user arena. The goal was to work through COS to formalize an effective way of communicating its priorities to the various user and vendor standards organizations. As of 1993, the User Alliance for Open Systems is no longer a part of COS, and appears to be defunct. [COS, 1994]

Mission

The mission of the Alliance was to focus on key issues within COS that were ignored in the past, such as the business process itself. It had four working groups:

- To create a model business case to justify the move to open systems using classic financial analysis

- To raise the awareness level of open systems and provide case studies via a task force on education and research

- To develop the requirements process, determining how users express their systems needs in order to be understood

- To assess the technological areas that need to be examined, such as EDI, E-mail, OLTP, and high-level frameworks [COS, 1991]

Membership

The Alliance was formed in September 1990. Its bylaws prohibit identification of members. [COS, 1991]

Address

User Alliance for Open Systems
c/o Corporation for Open Systems International
1750 Old Meadow Road, Suite 400
McLean, VA 22102
(703) 883-2723

Workflow Management Coalition

Description

The Workflow Management Coalition wants to make the work-flow market unified and to prevent the type of standardization disagreements encountered by messaging vendors. The APIs created by the consortium will focus on workflow computing, which addresses the intelligent routing of electronic data, documents and images. [Radosevich, 1993]

Mission

This group's objective is to promote interoperability between application programming interfaces (APIs), format specifications and protocols. [Radosevich, 1993]

Membership

Participating firms include Lotus Development Corp., NCR Corp. and Wang Laboratories Inc.

XAPIA—X.400 Application Program Interface Association

Description

XAPIA is an open, non-profit standards setting group comprised of messaging vendors and end-users that has developed programmatic interfaces to the X.400 international messaging standard and more recently a simple set of interfaces to be used with any message transport (Common Messaging Calls—CMC). [XAPIA, 1994]

Membership

American Express, Arabesque Software, Inc., Attachmate Canada Ltd., Boeing Computer Services, Bull HN Information Systems, Campbell Services Inc., CE Software Inc., Digital Equipment Corp., France Telecom, Hewlett Packard, Lotus Development Corp.,

Hitachi, Hughes Enterprise Information Systems, IBM, Linkage Office Information Solutions, Inc., Microsoft, Microsystems Software, Novell, On Technology, Oracle Corporation, OSIWare, Ram Mobile Data, Retix, Softswitch, Tandem, Wingra, Worldtalk, XcelleNet. [XAPIA, 1994]

Contact

Leslie Schroeder,
Leslie Schroeder PR & Marketing
10151 Western Drive
Cupertino, CA 95014
(408) 446-9158; Fax: (408) 257-1478

Miscellaneous

XAPIA announced that it will develop additional calls for the Common Messaging Calls (CMC). Common Messaging Calls are software elements that help move electronic mail between desktop applications running on different platforms, across different mail systems, and in different LAN environments. The XAPIA is also in the process of creating programmatic interfaces for Calendaring & Scheduling and Directory Synchronization. [XAPIA, 1994]

X Consortium

Description

The X Consortium is an independent, not-for-profit Delaware membership corporation. It was formed in 1993 as the successor to the MIT X Consortium. [X Consortium, 1994]

Membership

Adobe; AGE; Apple; ASTEC; ATR; ATT; BARCO; Congruent Corp.; Cray Research; CETIA; Diagnostic Retrieval; Digital Equipment Corp.; Dome Imaging Electronic Book; Fujitsu; Gallium Software, Inc.; Georgia Tech; Hewlett Packard; Hitachi; Hughes; Hummingbird Communications; Human Design Systems; IBM; Integrated Computer Solutions; Investment Management Services; Japan Computer; Jupiter; KAIST; Kubota Corp.; Labtam; Locus Computing; M3i; Megatek; Mercury; Metro Link; Motorola; NEC; NCD; NTT; OKI Electric; Omron; O'Reilly & Associates; Open Software Foundation, Inc.; ParkPlac; Performance Awareness; Petrotechnical Open Software; Phase X Systems, Inc.; Peritek Corporation; Quarterdeck; Santa Cruz Operations; Silicon Graphics; Siemans-Nixdorf; Sony Corp; Soum; Sun Microsystems; Tatung; Tech-Source, Inc.; Tektronix; UNIX Systems; User Interface Technologies; VisiCom; Visual Information Tech; Visionware;

Veritas Software; Visix Software; White Pines Software; Walker Richer & Quinn; Walker Richer & Quinn 1; XFree6 Project; X Inside Inc.

Address

Robert W. Scheifler; President
X Consortium
One Memorial Drive
Cambridge, MA 02142-1301
(617) 374-1000; Fax: (617) 374-1025

Mission

The purpose of the X Consortium is to foster the development, evolution, and maintenance of the X Window System, a comprehensive set of vendor-neutral, system-architecture neutral, network-transparent windowing and user interface standards. [X Consortium, 1994]

Miscellaneous

The X Consortium sponsors an annual technical conference, open to the public, to promote the exchange of information about the X Window System. The conference typically lasts three days, with one day devoted to tutorials and two days devoted to talks. [X Consortium, 1994]

X/Open Co. Ltd

Description

X/Open, founded in 1984, is a worldwide, independent company dedicated to bringing the benefits of open systems to market. The company markets products and services to computer system buyers, system suppliers, software developers and standards organizations. By integrating prioritized requirements and expertise from each of these groups, X/Open is able to evolve and manage a comprehensive set of publicly available open systems specifications, including de facto and international standards, called the Common Applications Environment (CAE). X/Open operates a test and verification process for products developed in line with its specifications, and awards its brand as the mark of compliance.

Mission

X/Open's mission is to increase the value of computing through the practical implementation of open systems. [X/Open, 1994]

X/Open's corporate sponsors have made a public commitment to deliver conformant X/Open branded systems, leading to:

- Portability across a wide and growing base of systems
- No dependence on a single source—freedom of choice
- Increased application software selection
- More security in software investments
- International support for the Common Applications Environment [X/Open, 1994]

Membership

X/Open Corporate Members include: [X/Open, 1994]

Amdahl; Bull; DEC; Fujitsu; Hewlett-Packard; Hitachi; IBM; ICL; NCR; NEC Corp.; Novell; Olivetti; Siemens Nixdorf; Sun Microsystems; Unisys.

In addition, over 80 of the world's largest IT users are found in X/Open's User Council plus close to 30 of the leading ISVs in the world. Finally, in addition to the system vendors listed above, there are 12 more to be found in the System Vendor Council. [X/Open, 1994]

Conformance Testing

X/Open uses the most stringent conformance testing procedures available. The XPG4 brand is awarded to products that conform with X/Open's current specifications. Products awarded XPG4 brands may include components such as: ISAM, SQL, Terminal Interfaces, COBOL, FORTRAN, Pascal, and Window Management. [X/Open, 1994]

Address

X/Open Company Ltd.
1010 El Camino Real, Suite 380
Menlo Park, Ca 94025
(415) 323-7992

Miscellaneous

To drive the transformation toward open systems, X/Open allows system vendors, software suppliers and standards organizations to create an internationally supported, vendor-independent Common Applications Environment (CAE) for open systems. X/Open then integrates these work products with existing standards. The resulting set of interface specifications is supported by all members and adopted by an increasing number of user organizations.

Applications written to operate in the CAE are portable at the source code level to a wide range of machines. This releases users from dependence on a single supplier, which reduces necessary investment in applications, increases the market for independent software, and opens up the market for systems suppliers. The foundations of the CAE are the interfaces specified in the IEEE 1003.1-1988 POSIX standard and the C language. Components of the CAE are categorized as BASE, EXTENSION and OPTIONAL. Every X/Open branded system implements all of the BASE components.

X/Open is the only organization that has Associate Membership Councils composed of users, system vendors and independent software vendors. The group also conducts the only ongoing international open systems user requirements study with published results. [X/Open, 1994]

XUC—X/Open User Council

Description

The X/Open User Council is the only international, cross-sector, non-vendor-aligned group of its kind in the computer industry. Members accomplish their mission by defining business requirements for open systems and identifying their relative importance and priority. [X/Open, 1994]

Mission

The mission of the X/Open User Council is to provide cross-industry and international user input to the development of a global information technology infrastructure that satisfies business needs. [X/Open, 1994]

Membership

Prospective members are organizations that:

- Seek to improve effectiveness of IT usage by implementing open systems

- Need to manage growth of multivendor solutions within a coherent enterprise-wide framework

- Commit to the open systems concept and accelerate its introduction

- Possess the ability and desire to contribute to X/Open's mission

Membership includes:

Automobile Association (U.K.); The Boeing Company; Commission of the European Communities; DuPont; Ford Motor Company; National Institute of Standards & Technology (NIST); Union Bank of Switzerland; US Defense Information Systems; US Department of Agriculture; US Treasury (IRS). [X/Open, 1994]

Address

X/Open User Council
1010 El Camino Real, Suite 380
Menlo Park, CA 94025
(415) 323-7992

XSVC—X/Open System Vendor Council

Description

The X/Open System Vendor Council gives emerging open systems vendors the opportunity to work with X/Open and its constituencies on the development of its open systems specifications. [X/Open, 1994]

Mission

The mission of the X/Open System Vendor Council is to provide a structure in which emerging or specialized open system vendors can contribute to the development of open systems specifications and strategic planning. [X/Open, 1994]

Membership

Membership is comprised of emerging computer systems vendors. The differentiating factors between X/Open corporate members and System Vendor Council members are size of the company's computer systems effort, as well as participation commitments and costs. [X/Open, 1994]

Address

X/Open User Council
1010 El Camino Real, Suite 380
Menlo Park, CA 94025
(415) 323-7992

X3J19 Committee

Description

The X3J19 committee, made up of approximately 40 Xbase developers and vendors, are setting out to develop a proposal for an Xbase language standard in conjunction with ANSI. The standard is expected to be broken down into several levels. The first level would involve documenting; level two would deal with the jump from DOS to a graphical user interface (GUI) and the third level would address object-oriented extensions. [Schaffhauser, January 1993]

APPENDIX

Standards and Technologies

This appendix contains a list of open standards and proprietary/open technologies. Group or vendor names indicated in the parenthesis after the full name of the standard/technology are those sponsoring or endorsing the standard/technology. The list is (obviously) incomplete and (probably) inaccurate. Please contact standards organizations and vendors for more complete and current information.

ABI—Application Binary Interface (UI). A specification that defines interfaces to make applications portable across different architectures at the binary level. [Datapro, May 1994]

ACE—Advanced Computing Environment (ACE). An initiative of the ACE consortium of hardware and software suppliers that promulgated standards for Intel 80X86-based and Mips-based computers and workstations. ACE has died with the apparently dissolved ACE Consortium. [DG/UX, 1991]

ANDF—Architecture Neutral Distribution Format (OSF). Announced by OSF and developed by the United Kingdom's defense Research Agency so that software vendors could develop a single version of an application that could run—without porting—on machines with different processors and operating systems. [Simpson, 1991]

Architecture Neutral Distribution Format (ANDF) supports developing portable applications. The developer generates an intermediate ANDF language that can be shrink-wrapped. The ANDF language is compiled into machine language at install time in the target machine. [Electronic Computer Glossary, March 1994]

313

ANDF enables developers to compile and distribute their applications in a form that can be installed and run on any hardware architecture that supports ANDF. ANDF establishes a software distribution method based on a compiler intermediate language which adequately balances the need for hardware independence and source code confidentiality. This method essentially divides the source code compilation process into two parts—one machine-independent and the other machine-dependent. Machine-independent processing is done with a tool, the ANDF producer, which software vendors use to produce the ANDF code for mass distribution. Another tool, the ANDF installer, performs the machine-dependent processing on the end user's system and produces executable code for that system at install time. [OSF, 1991]

The core components of the ANDF technology are the ANDF producer, which creates an ANDF representation of an ANSI C source code program; the ANDF installer, which creates executable object code for particular platforms from the ANDF representation; and the ANDF specification. [OSF, September/October 1991]

AT WORK—(Microsoft). Microsoft's office equipment architecture announced on June 9, 1993. Microsoft's idea is to put a set of software building blocks into both office machines and PC products, including:

- Desktop and network-connected printers

- Digital monochrome and color copiers

- Telephones and voice messaging systems

- Fax machines and PC fax products

- Handheld systems

- Hybrid combinations of the above

According to Microsoft, the Microsoft At Work architecture focuses on creating digital connections between machines (i.e., the ones above) to allow information to flow freely throughout the workplace. The Microsoft At Work software architecture consists of several technology components that serve as building blocks to enable these connections. Only one of the components, desktop software, will reside on PCs. The rest will be incorporated into other types of office devices (the ones above), making these products easier to use, compatible with one another and compatible with Microsoft Windows-based PCs. The components, according to Microsoft, are:

Microsoft At Work operating system. A real-time, preemptive, multi-tasking operating system that is designed to specifically address the requirements of the office automation and communication industries. The new operating system supports Windows-compatible application programming interfaces (APIs) where appropriate for the device.

Microsoft At Work communications. Will provide the connectivity between Microsoft At Work-based devices and PCs. It will support the secure transmission of original digital documents, and it is compatible with the Windows Messaging API and the Windows Telephony API of the Windows Open Services Architecture (WOSA).

Microsoft At Work rendering. Will make the transmission of digital documents, with formatting and fonts intact, very fast and, consequently, cost-effective; will ensure that a document sent to any of these devices will produce high-quality output, referred to as "What You Print Is What You Fax Is What You Copy Is What You See."

Microsoft At Work graphical user interface. Will make all devices very easy to use and will make sophisticated features accessible; will provide useful feedback to users.

Microsoft At Work desktop software for Windows-based PCs. Will provide Windows-based PC applications the ability to control, access and exchange information with any product based on Microsoft At Work. Desktop software is the one piece of the Microsoft At Work architecture that will reside on PCs. [Newton, 1993]

ARC—Advanced RISC Computing Specification (ACE). Open system specification based on the MIPS R3000 and R4000 CPUs. It includes EISA and TURBOchannel buses. [Electronic Computer Glossary, March 1994]

ARC defines the architecture for an industry-standard computing platform based on the MIPS family of microprocessors. The ARC Specification provides the baseline hardware requirements necessary to create RISC-based systems that are compatible with the Advanced Computing Environment (ACE).

ARC has died with the apparently dissolved ACE Consortium.

The Specification defines system hardware and firmware components, functions, interfaces, and data formats. The base functionality defined for ARC-compliant systems allows a wide range of suppliers of operating systems, applications, and peripherals to have a common development target among a large number of multivendor products. [88Open, 1991]

ASCII—(ANSI, NIST, FIPS) American Standard Code for Information Interchange. It's the most popular coding method used by small computers for converting letters, numbers, punctuation and control codes into digital form. Once defined, ASCII characters can be recognized and understood by other computers and by communications devices. ASCII represents characters, numbers, punctuation marks or signals in seven on-off bits. A capital "C," for example, is 1000011, while a "3" is 0110011. [Newton, 1993]

The term "ASCII" is normally taken to mean the code prescribed by the latest edition of this standard. [88Open, 1991]

ATIS—A Tool Integration Standard. A nonproprietary, object-oriented interface standard that supports portability across platforms. [DEC, 1991]

ATLAS (UI) Note: UNIX International has been disbanded, therefore ATLAS may be unsupported.

UNIX International "middleware." UI-ATLAS is a five-layer framework for a complete system software environment. For each component of ATLAS there is a reference technology direction and an API specification. Development of UI-ATLAS by UNIX International, its members, and UNIX System Laboratories began in 1989.

The UI-Atlas architectural framework is based on standard interfaces, rather than products. This allows business to choose from the many emerging technologies which address the business needs of the '90s while preserving their existing hardware and software investments. [UI, 1991a]

UI ATLAS

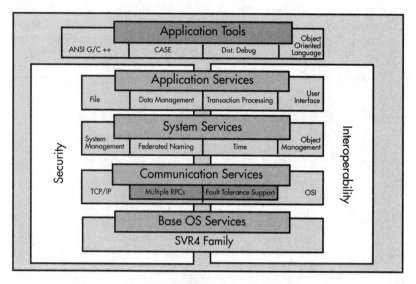

Source: UNIX International 1991

BCS™—Binary Compatibility Standard (88Open). The purpose of the Binary Compatibility Standard is to allow software vendors to compile a single version of an application that will run, without change or recompilation, on all certified Motorola 88000 microprocessor-based systems. The BCS applies to systems based on the Motorola MC88100 and future, related microprocessors. It has been endorsed as an Interim UNIX System V Application Binary Interface by AT&T for systems that are based on System V, Release 3.2 and/or support the System V Interface Definition (SVID) Issue 2. [88Open, 1991]

BSD sockets—Communications interface in BSD UNIX that lets an application access a protocol by "opening a socket" and declaring a destination. BSD sockets are popular because they provide a simple way to hook into the TCP/IP protocol. NetWare 3.x also supports BSD sockets as one of the common transport interfaces. [Electronic Computer Glossary, March 1994]

CAE—Common Applications Environment (X/Open). CAE is a broad conceptual framework for implementing open systems. As indicated in the figure below the CAE identifies those areas X/Open sees as critical for portability and interoperability. They include: systems management, object management, workstation data access, online transaction processing, mainframe data access, programming languages, data management, data interchange, security, and internationalization. This comprehensive environment covers all the standards, above the hardware level, that are needed to support open systems. XPG defines detailed specifications and interfaces for communicating within this framework. [X/Open, July 1994]

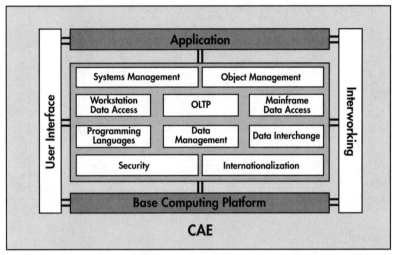

CGM—Computer Graphics Metafile (NIST). A graphics data interface standard which specifies a file format suitable for the description, storage and communication of graphical information in a device-independent manner. The purpose of the standard is to facilitate the transfer of graphical information between different software systems, graphical devices and computer graphics installations.

In this standard, a metafile represents illustration data in the form of a conforming basic metafile. In other words, it contains device-independent, system-independent, and implementation-independent form—the picture description data invoked through an application program interface.

CGM stores images primarily in vector graphics, but also provides a raster format. Earlier GDM and VDM formats have been merged into the CGM standard. [Electronic Computer Glossary, March 1994]

Harvard Graphics, Ventura Publisher, Microsoft Windows, and OS/2 are four common programs capable of reading and writing to CGM formats. [Nader, 1992]

CGM has been adopted and issued as Federal Information Processing Standard (FIPS) Publication 128 by the National Institute of Standards and Technology. [88Open, 1991]

CORBA—Common Object Request Broker Architecture (OMG). The Object Management Group sponsors standard-setting for the systems-software mechanism required to realize distributed object computing. This mechanism is called an Object Request Broker (ORB). OMG's first cut at open ORB standards, the Common Object Request Broker Architecture (CORBA) version 1.1, was released October 1991. The upgraded standard, CORBA 2.0, was released in 1994. [Shelton, May 1993; OMG, August 1994]

CMIP—Common Management Information Protocol (ISO). A protocol formally adopted by the International Standards Organization in Paris (ISO), used for exchanging network management information. Typically, this information is exchanged between two management stations. CMIP can, however, be used to exchange information between an application and a management station. CMIP has been designed for OSI networks, but it is transport independent. Theoretically, it could run across a variety of transports, including, for example, IBM's Systems Network Architecture. [Newton, 1993]

CMIS—Common Management Information Systems. OSI standard that defines the functions for network monitoring and control. [Electronic Computer Glossary, March 1994]

DAL—Data Access Language (Apple). Database interface that allows a Macintosh to access DAL-supported databases on Marcintosh or non-Apple computers. It is a superset of SQL. Database vendors license the specs and translate DAL calls to their database engines. [Electronic Computer Glossary, March 1994]

DCE—Distributed Computing Environment (OSF). The Open Software Foundation Distributed Computing Environment (DCE) allows programmers to build distributed applications that put standard protocols and services to work. DCE is a collection of tools and services that ease the development of distributed applications, which in turn, make information available throughout a network. This technology allows users to retrieve information easily—regardless of where it is stored—and distribute it to wherever it is needed. [OSF, August 1994]

OSF DCE

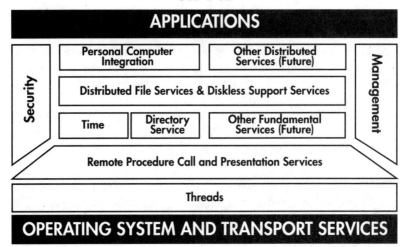

Source: OSF, 1991

DDE—Dynamic Data Exchange (Microsoft). Message protocol in Windows that allows application programs to request and exchange data automatically. A program in one window can query a program in another window. [Electronic Computer Glossary, March 1994]

DECnet—(Digital). Digital's communications network, which supports Ethernet-style LANs and baseband and broadband WANs over private and public lines. It interconnects PDPs, VAXs, PCs, Macs and workstations. In DECnet philosophy, a node must be an intelligent machine and not simply a terminal as in other systems.

DECnet/DOS allows DOS machines to function as end nodes in DECnet networks, and DECnet/OSI is the implementation of DECnet Phase V that supports OSI and provides compatibility with DECnet Phase IV and TCP/IP. [Electronic Computer Glossary, March 1994]

DES—Data Encryption Standard (NIST, FIPS). General security requirements for equipment using the Data Encryption Standard. Issued as Federal Information Processing Standard (FIPS) Publication 140-1.

DES was developed by a United States Government/Industry working group composed of both users and vendors. This working group identified requirements for four security levels for cryptographic modules to provide for a wide spectrum of data sensitivity and a diversity of application environments. [88Open, 1991]

DME—Distributed Management Environment (OSF). The OSF Distributed Management Environment (DME) provides a unified approach for managing systems, networks, and user applications in heterogeneous environments. Its purpose is to make systems and networks more efficient and cost effective. OSF is integrating several technologies to form a DME framework that supports the management of systems resources as well as the development of applications for distributed systems management. [OSF August 1994]

DPMI—DOS Protected Mode Interface (Microsoft). DOS extender specification for Intel x286s and up that allows DOS extended programs to cooperatively run under Windows 3.x. Developed by Microsoft, it keeps a DOS-extended application from crashing the computer and usurping Windows' control. It is not compatible with VCPI, the first DOS extender standard, but Windows 3.1 is more tolerant of VCPI applications than Windows 3.0.

XMS Versus VCPI/DPMI: XMS, VCPI and DPMI all deal with extended memory. However, XMS allows data and programs to be stored in and retrieved from extended memory, whereas the VCPI and DPMI interfaces allow programs to "run" in extended memory. [Electronic Computer Glossary, March 1994]

DRDA—Distributed Relational Database Architecture (IBM). SAA-compliant enhancement allows data to be distributed among DB and SQL/DS databases. Users or programs can access data from SAA or non-SAA systems that implement DRDA.

EDI—Electronic Data Interchange (NIST, ANSI). In EDI, data that would traditionally be conveyed on paper documents are transmitted or communicated electronically according to established rules and formats. [88Open, 1991]

EDI software translates fixed field or "flat" files that are extracted from applications into a standard format and hands off the translated data to communications software for transmission. EDI standards are supported (i.e., have been adopted) by virtually every computer company in the country and increasingly, by every packet switched data communications company. For example, you can use IBM VAN—IBM's Value Added Network for Electronic Data Interchange. [Newton, 1993]

EMS—Expanded Memory Specification (Lotus, Intel, Microsoft) Several years ago, three computer companies—Lotus, Intel and Microsoft—jointly developed EMS. This standard defines how an

MS-DOS program can access memory beyond 640KB while running under MS-DOS. Applications that conform to EMS (sometimes called LIM-EMS for Lotus/Intel/Microsoft Expanded Memory Specification) can take advantage of the computer's memory beyond 640KB of RAM. LIM-EMS uses a portion of the reserved memory area (between 640KB and 1MB) to access RAM beyond 1MB. Software that supports expanded memory uses this window to pass pages of data to and from expanded RAM as needed. [Newton, 1993]

Ethernet—A 10-megabit baseband, local area network that allows multiple stations to access the transmission medium at will without prior coordination, avoids contention by using carrier sense and deference, and resolves contention by using collision detection and transmission. Ethernet uses carrier sense multiple access with collision detection (CSMA/CD). [IBM Dictionary of Computing, 1994]

FDDI—Fiber Optic Data Distribution Interface (ANSI, GOSIP, ISO). FDDI is a layered standard for a 100 MB/s fiber optic token ring local area network (LAN). The FDDI network will allow up to 500 stations connected by up to 200 km of fiber. It is particularly suited as a "backbone" network interconnecting other, lower data-rate LANs, and for applications inherently requiring high bandwidth. These applications include image processing with engineering workstations, connecting storage servers to powerful computers, and other applications whose size and data transfer requirements exceed the capacity of other LANs.

The theoretical limit of Ethernet, measured in 64 byte packets, is 14,800 packets per second (PPS). By comparison, Token Ring is 30,000 and FDDI is 170,000 pps. FDDI LANs also work on twisted copper pairs. [Newton, 1993]

The FDDI standard covers the physical layer and lower portion of the data link layer of the OSI Basic Reference Model. It supports the DIS 88012 Logical Link Control (LLC) Standard, and fits within the framework of the Government Open Systems Interconnection Profile as one of several lower level standards supporting the LLC. [88Open, 1991]

Fiber Distributed Data Interchange II is proposed to be an update (i.e. faster, somewhere in the gigabit per second range) of FDDI.

For a complimentary copy of a 456-page book on FDDI called *The Fiber Optic LAN HANDBOOK*, contact Codenoll Corp., 1086 N. Broadway, Yonkers, NY 10701, 914/965-6300. [Electronic Computer Glossary, March 1994]

FIPS—Federal Information Processing Standard(NIST). The designation for a standard adopted by the U.S. government to be used in procuring computer systems. The POSIX.1 standard, for example, has been accepted (with some extensions) as a FIPS. [DG/UX, 1991]

FIPS 151-1—The U.S. government's version of the POSIX.1 standard. [DG/UX, 1991]

FTAM—File Transfer Access and Management (OSI/GOSIP). A communications protocol for the transfer of files between systems of different vendors [Freedman, 1991]. FTAM defines a file service and specifies a file protocol available within the application layer of the Open Systems Interconnection Basic Reference Model (ISO 7498 : 1984). [88Open, 1991]

FTP—File Transfer Protocol. In local area networking technology, a file-sharing protocol that operates at layers 5 through 7 of the Open Systems Interconnection (OSI) model. As specified in RFC-959, FTP provides full authentication of the user by requiring login on the remote host. It lets users transfer text and binary files to and from a PC, list directories on the foreign host, delete and rename files on the foreign host, and perform wildcard transfers between hosts [Newton, 1993]. It can also translate between ASCII and EBCDIC. [Electronic Computer Glossary, March 1994]

GKS—Graphical Kernel System (ISO, ANSI). A graphics system for applications that produce computer-generated, two dimensional pictures on line or raster graphics output devices. [Datapro, May 1994]

GOSIP—Government Open Systems Interconnect Profile. The U.S. government's version of the OSI protocols. GOSIP compliance is typically a requirement in government networking purchases. GOSIP addresses communication and interoperation among end systems and intermediate systems. It provides specific peer-level, process-to-process and terminal access functionality between computer system users within and across government agencies. [Newton, 1993]

GUM—"Grand Unified Management: the ideal system where one person at one console can manage all networks and the entire facility, including air-conditioning, power, and applications"—an idea developed by the Securities Industry Automation Corp. (SIAC), a stock exchange systems subsidiary. [Horwitt, 1991]

HDLC—High-level Data Link Control. ISO communications protocol used in X.25 packet switching networks. It provides error correction at the data link layer. SDLC, LAP and LAPB are subsets of HDLC, the U.S. government's version of the OSI protocols. GOSIP compliance is typically a requirement in government networking purchases. GOSIP addresses communication and interoperation among end systems and intermediate systems. It provides specific peer-level, process-to-process and terminal access functionality between computer system users within and across government agencies. [Newton, 1993]

HERMES—(Microsoft). Code name for Microsoft's enterprise wide network management system that will provide centralized control of resources and manage Windows and Windows NT environments. [Electronic Computer Glossary, March 1994]

IA5—International Alphabet Number 5 (CCITT, ISO). The standard character code defined by CCITT and recommended by ISO. It is almost identical to the ASCII code. [Halsall, 1992]

ICMP—Internet Control Message Protocol . A component part of the internet protocol (IP) in the TCP/IP suite that handles error and other control messages that are returned by internet gateways and hosts. [Halsall, 1992]

IDAPI—Idependent Database API (Borland, IBM, Novell, WordPerfect). Programming interface that provides a common language for applications to access databases on a network. It includes support for non-SQL and non-relational databases. [Electronic Computer Glossary, March 1994]

IEEE 488—(IEEE) IEEE 488 is the most widely-used international standard for computer-to-electronic instrument communication. It is also known as GPIB and HPIB. [Newton, 1993]

IEEE 802.1—(IEEE) A standard for local area networks.

>   802.1: covers network management and other aspects related to LANS
>   802.2: specifies the data link layer for access methods
>   802.3: specifies CSMA/CD, popularized by Ethernet
>   802.4: specifies a token passing bus
>   802.5: specifies a token passing ring, popularized by IBM's Token Ring. [Freedman, 1991]

IEEE 802.6—(IEEE) A standard for metropolitan-area networks (MANs) describes what is called a Distributed Queue Dual Bus (DQDB). The DQDB topology includes two parallel runs of cable—

typically fiber-optic cable—linking each node (typically a router for a LAN segment) using signaling rates in the range of 100 megabits per second. [Newton, 1993]

IGP—Interior Gateway Protocol. The routing protocol used in the gateways of a TCP/IP internetwork to obtain the shortest path routes through the internet. [Halsall, 1992]

INGRES—INteractive Graphics and REtrieval System (Ingres Corporation). Relational DBMS from Ingres Corporation, Alameda, CA, that runs on VAXs and UNIX workstations. It includes a 4GL, QBE and lets users create and manage a database as a series of forms. Its Knowledge Management extension allows rules to be programmed into the database.

Ingres Corporation was formerly Relational Technology, a company founded in 1980 to market a commercial version of INGRES, which was developed at the University of California at Berkeley in the early 1970s. [Electronic Computer Glossary, March 1994]

IP—Internet Protocol (ISO). The TCP/IP protocol that provides connectionless network service between multiple packet-switched networks interconnected by gateways. [Halsall, 1992]

IRDS—Information Resource Dictionary System. Specifies a computer software system that provides facilities for recording, storing and processing descriptions of an organization's significant data and data processing resources. It includes the functions performed by data dictionary systems or information repositories. It specifies two user interfaces: the full syntax and semantics of a Command Language, and the semantics of a menu-driven Panel Interface. NIST has adopted IRDS and issued it as FIPS Publication 156. [88Open, 1991]

JTM—Job Transfer and Manipulation. A protocol entity forming part of the application layer. It enables user application processes to transfer and manipulate documents relating to jobs (processing tasks). [Halsall, 1992]

KERBEROS—(MIT). Security system developed at MIT that authenticates users. It does not provide authorization to services or databases; it establishes identity at logon, which is used throughout the session. [Electronic Computer Glossary, March 1994]

LLC—Logical Link Control (IEEE). A protocol developed by the IEEE 802.2 committee for data-link-level transmission control. It is the upper sublayer of the IEEE Layer 2 (OSI) protocol that complements the MAC protocol. IEEE standard 802.2 includes end-system addressing and error checking. It also provides a common access control standard and governs the assembly of data packets and their exchange between data stations independent of how the packets are transmitted on the LAN. [Newton, 1993]

MAP—(GM) Manufacturing Automation Protocol. Communications protocol introduced by General Motors in 1982. MAP's goal is to provide common standards for the interconnection of computers and programmable machine tools used in factory automation. At the lowest physical level, it uses the IEEE 802.3 token bus protocol. Although MAP has provided vitally needed consolidation of standards, it continues to be in a constant state of revision.

MAP is often used in conjunction with TOP, an office protocol developed by Boeing Computer Services. TOP is used in the front office and MAP is used on the factory floor. [Electronic Computer Glossary, March 1994]

MAPI—Microsoft's Windows Messaging Application Programming Interface. Part of WOSA (Windows Open Services Architecture). When Microsoft announced its At Work architecture on June 9, 1993, it said one of At Work's benefits was its integration with Windows messaging. Microsoft said the At Work message protocol interfaces with the Windows Messaging API (MAPI). Consequently, users will be able to send and receive messages to and from Microsoft At Work-based devices through any MAPI-enabled e-mail software. Microsoft At Work-based message recipients are just a different recipient type whose address happens to be a name plus phone number. Another important benefit of this integration is that users will be able to send messages to e-mail and Microsoft At Work-based recipients. Finally, integration with MAPI means that all mail-enabled applications will be able to automatically make use of the Microsoft At Work message protocol with no modifications.

The same MAPI technology is implemented on Microsoft At Work-based devices as well, so we will be able to leverage advances in messaging that are added to MAPI on the desktop (e.g., the ability to have multiple communication "transports," or communications methods, operable at the same time) on Microsoft At Work-based devices. In addition, software developers will be able to leverage their understanding of MAPI on the desktop to develop applications for Microsoft At Work-based devices, according to Microsoft. [Newton, 1993]

MHS—Message Handling Service. Messaging system from Novell that supports multiple operating systems and other messaging protocols. Optional modules support SMTP, SNADS and X.400. It uses the SMF-71 messaging format. Standard MHS runs on a DOS machine attached to the server. Global MHS runs as a NetWare NLM. Under NetWare, MHS runs on top of IPX. [Electronic Computer Glossary, March 1994]

MHS—Message Handling System (ISO). An ISO standard Application Layer protocol that defines a framework for distributing data from one network to several others. It transfers relatively small messages in a store-and-forward manner (defined by CCITT as X.400 and by ISO as MOTIS/Message-Oriented Text Interchange Standard). [Newton, 1993]

MIPS ABI—MIPS Application Binary Interface (MIPS). A binary interface supporting binary compatibility across MIPS RISC processors manufactured by up to nine vendors under separate OEM agreements with MIPS Computer Systems, Inc. [Vacca, 1993]

MMS—Manufacturing Message Service (ISO/OSI, GOSIP). A protocol entity forming part of the application layer. It is intended for use specifically in the manufacturing or process control industry. It enables a supervisory computer to control the operation of a distributed community of computer-based devices. [Halsall, 1992]

Motif—(OSF). A graphical user interface (GUI), developed by OSF, that offers a PC-style behavior and appearance for applications running on any system that supports X Window, Version 11. It conforms to POSIX, ANSI C and X/Open's XPG3 standards. [Freedman, 1991]

NAS—Network Application Support (DEC). Digital's implementation of open systems, which provides standards-based software that allows a variety of workstations (VMS, ULTRIX, Sun, DOS, Windows, OS/2, Mac, etc.) to interface via VAX and ULTRIX servers. Connectivity to non-Digital server platforms is planned for 1992 and beyond. [Electronic Computer Glossary, March 1994]

NFS—Network File System (SUN). A protocol developed by Sun Microsystems to support file transfer over heterogeneous networks [Datapro, May 1994]. NFS implements a subset of UNIX file system semantics, and has been ported to a variety of UNIX and non-UNIX systems. For most UNIX file system operations, NFS gives users the ability to access files over a communications link as if they were resident on the user's local machine. [DG/UX, 1991]

NIS—Network Information Services (SunSoft). Naming service from SunSoft that allows resources to be easily added, deleted or relocated. Formerly called Yellow Pages, NIS is a de facto UNIX standard. NIS+ is a redesigned NIS for Solaris 2.0 products. The combination of TCP/IP, NFS and NIS comprise the primary networking components of UNIX. [Electronic Computer Glossary, March 1994]

OCCA—Open Cooperative Computing Architecture (NCR). NCR's UNIX SVR4-based network architecture that strongly supports IBM's Systems Network Architecture (SNA). OCCA also involves AT&T's Star-Group technology and LAN Manager for UNIX implementation. [Simpson, 1991]

OCS—Object Compatibility Standard (88Open). A standard for 88K-based computers, defined by the 88Open Consortium. OCS provides for object-level portability of application software by specifying interfaces among applications' object files and an operating system's libraries. [DG/UX, 1991]

ODA—Office Document Architecture (ISO, CCITT). A standard that facilitates the interchange of documents among different document systems. It specifies rules for describing the logical and layout structures of documents, as well as rules for specifying the character, raster and geometric content of documents. This standard was developed primarily by the International Organization for Standardization (ISO), and the International Telegraph and Telephone Consultative Committee (CCITT). [88Open, 1991]

ODBC—Open Database Connectivity specification (Microsoft). Provides a vendor-neutral application programming interface (API) that gives ODBC-enabled front-end applications equal access to most databases. The specification is based on the SQL Access Group's (SAG) Call-Level Interface (CLI) specification, which is also designed to provide a common interface to databases from multiple vendors. Application developers must create applications that adapt automatically to the various functions of database back-ends. Developing ODBC drivers is described based on the development of PageAhead's Simba interface for ODBC and Simba SQL Engine for ODBC, both of which are intended to help software vendors develop ODBC drivers quickly and efficiently for accessing open and proprietary data formats from custom and "off-the-shelf" applications and development tools. [Satterfield, 1993]

OLE—Object Linking and Embedding (Microsoft). Object Linking and Embedding is an approach for tying one piece of information in one form into a document in another form, such that a change in one piece of information will be automatically reflected in the other document. Here's an explanation from the New York Times: Business reports may contain information in a variety of formats, including text and numbers, charts, tables, images, graphics, sound and video. Typically, these are created in separate applications programs (e.g., spreadsheet, word processing, charting, database, etc.) and are merged into a single document (i.e. the report). But when the numbers used to create a chart are changed the chart must be updated as well. The executive then has to track down all the various components of the report, call up their respective applications, make the changes and stitch everything back together. OLE promises to keep track of those links and update the various components as they change. [Newton, 1993]

ONC—Open Network Computing (SunSoft). Family of networking products from SunSoft for implementing distributed computing in a multivendor environment. Includes TCP/IP and OSI protocols, NFS distributed file system, NIS naming service and TI-RPC remote procedure call library. ONC+ adds Federated Services, which is an interface for third-parties to connect network services into the Solaris environment. [Electronic Computer Glossary, March 1994]

OPEN BLUEPRINT—(IBM). An open architecture designed to replace IBM's Systems Application Architecture (SAA). Open Blueprint is much more open than SAA and provides a comprehensive view of distributed computing. The architecture's flexible infrastructure includes features that allow it to conduct distributed computing, such as connectivity, data access, presentation services, business logic and systems management. Open Blueprint supports existing IBM products as well as the OMG's CORBA and OSF's DCE. [Computer Weekly, 1994]

OPENDOC—(Apple, IBM, Novell, WordPerfect). Like OLE 2.0, OpenDoc is an architecture for creating compound documents (documents that combine information from different applications). And like OLE, OpenDoc is a blueprint for future object-oriented goals, such as cross-platform scripting (gluing applications together, even if they are on different operating systems) and distributed component software (pieces of code that work together seamlessly even though they reside on different computers). [Berst, July 1993]

OPENLOOK—(SUN). The trademarked name for a graphical user interface designed by Sun Microsystems for itself and USL. The look and feel of the Open Look interface can be exploited by programmers who adhere to the Open Look Style Guide and use one of two toolkits that implement Open Look concepts (one is based on X Windows, the other is based on NeWS). See also, Motif. [DG/UX, 1991]

OpenView—(HP). Network management software from HP. It supports SNMP and CMIP protocols, and third-party products that run under OpenView support SNA and DECnet network management protocols. OpenView is an enterprise-wide network management solution. [Electronic Computer Glossary, March 1994]

OSF/1—The name of the UNIX operating system sponsored by the Open Software Foundation. It is based on UNIX System V, release X, with BSD enhancements and Carnegie-Mellon's MACH kernel. OSF/1 conforms to the System V Interface Definition (SVID Release 2) and to the X/Open Portability Guide (XPG3). [DG/UX, 1991]

OSF/DCE—*See DCE.*

OSF/DME—*See DME.*

OSF/Motif—*See Motif.*

OSI—Open Systems Interconnection (ISO). OSI is a reference model, originally created by IEEE, and refined by ISO as a standard for worldwide communications. The standards agreed on at this level are very general and have many class options and parameters. OSI defines a framework for implementing protocols in seven layers:

OSI SEVEN LAYER FRAMEWORK

[Judge, 1988]

Control is passed from one layer to the next, starting at the application layer in one station, proceeding to the bottom layer, over the channel to the next station and back up the hierarchy. Similar functionality exists in all communications networks; however, existing non-OSI systems often incorporate two or three layers of functionality into one. [Freedman, 1991]

Layers 7 through 4 deal with end to end communications between the message source and the message destination, while layers 3 through 1 deal with network access.

Layer 1—The Physical layer deals with the physical means of sending data over lines (i.e., the electrical, mechanical and functional control of data circuits).

Layer 2—The Data Link layer is concerned with procedures and protocols for operating the communications lines. It also has a way of detecting and correcting message errors.

Layer 3—The Network layer determines how data is transferred between computers. It also addresses routing within and between individual networks.

Layer 4—The Transport layer defines the rules for information exchange and manages end-to-end delivery of information within and between networks, including error recovery and flow control.

Layer 5—The Session layer is concerned with dialog management. It controls the use of the basic communications facility provided by the Transport layer.

Layer 6—The Presentation layer provides transparent communications services by masking the differences of varying data formats (character codes, for example) between dissimilar systems.

Layer 7—The Applications layer contains functions for particular applications services, such as file transfer, remote file access and virtual terminals. [Newton, 1993]

PCTS—POSIX Conformance Test Suite (NIST). A test suite that is used to verify an operating system's conformance to POSIX (P1003.1). The best-known PCTS was developed by NIST (National Institute for Standards and Technology) for use in certifying compliance to FIPS 151-1. [DG/UX, 1991]

PEX—PHIGS Extension to X. An extension to the X server that provides support for three-dimensional graphics. PEX was originally developed to support PHIGS (Programmer's Hierarchical Interactive Graphics Standard), but has been expanded to provide support for more general three-dimensional graphics. [DG/UX, 1991]

POSIX—Portable Operating System Interface for UNIX (IEEE) IEEE 1003.1 standard that defines the language interface between application programs and the UNIX operating system. Adherence to the standard ensures compatibility when programs are moved from one UNIX computer to another. POSIX is primarily composed of features from UNIX System V and BSD UNIX. [Electronic Computer Glossary, March 1994]

The IEEE has several POSIX-related standards in the P1003.x family. The family of standards is discussed popularly as though they were UNIX standards. The P1003.1 committee's standard is known as POSIX.2, or just POSIX. The POSIX effort evolved from work initiated in the early 1980s by the UNIX user group (\usr\group, now called UniForum). [DG/UX, 1991]

A list of some of the related committees includes:

- P1003.0 is developing an overview guide to the POSIX Open Systems Environment.

- P1003.1 is the operating system interface used as the basis for a Federal Information Processing Standard (FIPS) and is embraced by the X/Open Standard.

- P1003.2 has begun work on a standard for shell commands and libraries

- P1003.3 is working on a standard for verifying compliance to the P1003 functional standards

- P1003.4 is discussing issues associated with real-time requirements. P1003.4a is preparing specifications for threads

- P1003.5 is working on an ADA language binding to the operating system interface defined by P1003.1

- P1003.6 is developing extensions to P1003.1 to address trusted and highly secure systems

- P1003.7 is discussing standards for UNIX system administration

- P1003.8 is discussing standards for networking

- P1003.9 is working on a FORTRAN language binding

- P1003.10 is working on a supercomputing Application Environment Profile (AEP)

- P1003.11 is the transaction processing AEP. [DG/UX, 1991]

PWI—Public Windows Interface (X/Open). *See WABI.*

RS-170—(NTSC) NTSC standard for composite video signals. [Electronic Computer Glossary, March 1994]

RS-232-C—(EIA) Also known as RS-232 and in its latest version EIA/TIA-232-E. A set of standards specifying various electrical and mechanical characteristics for interfaces between computers, terminals and modems. The RS-232-C standard, which was developed by the EIA (Electrical Industries Association), defines the mechanical and electrical characteristics for connecting DTE and DCE data communications devices. It defines what the interface does, circuit functions and their corresponding connector pin assignments. The standard applies to both synchronous and asynchronous binary data transmission. [Newton, 1993]

RS-328—(EIA) October, 1966 the Electronic Industries Association issued its first fax standard: the EIA Standard RS-328, Message Facsimile Equipment for Operation on Switched Voice Facilities

Using Data Communications Equipment. The Group 1 standard, as it later became known, made possible the more generalized business use of fax. Transmission was analog and it took four to six minutes to send a page. [Newton, 1993]

RS-422—(EIA) A standard operating in conjunction with RS-449 that specifies electrical characteristics for balanced circuits (circuits with their own ground leads). [Newton, 1993]

RS-423—(EIA) A standard operating in conjunction with RS-449 that specifies electrical characteristics for unbalanced circuits (circuits using common or shared grounding techniques). Another EIA standard for DTE/DCE connection which specifies interface requirements for expanded transmission speeds (up to 2 Mbps), longer cable lengths, and 10 additional functions. RS-449 applies to binary, serial, synchronous or asynchronous communications. Half- and full-duplex modes are accommodated and transmission can be over 2- or 4-wire facilities such as point-to-point or multipoint lines. The physical connection between DTE and DCE is made through a 37-contact connector; a separate 9-connector is specified to service secondary channel interchange circuits, when used. [Newton, 1993]

RS-449—(EIA) Another "standard" data communications connector. This one uses 37 pins and is designed for higher speed transmission. Each signal pin has its own return line, instead of a common ground return and the signal pairs (signal, return) are balanced lines rather than a signal referenced to ground. This cable typically uses twisted pairs, while a RS-232-C cable usually doesn't. [Newton, 1993]

RS-485—(EIA) Standard for multipoint communications lines. It can be implemented with as little as a wire block with four screws or with DB-9 or DB-37 connectors. By using lower-impedance drivers and receivers, RS-485 allows more nodes per line than RS-422. [Electronic Computer Glossary, March 1994]

RS-530—(EIA) Defines a 25-pin connector for RS-422 and RS-423 circuits. It allows for higher speed transmission up to 2Mbits/sec over the same DB-25 connector used in RS-232, but is not compatible with it. [Electronic Computer Glossary, March 1994]

RTF—Rich Text Format (Microsoft). Microsoft standard for encoding formatted text and graphics. It was adapted from IBM's DCA format and supports ANSI, IBM PC and Macintosh character sets. [Electronic Computer Glossary, March 1994]

SAA—System Application Architecture (IBM). Introduced in 1987, SAA is a set of IBM standards that provides consistent interfaces among all IBM computers from micro to mainframe. It is made up of user interfaces, programming interfaces and communications protocols, as follows:

1) Common User Access (CUA)—Interfaces based on the graphics-based Presentation Manager of OS/2 and the character-oriented interfaces of 3270 terminals.

2) Common Programming Interface (CPI)—A common set of application programming interfaces (APIs) that would, for example, allow a program developed on the PC to be easily moved to a mainframe. The standard database language is SQL.

3) Common Communications Support (CCS)—A common set of protocols, including LU 6.2 (APPC) and HLLPI. [Freedman, 1991]

SDLC—Synchronous Data Link Control (IBM). The primary data link protocol used in IBM's SNA networks. It is a bit-oriented synchronous protocol that is a subset of the HDLC protocol. [Freedman, 1991]

SMT—Station Management. The network management protocol of the FDDI fiber optic interface. It provides direct management, requiring only one node to have the network management software. [Freedman, 1991]

SMTP—Simple Mail Transfer Protocol (ARPA). In local area networking technology, protocol that operates at layers 5 through 7 of the Open Systems Interconnection (OSI) model. This TCP/IP protocol governs electronic mail transmissions and receptions. [Newton, 1993]

SNA—Systems Network Architecture (IBM). IBM mainframe network standards introduced in 1974. Originally a centralized architecture with a host computer controlling many terminals, enhancements, such as APPN and APPC (LU 6.2), have adapted SNA to today's peer-to-peer communications and distributed computing environment. Following are some of SNA's basic concepts:

- *Nodes and Data Links*: In SNA, nodes are end points or junctions, and data links are the pathways between them. Nodes are defined as Type 5 (hosts), Type 4 (communications controllers) and Type 2 (peripheral; terminals, PCs and midrange computers).

- *SSCPs, PUs and LUs*: The heart of a mainframe-based SNA network is the SSCP (System Services Control Point) software that resides in the host. It manages all resources in its domain.

  Within all nodes of an SNA network, except for Type 2.1, there is PU (Physical Unit) software that manages node resources, such as data links, and controls the transmission of network management information. In Node Type 2.1, Control Point software performs these functions.

  In order to communicate user data, a session path is created between two end points, or LUs (Logical Units). When a session takes place, an LU-LU session is established between an LU in the host (CICS, TSO, user application, etc.) and an LU in the terminal controller or PC.

  An LU 6.2 session provides peer-to-peer communication and lets either side initiate the session.

- *VTAM and NCP*: VTAM (Virtual Telecommunications Access Method) resides in the host and contains the SSCP, the PU for the host, and establishes the LU sessions within the host.

- NCP (Network Control Program) resides in the communications controller (front end processor) and manages the routing and data link protocols, such as SDLC and Token Ring.

- *SNA Layers*: SNA is implemented in functional layers with each layer passing control to the next layer. [Electronic Computer Glossary, March 1994]

SNMP—Simple Network Management Protocol (DOD). In 1988, the Department of Defense and commercial TCP/IP implementors designed a network management architecture for the needs of the average internet (a collection of disparate networks joined together with bridges or routers). Although SNMP was designed as the TCP's stack network management protocol, it can now manage virtually any network type and has been extended to include non-TCP devices such as 802.1 Ethernet bridges. SNMP is widely deployed in TCP/IP (Transmission Control Protocol/Internet Protocol) networks, but actual transport independence means it is not limited to TCP/IP. SNMP has been implemented over Ethernet as well as OSI transports. SNMP became a TCP/IP standard protocol in May 1990. SNMP operates on top of the Internet Protocol, and is similar in concept to IBM's NetView and ISO's CMIP. [Newton, 1993]

Data is passed from SNMP agents, which are hardware and/or software processes reporting activity in each network device (hub, router, bridge, etc.) to the workstation console used to oversee the network. The agents return information contained in a MIB (Management Information Base), which is a structure that defines what is obtainable from the device and what can be controlled (turned off, on, etc.).

SNMP 2 provides enhancements including security and an RMON (Remote Monitoring MIB), which provides continuous feedback without having to be queried by the SNMP console. Originating in the UNIX community, SNMP has spread to VMS, DOS and other environments. [Electronic Computer Glossary, March 1994]

Socket—The abstraction that serves as an endpoint for communication between processes or applications. [IBM Dictionary of Computing, 1994] *(See BSD Sockets)*

SPEC 1170—(X/Open). Spec 1170 defines a common set of APIs across multiple flavors of Unix. All Spec 1170-compliant Unix versions will interoperate, and any application written to the spec will run on any compliant Unix flavor without modification. Incompatibility at the binary level will remain...In March, 1994, X/Open announced the release of a draft specification or "snapshot" for the Spec 1170 API. The "snapshot" of Spec 1170 is the first step toward adopting the proposed Unix interface standard by X/Open's vendor and user members as part of the X/Open's CDE (Common Desktop Environment) effort. X/Open also plans to provide conformance testing for Spec 1170. According to Jeff Hansen, director of marketing communications for X/Open, "any UNIX flavor or application that wants to use the name "UNIX" must successfully pass Spec 1170 conformance tests through X/Open. [Digital News & Review, 1994; Datamation, 1994]

SPI—Service Provider Interface. Programming interface for developing Windows drivers under WOSA. In order to provide common access to services, the application (query, word processor, e-mail program, etc.) is written to a particular WOSA-supported interface, such as ODBC or MAPI, and the developer of the service software (database manager, document manager, print spooler, etc.) writes to the SPI for that class of service. [Electronic Computer Glossary, March 1994]

It defines how the network—anything from POTS to T-1, from a Northern Telecom to an AT&T PBX—shall interface to Windows Telephony, which in turn talks to the Applications Programming

Interface, which talks to the Windows telephony applications software. [Newton, 1993] *See Windows Telephony.*

SQL—(ANSI, NIST, FIPS). Structured Query Language. Pronounced "SQL" or "see kwill." A language used to interrogate and process data in a relational database. Originally developed by IBM for its mainframes, there have been many implementations created for mini- and micro-database applications. SQL commands can be used to interactively work with a database or can be embedded within a programming language to interface to a database. [Electronic Computer Glossary, March 1994]

STREAMS—Feature of UNIX System V that provides a standard way of dynamically building and passing messages up and down a protocol stack. NetWare 3.x and Windows NT also support the STREAMS interface. STREAMS passes messages from the application "downstream" through the STREAMS modules to the network driver at the end of the stack. Messages are passed "upstream" from the driver to the application. A STREAMS module would be a transport layer protocol such as TCP and SPX or a network layer protocol such as IP and IPX.

STREAMS modules can be dynamically changed (pushed and popped) at runtime, allowing the stack to be used for multiple protocols. Two important STREAMS components are the TLI and LSL interfaces, which provide common languages to the transport and data link layers. [Electronic Computer Glossary, March 1994]

Conceptually, STREAMS is similar to the pipe mechanism in establishing conventions for conveniently connecting logical units together and passing data between them. However, STREAMS offers some major benefits.

- By standardizing the kernel internals that protocol modules rely on, STREAMS makes possible the construction of protocol modules that are portable across various kernel implementations.

- By standardizing the means of communicating among protocol modules, STREAMS makes it possible to "plug" protocol modules together easily.

- The STREAMS mechanism supports dynamic streams configuration; i.e., without rebuilding and rebooting a kernel image, modules can be added to or removed from a STREAMS stack. [DG/UX, 1991]

SVID—System V Interface Definition (AT&T). A document which outlines interfaces a vendor must implement to claim System V compatibility, ensuring portability to other SVID conforming systems. [Datapro, May 1994]

TCP—Transmission Control Protocol (DARPA). Transmission Control Protocol. ARPAnet-developed transport layer protocol. Corresponds to OSI layers 4 and 5, transport and session. TCP is a transport layer, connection-oriented, end-to-end protocol. It provides reliable, sequenced, and unduplicated delivery of bytes to a remote or local user. TCP provides reliable byte stream communication between pairs of processes in hosts attached to interconnected networks. It is the portion of the TCP/IP protocol suite that governs the exchange of sequential data. [Newton, 1993]

TCP/IP—Transmission Control Protocol/Internet Protocol (DARPA). A set of protocols developed by the Department of Defense to link dissimilar computers across many kinds of networks, including unreliable ones and connected to dissimilar LANs. Developed in the 1970s by the U.S. Department of Defense's Advanced Research Projects Agency (DARPA) as a military standard protocol, its assurance of multivendor connectivity has made it popular among commercial users as well, who have adopted TCP/IP as an interim step while awaiting the availability of OSI products. Consequently, TCP/IP now is supported by many manufacturers of minicomputers, personal computers, mainframes, technical workstations and data communications equipment. It is also the protocol commonly used over Ethernet (as well as X.25) networks. It has been implemented on everything from PC LANs to minis and mainframes. Although committed to an eventual migration to an OSI architecture, TCP/IP currently divides networking functionality into only four layers:

- A Network Interface Layer that corresponds to the OSI Physical and Data Link Layers

- An Internet Layer which corresponds to the OSI network layer

- A Transport Layer, which corresponds to the OSI Transport Layer

- An Application Layer, which corresponds to the session, presentation and application layers of the OSI model [Newton, 1993]

TELNET—(ARPA) The process by which a person using one computer can sign on to a computer in another city, state or country. Terminal-remote host protocol developed for ARPAnet. Using Telnet, you can work from your PC as if it were a terminal attached to another machine by a hard-wired line. The TCP/IP protocol governing the exchange of character-oriented terminal data. [Newton, 1993]

TFTP—Trivial File Transfer Protocol. A simplified version of FTP that transfers files but does not provide password protection or user-directory capability. It is associated with the TCP/IP family of protocols. [Newton, 1993]

TIFF—Tagged Image File Format (Aldus, Microsoft). TIFF provides a way of storing and exchanging digital image data. Aldus Corp., Microsoft Corp., and major scanner vendors developed TIFF to help link scanned images with the popular desktop publishing applications. It is now used for many different types of software applications ranging from medical imagery to fax modem data transfers, CAD programs, and 3D graphic packages. The current TIFF specification supports three main types of image data: Black and white data, halftones or dithered data, and grayscale data. [Newton, 1993]

TI-RPC—Transport-Independent-Remote Procedure Call. Operating system and network-independent library of functions from Sun for executing procedures on remote computers. Allows development of distributed applications in multivendor environments. [Electronic Computer Glossary, March 1994]

TLI—Transport Level Interface (ISO). Common interface for transport services (layer 4 of the OSI model). It provides a common language to a transport protocol and allows client/server applications to be used in different networking environments.

Instead of directly calling NetWare's SPX for example, the application calls the TLI library. Thus, any transport protocol that is TLI compliant (SPX, TCP, etc.) can provide transport services to that application. TLI is part of UNIX System V. It is also supported by NetWare 3.x. [Electronic Computer Glossary, March 1994]

TOP—Technical Office Protocol (Boeing Computer Services). A communications protocol for office systems from Boeing Computer Services. It uses the Ethernet access method and is often used in conjunction with MAP, the factory automation protocol developed by

General Motors. TOP is used in the front office and MAP is used on the factory floor. [Freedman, 1991]

UDP—User Datagram Protocol. A transport protocol that guarantees only "best effort" delivery of individual information packets. Applications that use UDP instead of TCP must provide their own sequencing and retransmission support. UDP is, however, a cheaper protocol to use because it does not have the overhead of a reliable protocol such as TCP. UDP is used in applications where rapid delivery is more important than an occasional dropped packet or when the media being used is so inherently reliable that retransmission is better handled as an exception condition by the application instead of as a generic service of the transport layer. UDP uses IP to provide inter- and intranetwork routing. [DG/UX, 1991]

V.24/V.35—(CCITT)Standards for interfacing a digital device to a PTT-supplied modem. V.24 is also used as an interface standard for connecting a peripheral device, such as a visual display unit or printer to a computer. [Halsall, 1992]

V.42—(CCITT) Standard (1989) for modem error checking that uses LAP-M as the primary protocol and provides MNP Classes 2 through 4 as an alternative protocol for compatibility. [Electronic Computer Glossary, March 1994]

VFS—Virtual File System. The intermediate format used for data in transit from one system to another system. It is used as the transit format for FTAM and provides a set of common file operations that all FTAM systems understand. [Unisys, 1989]

VIM—Vendor Independent Messaging Interface (Lotus, Novell, IBM, Apple, Borland, MCI, Wordperfect, and Oracle). A programming interface that enables an application to send and receive mail over a VIM-compliant message system such as CC:Mail. [Electronic Computer Glossary, March 1994]

VTAM—(IBM). Virtual Telecommunications Access Method. Also called ACF/VTAM (Advanced Communications Function/VTAM). Software that controls communications in an IBM SNA environment. It usually resides in the mainframe under MVS or VM, but may be offloaded into an end processor that is tightly coupled to the mainframe. It supports a wide variety of network protocols, including SDLC and Token Ring. VTAM can be thought of as the network operating system of SNA. [Freedman, 1991]

WABI—Windows Application Binary Interface (Sun). WABI is a product, owned and developed by Sun's SunSelect arm, that allows Windows applications to run under Unix. Sun documented the Windows 3.1 API and published it as a developer document. Sun then submitted the document to the X/Open standards committee, through the fast-track process, and named it the Public Windows Interface (PWI). Technically, Sun describes the WABI as an implementation of PWI—and Windows 3.1 as another implementation of PWI. With WABI, Sun Microsystems is attempting to wrest control of the Windows standard from Microsoft Corp. and place it in the public domain. Sun founder and CEO Scott McNealy, argues that the changes to Windows APIs, which affect millions of users and thousands of developers, should be discussed in a public forum—not behind closed doors by Microsoft. Sun's WABI has been licensed to SunSoft, Novell, HP, and IBM. [Windows Sources, 1993; PC Week, 1993]

Windows—(Microsoft). Graphics-based windows environment from Microsoft that integrates with and interacts with DOS. It provides a desktop environment similar to the Macintosh, in which applications are displayed in re-sizable, movable windows on screen.

In order to use all the features of Windows, applications must be written for it. However, Windows also runs DOS applications.

Windows DDE (dynamic data exchange) and OLE (object linking and embedding) allow for information in one database to automatically update information in another. Windows multimedia provides a consistent way to manage audio and video. In general, Windows provides much more integration and standardization than DOS. [Electronic Computer Glossary, March 1994]

Windows 3.1, the first upgrade of Windows 3.0, introduced in 1992, provided a more stable environment for running 16-bit Windows and DOS applications than did Windows 3.0. It supports multimedia, TrueType fonts, compound documents (OLE) and drag & drop capabilities. Windows 3.1 also runs 32- bit Win32s applications by translating them into 16-bit calls. [Electronic Computer Glossary, March 1994]

Windows 4.0 is a major update of Windows 3.x, code named Chicago. It is a 32-bit operating system expected in late 1994 or early 1995, which will run 16-bit Windows and DOS applications as well as Win32s and Win32c applications. It is expected to be a self-contained operating system that does not use DOS. [Electronic Computer Glossary, March 1994]

Windows NT (New Technology), a 32-bit operating system from Microsoft, is designed to supplement and/or replace Windows and MS-DOS. As an operating system, Windows NT is targeted at the top 10% "power" users who need the power of a big, powerful operating system. Other less demanding souls will continue to run Windows and MS-DOS and possibly access Windows NT through a local area network to a server running Windows NT. Windows NT will require a minimum of 16 megabytes of RAM and 75 megs of free hard disk space. [Newton, 1993]

WOSA—Windows Open Services Architecture (Microsoft). According to Microsoft, WOSA provides a single system-level interface for connecting front-end applications with back-end services. Windows Telephony, announced in May 1993, is part of WOSA. According to Microsoft, application developers and users needn't worry about conversing with numerous services, each with its own protocols and interfaces, because making these connections is the business of the operating system, not of individual applications. WOSA provides an extensible framework in which Windows-based applications can seamlessly access information and network resources in a distributed computing environment. WOSA accomplishes this feat by making a common set of APIs available to all applications. WOSA's idea is to act like two diplomats speaking through an interpreter. A front-end application and back-end service needn't speak each other's languages to communicate as long as they both know how to talk to the WOSA interface (e.g., Windows Telephony). As a result, WOSA allows application developers, MIS managers, and vendors of back-end services to mix and match applications and services to build enterprise solutions that shield programmers and users from the underlying complexity of the system. [Newton, 1993]

WINDOWS TELEPHONY—(Microsoft, Intel). Introduced in the spring of 1993 jointly by Microsoft and Intel, Windows Telephony is actually a piece of software called a Windows Telephony DLL and two standards. The first standard is the Service Provider Interface (SPI). If a hardware manufacturer's product honors that SPI, that product can happily talk to the Windows Telephony DLL. The second standard is called the Application Programming Interface and it is directed at software developers who write applications programs. If those developers' programs adhere to the API, they can take advantage of the Windows Telephony DLL to drive whatever telephony devices or services adhere to the SPI. DLL stands for

Dynamic Link Library. It is a Windows feature that allows executable code modules to be loaded on demand and linked at run time.

Windows Telephony should bring about an explosion of shrink-wrapped Windows-based telephone software applications—from simple personal rolodexes to power dialers, to customized phone systems for banks and for bakers. It should also bring about an explosion of new telephony hardware devices—from telephones that look more like PCs than phones, to PCs that are phones, to black-box telephony devices that hook to laptops and transform hotel phones. [Newton, 1993]

Win32—(Microsoft). Programming interface (API) for the 386's 32-bit mode fully supported in Windows NT. Many functions are also supported in Windows 3.1, and applications can be written to the Win32 subset (Win32s) to gain improved performance on a 386 or up running Windows 3.1 or higher. Windows 3.1 translates the 32-bit calls in a Win32s application into its native 16-bit calls.

The Win32c subset includes almost all Windows NT functions except for security. Win32s and Win32c applications are native Windows NT applications. Windows NT runs 16-bit Windows applications via a translation layer. Windows 4.0 will also do the same.

API	**Supported by**
Win16 Windows NT,	Windows 3.0 and up
Win32s Windows NT,	Windows 3.1 and up
Win32c Windows NT,	Windows 4.0 and up
Win32 Windows NT	

[Electronic Computer Glossary, March 1994]

X.25—(CCITT). The standard device-independent interface between packet networks (DCE) and user devices (DTE). X.25 is promulgated by CCITT and is often used in Wide Area Networks (WANs) [DG/UX, 1991]; an internationally agreed upon standard protocol defined for the interface of a data terminal device, such as a computer, to a packet-switched data network. [Halsall, 1992]

X.400—(CCITT). X.400 is an international standard which enables disparate electronic mail systems to exchange messages. Although each e-mail system may operate internally with its own, proprietary set of protocols, the X.400 protocol acts as a translating software making communication between the electronic mail systems possible. The result is that users can now reach beyond people on their same e-mail system to the universe of users of interconnected systems. [Newton, 1993]

X.500—(CCITT). Directory Services. Recommendation X.500, together with other recommendations in this series, was produced to facilitate the interconnection of information processing systems to provide directory services. The set of all such systems, together with the directory information they hold, can be viewed as an integrated whole, called the "Directory." The information held by the Directory, collectively known as the Directory Information Base (DIB) is typically used to facilitate communication between, with, or about objects such as application entities, people, terminals, and distribution lists.

Recommendation X.500 introduces and models the concepts of the directory and of the DIB, and overviews their services and capabilities. Other recommendations make use of these models in defining the abstract service provided by the Directory, and in specifying the protocols through which this service can be obtained or propagated.

The Directory plays a significant role in the Open Systems Interconnection. It provides the directory capabilities required by OSI applications, management processes, other OSI layers, and telecommunications services. [88Open, 1991]

XPG—X/Open Portability Guide (X/Open). X/Open designed the XPG as the vehicle for implementing open systems in the field. XPG is an evolving portfolio of applications programming interfaces (API), protocols, and other specifications that are supported with an extensive set of conformance tests and a distinct trademark carried only on products that comply with the X/Open definitions. There have been many releases of the XPG, beginning with XPG1 in 1985 that specified a core set of interfaces and services. The most recent release, XPG4, has expanded dramatically into the area of communications and networking. By using the XPG, vendors can build products that conform to the most complete and practical set of open systems definitions available. [X/Open, July 1994]

XPG3—*See XPG.*

XPG4—*See XPG.*

X Window System—(MIT). The windowing technology developed by MIT, providing a portable windowing environment for use on a variety of hardware platforms. [Datapro, May 1994]

APPENDIX

Open Systems Terminology

AIM—An independent UNIX testing and performance analysis service, provided by AIM Technology. AIM Technology publishes benchmark results for many UNIX computer systems, which allows "comparison shopping." The AIM III tests, for example provide several metrics, such as AIMs (a performance rating relative to a VAX 11/780), maximum user load, a utilities index (how fast a system runs utilities in the foreground and background), and maximum multitasking throughput. [DG/UX]

ANSI—American National Standards Institute—The principal organization responsible for standards coordination in the United States. [HP]

API—Application Programming Interface. A documented programming interface to a product operating system or piece of code. An API allows "foreign" applications to work functionally supported by the API.

Applications interface—The common "rules" that enable a computer's operating system and applications software to communicate. A standard applications interface provides application developers with a common programming environment for writing applications that can run interchangeably on different vendors' computers. [HP]

Application layer—The layer that provides means for application processes residing in open systems to exchange information and that contains the application-oriented protocols by which these processes communicate in the Open Systems Interconnection reference model. [IBM]

347

Applications programming interface—*See API.*

Architecture—The underlying design that defines the computing environment. Architecture may consist of a Business Information Systems and a technology stack or computing architecture.

ARPA—Advanced Research Projects Agency—The former name of DARPA, the U.S. government agency that funded the creation of the ARPANET and the Internet.

ARPANET—The part of the Internet funded by ARPA/DARPA that links many universities and research and defense establishments throughout the United States and other countries. In addition to carrying live traffic, it has been used as a development test for research into inter-networking.

ASCII—American National Standard Code for Information Interchange—The standard code, using a coded character set consisting of 7-bit coded characters (8 bits including parity check), that is used for information interchange among data processing systems, data communications systems, and associated equipment. [IBM]

Athena—A multifaceted MIT computer project. One of its best known results is the X Window System, which has been placed in the public domain and is a *de facto* windowing standard for UNIX workstations. [DG/UX]

ATM—Asynchronous Transfer Mode—Very high speed telecommunication transmission technology. ATM is a high bandwidth, low-delay, packet-like switching and multiplexing technique, which segments usable capacity into fixed-size cells consisting of header and information fields allocated to services on demand. [Newton]

B1—A trusted operating system security level, which the optional trusted version of the DG/UX 5.4 operating system supports. The B1 level is defined by the Department of Defense Trusted Computer System Evaluation Criteria 5200.28-STD (DoD TCSEC). The B1 level provides Mandatory Access Controls (MAC) and is designed for use in classified or sensitive data processing environments. Another version of the DG/UX 5.4 operating system provides C2 level security (C2 is less secure than B1). [DG/UX]

BSD—Berkeley Software Distribution—The name used by the University of California at Berkeley to identify its version of the UNIX operating system. Many important UNIX innovations have come from work done at Berkeley, such as virtual memory support, a fast file system, sockets, and tools like the C-shell and the vi editor. Many versions of UNIX include BSD features. [DG/UX]

Bus—A facility for transferring data between several devices located between two end points, only one device being able to transmit at a given moment. [IBM]

C2—A trusted operating system security level. The C2 level is defined by the Department of Defense Trusted computer System Evaluation Criteria 5200.28-STD (DoD TCSEC). The C2 level provides Discretionary Access Controls (DAC) and is designed for use in sensitive but unclassified data processing environments. [DG/UX]

CAE—Common Applications Environment—X/Open's broad conceptual framework for implementing open systems. The CAE identifies those areas X/Open sees as critical for portability and interoperability. They include: systems management, object management, workstation data access, on-line transaction processing, mainframe data access, programming languages, data management, security and internationalization. This comprehensive environment covers all the standards above the hardware level, that are needed to support open systems. [X/Open]

CASE—Computer Aided Software Engineering—A set of software tools that automate the conventional application development life cycle.

CDS—Cell Directory Service—A product which tracks names and resources within a cell, allowing users to locate resources for themselves and for users in other cells. CDS is usually integrated with DFS (Distributed File Service) and GDS (Global Directory Service) to enable client communication. [Gallagher]

Client/Server—A distributed computing architecture that splits computing functionality such that the pieces can run on different pieces of hardware (e.g., desktop or workstation and network server or mainframe). It is a model of interaction in distributed computing in which a program at one site sends a request to a program at another site and then awaits a response. The requesting program is called a "client," and the responding program is called a "server."

CLNS—Connectionless Network Service—A packet-switched network where each packet of data is independent and contains complete address and control information. A connectionless network can minimize the effect of individual line failures and can distribute the load more efficiently across the network. [Unisys]

CONS—Connection-Oriented Network Service—A packet-switched network that exchanges information over a virtual circuit (a circuit where all the connections and protocols have been agreed upon and established); address information is exchanged only once. It requires a virtual circuit between the sending and receiving systems before it can send message packets. The two networks exchange address information only while the connection is being established. A connection-oriented network can provide accounting and management information for each connection. [Unisys]

CPU—Central Processing Unit—The hardware (and perhaps microcoded software) that fetches, decodes, and executes instructions, and performs arithmetic and logical operations. [DG/UX]

CSMA/CD—A bus network in which the medium access control protocol requires carrier sense and where a station always starts transmission by sending a jam signal. If there is no collision with jam signals from other stations, it begins sending data; otherwise, it stops transmission and then tries again later. [IBM]

CUT—Coordinated Universal Time—A world time standard based on atomic time. [Unisys, 1989]

DARPA—Defense Advanced Research Projects Agency—DARPA funds research activities that can lead to commercial products. For example, DARPA funded the original work at Berkeley that led to the 4.2 BSD version of the UNIX operating system. DARPA also funded work that led to TCP/IP and Internet communication protocols. [DG/UX]

Data link layer—The layer that provides services to transfer data between entities in the network layer over a communication link in the Open Systems Interconnection reference model. The data link layer detects and possibly corrects errors that may occur in the physical layer. [IBM]

Database management system CDBMS—A product that systematizes the storing, updating, and retrieving of information stored as data items (usually in the form of records in a file).

DCA—Distributed Communications Architecture—A Unisys proprietary network architecture that provides lower OSI layer services, including specialized features and functionality. [Unisys]

"De facto" standard—A product or standard that is so widely used it becomes an unofficial industry standard.

DFS—Distributed File Service—A product which provides uniform name spaces within a distributed computing environment. Integrated with CDS (Cell Directory Service) and GDS (Global Directory Service), DFS enables transparent, secure file access across local or wide area networks. [O'Brien]

Distributed computing—The dispersion of discrete computing functions, such as processing, storage and network management, among the various computers on a network, as determined by their specialized capabilities or availability. [Sun]

Distributed system—A system consisting of a group of connected, cooperating computers. [Unisys]

DS—Directory Service—An application service element that translates the symbolic names used by application processes into the complete network addresses used in an OSI environment. [IBM]

Electronic mail—A technology that allows a user to exchange correspondence, documents, and files with other electronic mail users.

End-to-end services—The services collectively offered by the lower three layers of the OSI model. [Rose, 1991]

Ethernet—A 10-megabit baseband local area network that allows multiple stations to access the transmission medium at will without prior coordination, avoids contention by using carrier sense and deference, and resolves contention by using collision detection and transmission. [IBM]

FDDI—Fibre Distributed Data Interface—An optical fibre-based ring network that can be used as a high-speed LAN or MAN. It provides a user bit rate of 100Mbps and uses a control token medium access control method.

FSF—Free Software Foundation—Supplier of the "Gnu" family of software, such as Gnu EMACS and the Gnu C compiler. The FSF licenses its Gnu software free of charge, requiring only that the licensee not charge for the software and that improvements to the software be returned to the FSF so that the improvements can propagate to other licensees. [DG/UX]

Gateway—A functional unit that interconnects two computer networks with different network architectures. [IBM]

Gnu—*See FSF-Free Software Foundation.* [DG/UX]

Graphical User Interface (GUI)—The software that creates a physical or pictorial means for the user to interact with a computer system and applications software separate from the functionality of an application program. [HP]

IEEE—Institute of Electrical and Electronics Engineers—An electronics industry professional society commissioned by ANSI to define or specify standards. One of IEEE's many committees, P1003, is working to define the POSIX standards. [HP]

Implementation—The means by which a standard, specification, or reference is applied or put into practical use; for example, OSF's OSF/1 operating system is an implementation of POSIX and X/Open standards. [HP]

Industry standard, computer—A detailed specification for the structure and functions of hardware and software based on agreement reached by a public standards organization. [HP]

Interconnectivity—*See Interoperability.*

International standards—Standards which have been finalized and published by an international standards organization.

Internet—The global collection of publicly addressable data communication networks that are able to exchange data through a common set of protocols (such as TCP/IP) and gateways. The actual size of the Internet is not known. It consists of thousands of networks worldwide, containing possibly hundreds of thousands of computers.

Interoperability—The ability of computer systems made by different vendors to exchange information, interpret it correctly, and act on it appropriately.

IS—Intermediate System—The name used by ISO to describe a router or a gateway.

ISDN—Integrated Services Digital Network—A new generation of worldwide telecommunications networks which utilize digital techniques for both transmission and switching to support both voice and data communications.

ISO—International Organization for Standardization—An organization that coordinates international standards activities, including Open Systems Interconnection standards for multivendor networking.

Kernel—The core of the UNIX operating system; the code that implements system calls. [HP]

LAN—Local Area Network—1. Any one of a number of technologies providing high-speed, low-latency transfer [Rose, 1991]. 2. A data communications network that provides service within a building or small collection of buildings. There are competing technologies and standards in use for LANs; Ethernet, Token Ring, and serial lines are all commonly used in LANs. See also MAN (Metropolitan Area Network) and WAN (Wide Area Network). LANs, MANs, and WANs differ enough in their requirements that they use significantly different technologies. [Unisys]

Language—The means by which a program tells a computer how to perform a given task. Machine language is in the form of binary code (0's and 1's). Third generation programming languages (such as Ada or FORTRAN) are translated into machine languages by a compiler. Higher level fourth generation languages (4GL) reduce the amount of code programmers must write.

MACH 2.5—The name for a UNIX operating system developed at Carnegie-Mellon University. MACH 2.5, which uses the MACH kernel, supports threads and a software layer called Camelot that provides transaction processing capabilities. MACH 2.5 also supports a UNIX interface. [DG/UX]

Mach kernel—The name for the operating system kernel developed at Carnegie-Mellon University. The MACH kernel provides low-level services, such as virtual memory management and threads (similar to what is known as multitasking in AOS/VS). The MACH 2.5 operating system and OSF/1 operating system are built on the MACH kernel. [DG/UX]

Message—A block of information sent from a source to one or more destinations. [Unisys]

MILNET—Military Logistics Network. (TCP/IP) Part of the US Defense Data Network. [Unisys]

MNLS—Multi-National Language Support—Support, such as libraries and commands, for user selection of a preferred locale. A locale allows specification of language, character set, time format, date format, and monetary symbols (among other things). [DG/UX]

Modem—A functional unit that modulates and demodulates signals. One of the functions of a modem is to enable digital data to be transmitted over analog transmission facilities. [IBM]

MS-DOS—The personal computer operating system developed by Microsoft Corporation. [Unisys]

Multiplexer—A device that takes several input signals and combines them into a single output signal in such a manner that each of the input signals can be recovered. [IBM]

Multivendor network—A computer network with hardware and software from more than one vendor. [Unisys]

NCP—Network Control Program. A program that controls the traffic between multiple terminals and a mini or mainframe. NCP typically resides in a front-end processor and performs such operations as polling the terminals.

NCSC—National Computer Security Center—A directorate of the NSA (National Security Agency). The NCSC is charged by the DoD to establish and maintain: "...technical standards and criteria for the security evaluation of trusted computer systems that can be incorporated readily into the Department of Defense component life-cycle management process..." [DG/UX]

Network layer—The layer that provides for the entities in the transfer layer the means for routing and switching blocks of data through the network between the open systems in which those entities reside in the Open Systems Interconnection reference model. [IBM]

Networking—The interconnection of two or more computers. [Sun]

Network management—The process of planning, organizing, and controlling a communications-oriented system. [IBM]

NeWS—Network Extensible Windowing System—The windowing system from Sun Microsystems. NeWS is similar to the X Window System in that it is a server-based windowing system that supports networked applications. NeWS-based applications send requests to the NeWS server in the form of PostScript programs, which are interpreted by the server and the results displayed on the graphics display. Using PostScript is a compact way of transmitting graphics information instead of transmitting pixel-level information—this can be especially valuable for networked applications that display a large amount of graphical information. PostScript interpreters are a popular way of driving many laser printers and other graphics devices; this means that the same PostScript programs used to drive the graphics display can be captured and redirected to hardcopy devices. A version of NeWS hosts X (version 11) applications. [DG/UX]

NewWave—An object manager, marketed by Hewlett-Packard, which runs on a window manager. NewWave enables a user to store, retrieve, and connect objects, such as files. [DG/UX]

NextStep—The name of Next Inc.'s GUI (Graphical User Interface) for the Mach-based version of UNIX that runs on Next machines (such as the NextStation). NextStep includes a toolkit to build 3D interfaces. NextStep also incorporates voice and sound features. The NextStep GUI is not based on the X Window System. [DG/UX]

ONC—Open Network Computing—Sun Microsystems' name for their distributed services architecture. Data General licenses ONC from Sun. ONC includes basic components like XDR and RPC, as well as higher level services like NFS, NIS, and REX, which are built using XDR and RPC. [DG/UX]

Open Look—The trademarked name for a graphical user interface designed by Sun Microsystems for itself and USL. The look and feel of the Open Look interface can be exploited by programmers who adhere to the Open Look Style Guide and who use one or two tool-kits that implement Open Look concepts (one is based on X Windows, the other is based on NeWS). [DG/UX]

Open system—1. A computer environment in which the operating system and applications software are portable and interoperable. In an open system, different vendors' hardware, operating systems, applications, and user interfaces can work together in an integrated environment. [HP] 2. Computing devices that, due to their reliance on industry-standard technologies and availability from multiple sources, are versatile, compatible and relatively inexpensive to produce. [Sun] 3. A computer system that allows application portability by adhering to and implementing industry standards. In contrast to a closed system, which is implemented against a particular vendor's proprietary software and hardware technology. [DG/UX]

Operating system—1. A group of programs that manages the resources of a computer system. The operating system handles such things as memory, input/output procedures, process scheduling, and file management. [HP] 2. The basic software that runs the inner workings of a computer; the intermediary between the application software and the computer. [Sun] 3. A group of programs operating under the control of data processing monitor program. It manages such functions as memory, processing tasks, and interprocess communication in a computer system. [Unisys]

OSF—Open Software Foundation—A nonprofit, industry-supported research and development organization formed to define source code reference implementations and specifications, develop a leading operating system, and promote a portable applications environment. [HP]

OSF/1—The first operating system implementation developed by OSF, based on X/Open and POSIX standards. [HP]

OSF/Motif—A user interface developed by OSF based on submissions by Hewlett-Packard, Digital Equipment Corporation, and Microsoft. [HP]

OSI—Open Systems Interconnection—An international effort to facilitate communications among computers of different manufacture and technology. [Rose]

OSI reference model—The International Standards Organization's Open Systems Interconnection model that is the basis for multivendor networking. [HP]

P1003—The IEEE standards committee responsible for developing interface standards to promote applications portability. [HP]

Packet switching—The process of routing and transferring data by means of addressed packets so that a channel is occupied only during transmission of a packet and becomes available for the transmission of other packets upon completion of the transmission. [IBM]

PAD—Packet Assembler/Disassembler—The mechanism for disassembling packets at the sending end and assembling them to form the complete message at the receiving end. It is traditionally used in X.25 networks. [Unisys]

PDN—Public Data Network—A network providing communication services for a fee to anyone who desires such services and has access to the appropriate equipment. [Unisys]

PDU—Protocol Data Unit—The message units exchanged between protocol entities.

Physical layer—The first layer of the OSI Reference Model. It governs hardware connections and byte-stream encoding for transmission. It is the only layer that involves a physical transfer of information between network nodes. [Unisys]

Pipe—A UNIX interprocess communication (IPC) mechanism that connects two processes. The output from one process is used as input to the other, without the user having to manage temporary files. A pipeline can include two or more processes. The pipe mechanism can be used at the shell command-level to string commands together on a command line. A procedural interface is also available for use within programs. [DG/UX]

Portability—The ability to use an operating system or applications software on different vendors' computer systems. [HP]

POSIX—Portable Operating System Interface for Computer Environments—The IEEE standard definition for the interface between applications and the operating environment. POSIX permits the portability of applications at the source code level. [HP]

PowerOpen—The name for the UNIX operating system being designed jointly by IBM and Apple to run on the new PowerPC processors. The current plan for PowerOpen is that it will combine features of the IBM AIX operating system with features of the Apple Macintosh interface. PowerOpen is scheduled to be ready in the "next two or three years." [DG/UX]

PowerPC—The name for the single-chip family of RISC CPUs being designed jointly by IBM and Motorola. PowerPC, which Motorola plans to second source and OEM, is based on the RISC architecture used currently in the IBM RS/6000 workstations. [DG/UX]

Presentation layer—The layer that provides for the selection of a common syntax for representing information and for transformation of application data into or from this common syntax in the Open Systems Interconnection reference model. [IBM]

Protocol—A set of semantic and syntactic rules that determines the behavior of functional units in achieving communication. [IBM]

Protocol entity—The code that controls the operation of a protocol layer.

PTT—Postal, Telegraph and Telephone—The government agency that controls all the postal and public telecommunications networks and services in a country.

Repudiation and non-repudiation—Denial of the authenticity or correctness of a transaction or message.

RFS—Remote File Sharing—The System V distributed file system capability. RFS differs from NFS in that it implements full UNIX file system semantics, making it functionally more robust. However, RFS, because of its full support of the UNIX file system capabilities, is not as amenable to implementation on non-UNIX systems, as NFS is. [DG/UX]

RFT—OSF's Request for Technology—A vendor-neutral process whereby OSF issues a public request (within the computer industry) for submissions in a specified technological area. Submissions are then evaluated and adopted by OSF. [HP]

RISC—Reduced Instruction Set Computer—A name for a class of computer designs characterized by a regular and uncomplicated instruction set (typically fewer that 100 instructions). For example, the Motorola MC88100 has 51 instructions. The uncomplicated RISC instruction set simplifies hardware design, allowing fast, highly-pipelined implementations. Because of the instruction set simplicity, the instruction execution rate of a RISC machine (such as the Motorola 88K) is faster than that of a CISC machine (such as the Motorola 68K).

Most RISC machine architectures implement their instructions in silicon (hardwired logic), rather than in microcode, which provides even better performance when compared to a microcoded CISC machine. (Note that some entry level RISC machines use a combination of hardwired and microcoded instructions). RISC machines require more sophisticated compiler optimizations to achieve high levels of performance. [DG/UX]

RPC—Remote Procedure Call—A layer of distribution service that intercepts a service request on one system in a network, packages the request for transmission over the network, and unpackages the request on another system in the network for execution, then passes back the results to the original requester. RPC is one of the bases on which a service such as NFS is built. Other system services can be built using RPC, and distributed applications may choose to use RPC. [DG/UX]

SAA—System Application Architecture—A superset of SNA (System Network Architecture). While SNA deals solely with data transport issues, SAA deals with portable application interface standards and subsumes SNA as its standard for data transport services. [DG/UX]

Scalability—The ability to use the same software on different classes of computers, ranging from personal computers to supercomputers. [HP]

Session—A cooperative relationship between two communicating application entities. [Unisys, 1989]

Session layer—The layer that provides the means necessary for two end users to organize and synchronize their dialogue and to manage their data exchange in the Open Systems Interconnection reference model. [IBM]

Shell—A command line interpreter that provides users a means of executing programs and manipulating their file systems. Several shells are available on UNIX systems. the most common are the Bourne shell (the **sh** command) from System V and the C shell (the **csh** command) from BSD. Another shell, known as the Korne shell (the **ksh** command), is gaining in popularity.

Server—A computer that manages and coordinates the sharing of computing resources. [Sun]

SNA—System Network Architecture—IBM's overall data communications architecture. [DG/UX]

*SNA Layers—SNA is implemented in functional layers with each layer passing control to the next. This layering is called a protocol stack. [Freedman]

Sniffer—A network management tool for monitoring traffic characteristics and content. Along with its many positive uses, this device can be also used to intercept passwords, IDs and routing information. A good reason for encryption.

Socket—The BSD programming interface to data communications facilities, which is now available in System V. Sockets provide a mechanism for an application to build a linkage to a transport service and deliver/receive blocks of information to/from the transport service. Sockets are kernel-based in DG/UX and BSD-derived operating systems—they are implemented as a set of library routines in SVR4-based operating systems. [DG/UX]

Solaris—The name of the operating environment developed by SunSoft (a Sun Microsystems company). Solaris, which is shipping currently at version 1.0, is based on SunOS and ONC (Open Network Computing). Solaris uses the X Window System with the

Open Look GUI (instead of Motif). Version 1.0 runs on SPARC machines. Plans are for version 2.0 to run on both SPARC and 80X86 machines. Version 2.0 is projected to ship in 1992. [DG/UX]

Source code—Software programs that have not been compiled (that is, they are in textual, rather than binary, format). Source code can be portable if it complies with interface standards, such as POSIX and X/Open's CAE. [HP]

SPARC—The name of the RISC chipset used by and licensed by Sun Microsystems. The SPARC architectural definition is maintained by SPARC International and is described in its SPARC Compliance Definition (SCD). Other parts of the SCD describe the software and interfaces (such as bus interfaces) that a system must meet to be "SPARC compliant." [DG/UX]

Specification—In reference to programming, a precise definition of the records and programs needed to execute a standard or a particular processing function. [HP]

Spoofing—Falsely representing oneself or a process acting for oneself as an authorized user or process by capturing and using legitimate access control information such as a password or by invading and piggybacking on a legitimate, unclosed or improperly closed session.

Standard—1. A specification or technology that has widespread acceptance within an industry. Standards may be promulgated by a licensed body charged with defining and integrating standards (*de jure* standards) or may arise from products that have such widespread use as to become *de facto* standards. 2. A specification, a set of functions, or a specific implementation that has been widely accepted either formally or informally as the preferable method or interface. [Cerutti]

Star—A type of network topology in which there is a central node that performs all switching (and hence routing) functions for a radial configuration of nodes.

Streams—A standard interface for character and message-based I/O within the kernel and between the kernel and the rest of the UNIX system. Conceptually, streams is similar to the pipe mechanism in establishing conventions for conveniently connecting logical units together and passing data between them.

Subsystem—A set of software modules that executes a portion of the functions performed in an operating environment. Examples include a database management subsystem and a graphics subsystem. [HP]

SunOS—The name for Sun Microsystems' UNIX implementation. This product was derived originally from a BSD base, but many major modifications have been made, such as to support NFS, windowing systems, and shared libraries.

SVID—System V Interface Definition—The AT&T (USL) specification for a portion of their System V UNIX product. The SVID is divided into base and extension sections. Conforming systems must support the base and may support one or more of the extension sections. The SVID does not define everything in a specific UNIX release like System V Release 4; this is because there are some things that may be specific to a specific hardware line and therefore not appropriate for inclusion in the generic System V definition. [DG/UX]

SVR4—System V Release 4—A UNIX operating system released in 1989. SVR4 was created by an alliance between AT&T and Sun Microsystems to consolidate System V, Berkeley 4.XBSD, SunOS, and Xenix in SVR4. [Datapro]

SVR4 MP—UNIX Software Laboratories' Summer '91 multiprocessor release, based on SVR4. Compared to DG/UX 5.4, SVR4 MP is not yet fully symmetrical, nor is it very fine grained, especially in some parts of the virtual memory and file system code. Also, SVR4 MP is not a completely preemptible design; that is, the operating system code can be preempted only at designated "preemption points," rather than anywhere in the kernel—as in DG/UX. [DG/UX]

SVVS—System V Verification Suite—A test suite licensed by USL (UNIX Software Laboratories), which is used to verify conformance to a portion of the SVID (System V Interface Definition). [DG/UX]

Synchronous transmission—Data transmission in which the time of occurence of each signal representing a bit is related to a fixed time base. [IBM]

System V—AT&T's source code reference implementation of the UNIX operating system. [HP]

TCB—Trusted Computing Base—The combination of hardware and software subsystems that combine to support a particular level of security. Typically includes parts of the kernel and code outside of the kernel. [DG/UX]

TCP/IP—A set of communication protocols that support peer-to-peer connectivity functions for both local and wide area networks. [IBM]

TCSEC—Trusted Computer System Evaluation Criteria—A technical standard against which the NCSC (National Computer Security Center) evaluates a computer system to see that it meets the minimum standards for particular security levels, such as C1 and B1. The TCSEC is colloquially known as the "orange book." [DG/UX]

Technology—Innovations in computing hardware, software, tools, languages, and databases including fundamental concepts, structure, uses, approach, and management methods.

Thread—A single flow of control within a process. Threads are the concurrent programming paradigm advanced for UNIX-based systems. Threads enable programmers to manage flow of control within a process so that different parts of a process can run simultaneously on multiple processors.

A thread is created within a process, never leaves the process, and does not "see" threads in other processes. Threads use the resources of the kernel's Light Weight Process (LWP) abstraction. Multiple threads may be implemented as one or more LWPs. [DG/UX]

Time Bomb—A hostile piece of software (often hidden or posing as benign—*See Trojan Horse* which is triggered by a specific time, event or number of process iterations. The Friday the Thirteenth virus is also a time bomb. Some software suppliers cripple their software's function at the cessation of the lease period. Depending on how gracefully it is executed and with how much advance warning, this could be a time bomb. One overeager supplier installed file destruct mechanisms into its applications to punish delinquent payment.

Token bus—1. A type of local area (data) network. All the devices are connected in the form of a (physical) ring and messages are transmitted by allowing them to circulate around the ring. A device can only transmit a message on the ring when it is in possession of a control (permission) token. A single token is passed from one device to another around the ring. [Halsall, 1992] 2. As defined in IEEE 802.4, a master controller that has a list of addresses for all computers on the LAN and controls a token (a packet of control information). When a computer on the LAN receives the token from the master controller, it can transmit. When it has nothing more to transmit, it returns the token to the master controller. [Unisys]

Token ring—As defined in IEEE 802.5, a communication method that uses a token to control access to the LAN. The difference between a token bus and a token ring is that a token ring LAN does not use a master controller to control the token. Instead, each computer knows the address of the computer that should receive the token next. When a computer with the token has nothing to transmit, it passes the token to the next computer in line. [Unisys]

Transport layer—The layer that provides a reliable end-to-end data transfer service in the Open Systems Interconnection reference model. [IBM]

Trojan Horse—A hostile piece of software which poses as benign or hides within another benign program. It may be triggered in many different ways.

TRON—The Realtime Operating System Nucleus. An advanced real-time computer architecture and operating system under development by Japanese universities and corporations. Its ultimate goal is common architecture and user interface from the smallest consumer appliance to the largest supercomputer. TRON-based intelligent cars are also under research and development.

C-TRON is the OSI-compliant communications system; B-TRON is for business applications; and I-TRON is the version for industrial applications.

There is considerable controversy over TRON, as its adoption may exclude foreign vendors from competing in the Japanese market. [Freedman]

Trusted system—A computer system that employs sufficient hardware and software integrity measures to allow its use for processing a range of sensitive or classified information for a diverse set of users, without violating access privileges. Levels of security for trusted systems are described in the Department of Defense Trusted Computer System Evaluation Criteria 5200.28-STD (DoD TCSEC). Security levels, from most secure to least secure include A, B3, B2, B1, C2, C1. The DG/UX 5.4 operating system supports security levels B1 and C2. [DG/UX]

UNIX operating system—1. A computer operating system rapidly gaining worldwide acceptance as a standard for both technical and commercial applications. [Sun, 1991] 2. A trademark of AT&T; also inappropriately used as a generic term for various versions of the UNIX operating system (e.g., Hewlett-Packard's HP-UX operating system, Microsoft's XENIX operating system, UC Berkeley's BSD operating system, and DEC's Ultrix operating system). [HP]

User interface—1. Software that governs the ease with which a user can interact with the computer. [Sun, 1991] 2. The software, including screens, menus, and windows, that controls the interaction of the user with a computer system. [HP]

\usr\group—A nonprofit trade association (now called UniForum) founded in 1980 and dedicated to promoting the UNIX operating system; a \usr\group standards committee was the precursor to the IEEE P1003, or POSIX, committee. [HP]

Viruses— Software programs which produce results which are frequently destructive and always annoying. The distinctive characteristics of a virus include self-replication and elusive defense mechanisms. A virus can be a Trojan Horse or a Time Bomb or both. Not all Trojan Horses or Time Bombs are viruses since they may not replicate.

Virtual terminal—A protocol entity forming part of the application layer. It enables an application process to have a dialogue with a remote terminal in a standard way, irrespective of the make of the terminal. [Halsall]

VSX—X/Open Conformance Test Suite—A test suite, provided by the X/Open Co. Ltd., which is used to verify conformance to the X/Open standards. [DG/UX]

WAN—Wide Area Network—A data communications network that serves a (potentially) very large area. WANs are sometimes referred to as "long haul" networks, in contrast to Local Area Networks (LANs) or Metropolitan Areas Networks (MANs). Currently, most WANs are based on high speed serial I/O techniques, such as X.25. [DG/UX]

Workstation—A high-speed desktop computer with a powerful multitasking operating system, a high-resolution graphics display, integrated networking functions and connectivity to different computer systems. [Sun]

Worms—A specialized virus-like program which replicates and sends itself repeatedly to all the locations on a network that it can reach. It does not hide. It does its damage by creating major bottlenecks and network crashes through the traffic overload caused by its geometric replication and retransmissions.

X client—The application process that needs to use a graphics display in the X Windows system. A client may be a user-written application that calls library routines in slib. A client may be a utility provided with the X Windows system that provides an interface for the interactive user; such a client is called a window manager. The client communicates to the server using xlib functions that produce requests expressed in the X protocol. Since these requests are passed to the server over a socket connection, the client and the server may actually be running on different systems. A client, for example, might run on a high performance server that has no graphics display and renders its results on a lower performance graphics server. [DG/UX]

XENIX—The name for a version of UNIX (developed by Microsoft) with commercial extensions. XENIX runs on a number of Intel 80X86 machines. AT&T has incorporated XENIX functions into its base System V software as part of an effort to create a single UNIX standard. [DG/UX]

xlib—The library that comprises the basic functions that the X Windows system offers to user programs. xlib functions translate the clients' logical requests into the X protocol, the form the X server interprets. [DG/UX]

X11R5—X Window System Version 11 Release 5—The current version of the X Window System which was released September, 1991. [Freedman]

X/Open—An international consortium of computer vendors working to create an internationally supported, vendor-independent, Common Applications Environment based on industry standards. [HP]

XPG—X/Open Portability Guide—A series of publicly available reference documents that defines the steps applications developers must take to ensure applications portability at the source code level. [HP]

X server—The process that mediates across to a graphics device in the X Window System. The server's primary job is to drive the graphics display from client's requests and to manage keyboard and mouse input.

Clients communicate requests to the server by making calls to xlib library routines, which in turn convert the clients' requests into the X protocol before they are handed over to the server, which integrates the requests of the various clients and performs services like signaling clients whose windows become obscured or uncovered. Because the X server communicates with its clients via a socket connection, the client may actually be running on a machine remote from the server. [DG/UX, 1991]

X terminal—A terminal with a built-in processor that supports the standard elements of the X Window system (widgets), such as windows, borders, and buttons. X terminals are analogous to "dumb" ASCII terminals in that application program computation is handled by an X server. However, X terminals off-load much of the window management functions from the server.

X terminals are typically less expensive ($1,500-$4,000) than diskless workstations, but there is overlap between the two implementations. X terminals contrast to diskless workstations in that they are not designed to run application software. [DG/UX, 1991]

X Window System—A public domain window management system developed as part of Project Athena at MIT. The X Window System (X) provides fully hierarchical windows (windows can be nested within windows to arbitrary levels). X provides the tools for building Graphical User Interfaces (GUIs). Motif and Open Look are two examples of GUIs that run on X. X is not tied architecturally to UNIX or to a particular hardware implementation. AViiON computers support X, and there are versions of X that run on other platforms such as the Apple Macintosh and on 386-486 PCs. [DG/UX, 1991]

REFERENCES

Introduction

Benjamin, Robert and Blunt, Jon. "Critical IT Issues: The Next Ten Years." *Sloan Management Review.* Summer 1992.

Design News. "Building Printers 'The HP Way.'" March 7, 1994, p. 96.

Donovan, John J. *Business Re-engineering with Technology.* Cambridge Technology Group. 1993.

Huey, John. "Nothing is Impossible." Fortune. September 23, 1991. Volume 124, No. 7, p. 134.

Rukeyser, Louis. *Louis Rukeyser's Business Almanac.* Simon & Schuster. 1991.

Verity, John W. "Computer Confusion," *Business Week.* June 10, 1991, p. 73.

Information Systems in Perspective

Cerutti, Daniel. *Distributed Computing Environments.* McGraw-Hill. 1993.

Hoff, Benjamin. *The Tao of Pooh.* 1982.

Investor's Business Daily. "Catalog Retailers Ponder A Future Without Paper." Page 4. February 9, 1994.

Kidder, Tracy. *The Soul of New Machine.* 1982.

Interop. Millikin, Michael D. Vice President, Patricia Seybold's Office Computing Group. "Distributed Computing Environments." Interop 90 Conference Proceedings. October, 1990.

Springfield Business Journal. January 25, 1993.

Definitions and Disinformation

The American Heritage Dictionary. Second College Edition. Houghton Mifflin. 1985.

AT&T Global Information Solutions. Tim Davis. 1994.

Bull HN Information Systems. Peter Stavropulos. 1994.

Computer Associates. Bob Gordon. 1994.

Data General Corporation. Margaret N. Taylor. 1994.

Digital Equipment Corporation (DEC). Kate Thompson. 1994.

Hewlett Packard. Sanjay Srivastava. 1994.

IBM. Helen Trollman. 1994.

Lotus Development Corporation. Bryan Simmons.1994.

Microsoft. Cristine Wittriss, 1994.

Open Software Foundation (OSF). Jane Saneloff. December, 1993.

Oracle Corporation. Brett Bachman. 1994.

Rose, Marshall T. *The Open Book—A Practical Perspective on OSI.* Prentice-Hall. 1990.

Safire, William. *Quoth the Maven—More on Language.* Random House, 1993.

SUN. Eric Jaeger. 1994.

Sybase. Berl Hartman. 1994.

Unisys. Bruce Halvorsen. 1994.

X/Open Company Ltd. Organization Overview. 1994.

Benefits, Opportunities, Costs, Risks AND Barriers

Dataquest X/Open XTRA 1993 Survey. *Olivetti presentation.* X/Open Xtra Conference. December, 1993.

Standards Organizations

ANSI, November 1993. Ms. Bernadette St. John, Director of Member Relations, ANSI, November 16, 1993.

COS. 1994. Company Distributed Information.

Gray, Pamela A. Open Systems, A Business Strategy for the 1990's. McGraw Hill. 1991.

Heffernan, Henry. "IBM Lends a Standard; OIW Adopts CPI-C as First Non-OSI API." *Software Magazine.* December, 1992.

IEEE, December 1993. Institute of Electrical and Electronics Engineers. Company Distribution Materials. December 9, 1993.

ISO, November 1993. International Organization for Standardization. Roger Frost, Press Officer, November 12, 1993.

McMullen, June. "User Groupies" LAN Magazine. Volume 8, number 6, p. 103. June 1993.

OMG, November 1993. Chris Stone, Object Management Group, November 5, 1993.

OSF, December 1993. Open Software Foundatation, Jane Saneloff, December 9, 1993.

Rose, Marshall T. *The Open Book: A Practical Perspective on OSI.* New Jersey. Prentice Hall, 1991.

UniForum, November 1993. Dick Shippee, UniForum, November 2, 1993.

X/Open, 1994. Company Distribution Materials, 1994. Robert Noyes, August, 1994.

Standards

88Open Consortium. *The World of Standards. An Open Systems Reference Guide.* San Jose, CA, 1991.

Crystal, David. *The Cambridge Encyclopedia of Language.* Cambridge University Press. 1987.

Data General's UNIX Development Group (DG/UX). Open Systems Technology, Technical Brief. 1991.

Data Pro Reports on UNIX Systems & Software, May, 1994.

Datamation. "Where's UNIX Headed?" Datamation. April, 1994.

Digital, 1994. *Digital News & Review,* 1994.

Economist, 1987. "Can high-tech save Esperanto?" May 23, 1987. Page 47.

Electronic Computer Glossary. March, 1994. (Excerpted from the Electronic Computer Glossary. Reprinted with kind permission from Computer Language Company. Copyright, 1994. 5521 State Park Road. Point Pleasant, PA 18950)

Genesis II, Genesis 11:1-9

Katzner, Kenneth. *The Languages of the World.* Funk & Wallis. 1975.

Lee, John and Shapiro, Joseph P. "In search of a common language." *U.S. News and World Report.* March 2, 1987, page 72.

Newton, Harr, 1993. (Reprinted with kind permission from Newton Telecom Dictionary. Harry Newton Flat Iron Publisher, (212) 691-8215.)

Open Software Foundation (OSF). *Distributed Management Environment.* 1991.

Open Software Foundation (OSF). *Open Line.* September/October 1991.

OSF, July 1994. Jack Dwyer, Open Software Foundation, July 12, 1994.

Shelton, Robert E. "OMG's CORBA 2.0; Industrial-Grade Standard for Distributed Object Computing?" *Distributed Computing Monitor.* Volume 8, number 5, page 3. May 1993.

Shenker, Israel. "Doing away with all babble from the Tower of Babel". *Smithsonian.* Volume 17. January 1987.

Windows-DOS Developers Journal. December, 1993.

X/Open, July 1994. Robert Noyes, July 14, 1994.

Vendor Directions

Digital Equipment Corporation (DEC). Corporate literature, product materials. Kate Thompson, *Business Management and Competitive Analysis Manager.* 1994.

Hewlett Packard (HP). Corporate literature, product materials. Sanjay Srivastava, *Market Communication Manager.* 1994.

International Business Machines (IBM). Corporate literature, product materials. Helen Trollman, *Manager, Open Distributed Systems Market.* 1994.

MCS. *MCS 1993 Evaluation: Open Systems—Interoperability and Portability.* Gartner Group, 1993.

Microsoft Corporation. Corporate literature, product materials. Cristine Wittress, *Microsoft Systems Product Manager.* 1994.

Sun Microsystems (Sun). Corporate literature, product materials. Eric Jaeger, *Director of Strategic Standards.* 1994.

Impact On Everyone

Gartner Group. "Five Year IT Spending Scenario." *IS Research Note.* December 17, 1993.

Lorin, Harold. "Limits to Distributed Computing: Problems include old software, new development and human nature." *Computerworld,* October 28, 1991.

Strassmann, Paul A. *Business Value of Computers.* Information Economics Press. New Canaan, Connecticut. 1990.

X/Open Market Research Report. 1993.

Case Studies

Abbott, Edwin A. *Flatland; A Romance of Many Dimensions.* Dover Publications. 1992.

Home Depot. Dave Ellis, *Director of Network Services* and Beach Clark Jr., *Senior Manager—Network Architecture.* 1994.

Honeywell. Bill Saunders, *Vice President of Information Systems* and John White, *Manager of Technology Supplier Relations.* 1994.

Hyatt Hotels. Gordon Kerr, *Senior Vice President* of Regency Systems Solutions. 1994.

Merck. Charles Popper, *Vice President of Corporate Computer Resources*; Ian Miller, *Senior Director of Architecture and Emerging Technology*; Richard Bakunas, *Director of Infrastructure: Automation & Information Technology Department.* 1994.

Opening Systems

CSC Consulting Group. *Critical Issues of Information Systems Management for 1994.* The Seventh Annual Survey of I/S Management Issues. North American and European Edition.

Deloitte & Touche LLP. *Leading Trends in Information Services.* Information Technology Consulting Services Sixth Annual Survey of North American CIOs 1994.

Insights. *Insights Quarterly*, CSC Index. Winter, 1993.

Milne, A. A. *Winnie the Pooh.*

Closing

McConnell. "Fax, Digital Facsiumile Technology, and Applications." *The Artech House Telecommunication Library.* 1989.

Appendix—Standards Groups

88Open Consortium. *The World of Standards: An Open Systems Reference Guide Ltd.* San Jose, CA, 1991.

Ambrosio, Johanna. "Open systems user groups lead the way." *Computerworld.* August 26, 1991. Page 27.

ANSI, November 1993. Ms. Bernadette St. John, Director of Member Relations, ANSI. November 16, 1993.

AOW, November 1993. K. Miyao, AOW Secretariat. November 8, 1993.

Baker. "The Network Lament: Routing and Addressing Problems on the Internet." *Unix Review.* November, 1992. Volume 10, number 11, page 15.

Brandel, William. "New Alliance of 20 Messaging, Scheduling, and Gateway Vendors Showcases Message Handling Service Interoperability." *LAN Times.* January 25, 1993. Volume 10, number 2, page 9.

Breitenburg, Maureen. *Directory of International and Regional Organizations Conducting Standards Related Activities.* 1990.

CBEMA, November 1993. *Computer and Business Equipment Manufacturers Association.* Janet Geobel. November 5, 1993.

CEN, November 1993. Sharon Larson. CEN, November 9, 1993.

Computergram, September 1991. "New U.S. standards body may threaten X/Open." *Computergram International Issue.* September 2, 1991, number 1752.

Computergram. May, 1992. "SQL Access Group suspends work on key access specifications as cash, backers run out." *Computergram International*. May 22, 1992.

COS, 1991. Company Distributed Information.

COS, 1994. Company Distributed Information.

Datapro. "COSE Accelerates Open Systems Compatilibity." *Datapro Reports on UNIX Systems & Software*. Mary Hubley. October, 1993.

Datapro. "UNIX International: Mapping System V and Beyond." *Datapro*. Mary Hubley. August 1993. UX31-090-101.

Desmond, John. "MOSES leads the way to Open Requirements." *Software Magazine*. March, 1993. Volume 13, number 4, page 67.

Devoney, Chris. "The Promise of PCMCIA." *Computer Shopper.* December, 1992. Volume 12, number 12, page 74.

Digital News & Review. "Consortium to Develop Standard for Multimedia X.400 Transmission." *Digital News & Review*. December 7, 1992. Volume 9, number 23, page 23.

DMTF, 1993. Desktop Management Task Force. Organization Distribution Materials. 1993.

DSIS Group, 1994. Organization Informational Material.

ECMA, July 1994. Mr. Jan van den Beld. European Computer Manufacturers Association, July 14, 1994.

EDGE On & About AT&T. "Speech Recognition: SCSA Workgroup Formed to Develop API." *EDGE On & About AT&T*. July 26, 1993. Volume 8, number 261, page 11.

EDGE: Work-Group Computing Report. "Desktop Management Standard: DMTF Sponsors Developer's Conference 'Building the Intelligent Desktop' Set for October 18." *EDGE: Work-Group Computing Report*. July 26, 1993. Volume 4, number 166, page 28.

EDGE: Work-Group Computing Report. "Multimedia Kaleida Labs Announces Manufacturers' Alliance: Charter Members Named." *EDGE: Work-Group Computing Report*. May 31, 1993. Volume 4, number 158, page 16.

Eibisch, James and Jubley, Mary. "Advanced Computing Environment (ACE) Initiative." *Datapro Reports on UNIX Systems & Software*. Number UX31-210-101. December 1991.

Fibre Channel Association, 1993. Organization Distribution Materials.

Fredric, Paul. "UNIX International Spells Out Future of UNIX System 5." *Network World*. February 15, 1993. Volume 10, number 7, page 5.

Freedman, Alan. The Computer Glossary: *The Complete Illustrated Desk Reference*. New York: AMACOM. 1991. Reprinted with kind permission.

Garry, Greg. "Twelve Say They'll Back MIPS Interface Spec." *Digital News & Review*. March 15, 1993. Volume 10, number 6, page 25.

Garry, Greg. "Eight Hope to Standardize 32-bit Development." *Digital News & Review*. March 15, 1993. Volume 10, number 6, page 15.

Gerishanker, "Authority Shifts for Internet Standards." *Communication Week*. November 23, 1992.

Gillen, Al. "Power to the Platforms: Computer Makers Rally Around PowerPC Chip with New Consortium." *MIDRANGE Systems*. April 13, 1993. Volume 6, number 7, page 1.

Heffernan, Henry. "IBM Lends a Standard; OIW Adopts CPI-C as First Non-OSI API." Software Magazine. December, 1992. Volume 12, number 17, page 27.

Heffernan, November 1992. "U.S. Looks to ECMA: Federal Agencies, NIST Pushing PCTE Adoption," *Software Magazine*, Henry Heffernan, November 1992, Volume 12, page 33.

Hickerson, L. Brooks, Pervier, Cheryl S., and Valdes, Peter. "Managing networked workstations." *IEEE Spectrum*. April 1992.

Houser, Walter R. "NIST's Making History with Open Systems." *Government Computer News*, December 9, 1991. Volume 10, number 25, page 65.

IEC, November 1993. International Electrotechnical Commission. Charles T. Zegers, Secretary, November 2, 1993.

IEEE, December 1993. Institute of Electrical and Electronic Engineers. Distribution Materials. December 9, 1993.

ISO, November 1993. International Organization for Standardization. Roger Frost, Press Officer. November 12, 1993.

ITU, September, 1993. International Telecommunication Union. Distribution Materials. September 11, 1993.

Johnson, Jim and Gray, Jim. "Benchmarks Help with Server Platform Buys." *Software Magazine.* September, 1993. Volume 13, number 13, page 93.

LaCroix, Catherine. "Open User Recommended Solutions: Industry Briefs." *LAN Technology.* Volume 8, number 1, page 17. January 1992.

LAN Computing. "Standards Watch." *LAN Computing.* February, 1993. Volume 4, number 2, page 3.

LAN Computing. "PPP Group Fosters Interoperability." *LAN Computing.* December, 1992. Volume 3, number 12, page 7.

Lavin, Paul. "Ace is High." *Computer Weekly.* May 13, 1993. Page 42.

Levine, Ron. "A Standard for Service." *DEC Professional.* August, 1993. Volume 12, number 8, page 66.

Macpherson, Andrew. *International Telecommunication Standards Organizations.* Boston: Artech House. 1990.

Masud, S.A. "Defense's One-Stop GOSIP Shop: JITC to Become Site for European, U.S. Interoperability Testing." *Government Computer News.* May 10, 1993. Volume 12, number 10, page 37.

McMullen, June. "User Groupies." *LAN Magazine.* June 1993. Volume 8, number 6, page 103.

Moser, Karen D. "IDAPI Group Releases First Draft of Spec: Will Compete with Microsoft-sponsored ODBC Standard." *PC Week.* March 1, 1993. Volume 10, number 8, page 12.

"New US standards body may threaten X/Open." *Computergram International Issue.* September 2, 1991, number 1752.

NIST, November, 1993. National Institute of Standards and Technology. Sharon Kemmerer. November 12, 1993.

OMG, November 1993. Chris Stone, Object Management Group, November 5, 1993.

OMG, August 1994. Organization representative, Object Management Group, August 1994.

OSF, December, 1993. Open Software Foundation. Distribution Materials.

OSF, August, 1994. Open Software Foundation. Jack Dwyer. August 1994.

The OSINetter Newsletter. "IETF Meets for First Time in Europe." *The OSINetter Newsletter*. August, 1993. Volume 8, number 8, page 6.

OSINET. Carol A. Edgar, OSINET, November 9, 1993.

The OSINetter Newsletter. "XZPIA to Develop Additional Calls for CMC Program." *The OSINetter Newsletter*. July, 1993. Volume 8, number 7, page 13.

POSC, 1994. Corporate Informational Material.

PowerOpen Association, 1994. Corporate Informational Material.

PCCA, 1994. Organization Informational Material.

Press, Larry. "The Net: Progress and Opportunity." *Communications of the ACM*. December, 1992. Volume 35, number 12, page 21.

Rada, Roy. "The Power of Standards." *Communications of the ACM*. August, 1993. Volume 36, number 8, page 11.

Radosevich, Lynda. "Vendors Unite to Promote Workflow." *Computerworld*. August 2, 1993. Volume 27, number 31, page 16.

Rose, Marshall T. *The Open Book: A Practical Perspective on OSI*. New Jersey. Prentice-Hall, 1990.

Seybold, Patricia. "The Alphabet Soup of Standards Bodies: A Primer on Setting Standards." *Patricia Seybold's Office Computing Report*. October, 1992. Volume 15, number 10.

Schaffhauser, Dian "Xbase Standards Effort Lurches Ahead." Data Based Advisor. January, 1993. Volume 11, number 1, page 99.

SGML, 1994. Consortium Informational Material.

Sherer, Paul M. "Consortium Plans to Promulgate Spec for Multiuser DOS." *PC Week*. November 9, 1992. Volume 9, number 45, page 84.

Software Magazine. "SQL Access Group Unveils First Specs." *Software Magazine*. May, 1993. Volume 13, number 7, page 16.

Software Magazine. "Novell Creates UNIX Group." *Software Magazine*. September 1993. Volume 13, number 13, page 14.

TPC, 1994. Corporate Informational Material.

UniForum, November 1993. Dick Shippee, UniForum, November 2, 1993.

Unisys Corporation. *How to Speak Open Systems.* 1989.

UNIX Review. "MIPS." *Unix Review.* June, 1993. Volume 11, number 6, page 120.

UNIX International (UI). "UNIX International Overview." *Working Together for Open Systems, UNIX International General Information.* Distribution Material.

UNIX International (UI). *UNIX International Member List as of 10/1/91.* Company distribution material. 1991.

UNIX World's Open Computing. "Bye Bye, UI." *UNIX World's Open Computing.* March, 1994. McGraw-Hill. Volume 11, number 3, page 3.

USENIX, 1994. Organization Informational Material.

Vizard, Michael. "Consortium May Loosen OLE's Grip on Market." *Computerworld.* September 20, 1993. Volume 27, number 38, page 1.

XAPIA, 1994. Organization Informational Material.

X Consortium, 1994. Corporate Informational Material.

X/Open, 1994. Company Distribution Materials.

X/Open, July 1994. X/Open XPG Technical Background Information, received from Robert Noyes, July14, 1994.

X/Open, August 1994. Robert Noyes.

Appendix—Standards And Technologies

88Open Consortium. *The World of Standards. An Open Systems Reference Guide.* San Jose, CA, 1991.

Berst, Jesse. "Coalition Announces OLE Alternatives." *The CompuThink Windows Watcher.* July, 1993. Volume 3, number 7, page 4.

Computer Weekly. "IBM Unveils blueprint for Distributed Future." *Computer Weekly.* February 3, 1994, page 2.

Data General's UNIX Development Group (DG/UX). *Open Systems Technology, Technical Brief,* 1991

Datamation. "Where's Unix Headed?" *Datamation.* April 1, 1994. Volume 40, number 7, page 24.

Datapro. *Datapro Information Services Group.* May, 1994.

Digital Equipment Corporation (DEC). *Open Systems Definitions and Strategy.* 1991a.

Digital Equipment Corporation (DEC). *The NAS Handbook.* 1991b.

Digital News and Review. "Spec 1170, CDE Snapshots Advance Unix Progress." *Digital News and Review.* April 4, 1994. Volume 11, number 7, page 5.

Electronic Computer Glossary. From "Computer Select CD-ROM." March 1994.

Freedman, Alan. *The Computer Glossary: The Complete Illustrated Desk Reference.* New York: AMACOM, 1991. Reprinted with kind permission.

Halsall, Fred. *Data Communications, Computer Networks, and Open Systems, 3rd edition.* Addison-Wesley. 1992.

Horwitt, Elisabeth. "Users Joint Open Systems Forum." *Computerworld.* February 18, 1991.

Judge, Peter. *Open Systems: The Guide to OSI and Its Implementation.* Reed Business Publishing. 1988.

IBM Dictionary of Computing. McGraw-Hill. 1994.

Nader, Jonar C. *Prentice Hall's Illustrated Dictionary of Computing.* 1992.

Newton, Harry. *Telecom Library.* 1993.

OMG, August, 1994. Organization representative, Object Management Group.

Open Software Foundation (OSF). *ANDF, Application Portability, and Open Systems.* June, 1991.

Open Software Foundation (OSF). *Distributed Management Environment.* 1991.

Open Software Foundation (OSF). *Open Line.* Sept/Oct 1991.

Open Software Foundaiton (OSF). July, 1994.

Satterfield, Mile. "Introduction to ODBC Driver Development." *Windows-DOS Developer's Journal.* December, 1993.

Shelton, Robert E. "OMG's CORBA 2.0; INdustrial-Grade Standard for Distributed Object Computing?" *Distributed Computing Monitor.* Volume 8, number 5, page 3. May, 1993.

Simpson, David. "What's ahead for UNIX in '92." *Systems Integration.* November, 1991.

Unisys Corporation. *How to Speak Open Systems.* 1989.

Unix International (UI). *Sustaining the Promise of Open Computing.* 1991a.

Unix International (UI). *Working Together for Open Systems.* 1991b.

Vacca, John. "Unix variants adhere to standards, but also provide proprietary extensions." *Software Magazine.* Page 84, November, 1993.

Windows Sources. "Scott McNealy on Sun's WABI." *Windows Sources.* December, 1993. Volume 1, number 11, page 109.

PC Week. "Something about Wabi and Unix." *PC Week.* December 6, 1993. Volume 10, number 48, page 12.

X/Open, July 1994. X/Open XPG Technical Background Information, received from Robert Noyes, July 14, 1994.

Appendix—Open Systems Terminology

The Datapro Reports on UNIX Systems and Software, 1993.

Freedman, Alan, *The Computer Glossary: The Complete Illustrated Desk Reference*. New York: AMACOM, 1991. Reprinted with kind permission.

Gallagher, Bob, "Can DCE Fulfill Its Promise?" in *PC Week*, version 11, number 20, May 23, 1994.

Newton, Harry, *Newton's Telecom Dictionary*, 1994.

O'Brien, Timothy, "Hewlett-Packard's Client/Server Strategy" in *Distributed Computing Monitor*. Version 9, number 4, April 1994.

Index

A

Abbott, Edwin, 195-97, 223
ABI (Application Binary Interface), 97
Access management, protection and, 148
Accountability
   information protection design and, 163, 164
   protection and, 150
Acquisition. *See also* Vendors
   I&T planning and, 247
   roles in, 245
Acquisition process, 34
   procurement policies, 186-87
Administration, information protection design and, 162-64
Adopters/integrators of standards, 67-69, 76
   criteria influencing standards development and, 74-75
Aggressive, controlled approach to Open Systems, 250
Alarms, 164
Alpha chip, 117
American National Standards Institute (ANSI), 62, 66, 91
ANDF (Architecture Neutral software Distribution Format), 97
ANSI (American National Standards Institute), 62, 66, 91
API. *See* Applications programming interface
Apollo's Network Computing System (NCS), 120
Apple Data Access Language (DAL), 92
Applications layer of computing environment, 81, 83
Applications programming interface (API)
   competition and, 90
   control of, 86-87
   maturity of, 89
   Microsoft, 107, 109
   origins of, 89
   selecting, 89-90
   support for, 89-90
Applications services layer of computing environment, 83
   standards for, 91-93

Applications tools layer of computing environment, 83
   standards for, 91
Architecture. *See also* Computing architecture; Information architecture; *and specific topics*
   of information protection systems, 158-63
   building blocks, 160-63
   value of, 237-38
Architecture, standards, and data group of IS organization, 191
Artificial languages, 78-79, 80
AS/400 series, 126
Asymmetric encryption techniques, 167
AT&T, 2
   Global Information Solutions, open systems as defined by, 37
   SVID (System V Interface Definition), 96
Auditability, 163, 164
   protection and, 150
Authentication (verification)
   basic modes of, 148
   information protection design and, 161
   protection and, 148
Authorization
   information protection design and, 161-62
   protection and, 147-48
Automobile industry, 1-2, 17
   standards and, 34-35
Availability of products, 57

B

Backwards compatibility, 31-32
Banking industry, 17
Barriers to implementing open systems, 58-59
Benefits of open systems, 44-47
Benjamin, Robert, 9
Branding, 48-49
   standards and, 90-91
British Standards Institution (BSI), 62
Budget, IS, 184, 226
Bull, open systems as defined by, 36-37
Business
   convergence of technology and, 10